MAKING RAIN

"What I like about this book is that it has challenged me to face the fact that many of the tips, I already knew, but in the daily routine of business had forgotten their importance. It seems to me any aspiring businessperson could do a lot worse than keeping this book on their desk as a constant reminder of what they should be doing."

Glen Manship – Red Hot Media

"We can sometimes forget that there is a logical process for building relationships in business that are not only capable of building your reputation and brand but also creating enduring relationships that result in multiple sales opportunities and referrals. To give you the edge, read this book!"

Adrian Brooks – Chatsbrook

"I don't get much time to read books but have recently started the process of designing and launching my own business, three things have played an important part in that process, my membership of the Rainmakers Club, the mentoring program included in my membership and this book, that is written in such a way that I can just dip in and out when I need a quick fix!"

Greg Parkin - Vala Evolution

"As a member of the Rainmakers Club I was looking forward to reading the latest book. I was not disappointed. It's not just an informative read but a challenge to us all to become better versions of ourselves in business. Many of the messages in this book resonated with me personally."

Steve Whiteside

MAKING RAIN

Becoming A Rainmaker The definitive guide to improving your results in business and sales

Chris Batten

authorHOUSE®

AuthorHouse™ UK
1663 Liberty Drive
Bloomington, IN 47403 USA
www.authorhouse.co.uk
Phone: 0800 047 8203 (Domestic TFN)
+44 1908 723714 (International)

Published by AuthorHouse 11/12/2019

ISBN: 978-1-7283-9442-8 (sc)
ISBN: 978-1-7283-9443-5 (hc)
ISBN: 978-1-7283-9444-2 (e)

Print information available on the last page.

This book is printed on acid-free paper.

Dedication

I dedicate this book to all those brave souls who take the plunge and start their own business ventures, sometimes despite the barrage of naysayers who would have them comply and seek 'A Proper Job!' To all those enterprising people and entreprenuers who understand that learning is a lifelong activity. To all those who work the Rainmakers way – Learn, Share, Develop. Hats off to you all, this is for you.

Contents

What is a Rainmaker

A *Rainmaker* in the context of this book is derived from the native North American Indians, each tribe would have an elder who was alleged to have powers that could cause rain to fall on the land of the village to ensure the crops would flourish and feed the tribe through the harsh winter months. The term has been adopted by the world of business in North America to describe a person who generates income or opportunities for businesses to grow, through new deals, attracting new clients or funds for businesses to grow.

A few years ago, I wrote a book called Sales Alchemy, in the few short years that have passed since then, much has changed in the world of business and continues to do so. Making Rain is my turbo charged version of that original book and also the inspiration for some of the core development programs provided by the Rainmakers Club.

Although things have changed, the core rules for building enduring relationships and creating sales opportunities have not, they still come down to ten very key rules. If you do nothing else with this book, read and learn these rules and incorporate them into your daily routine, no matter what business you are in, its size or the stage of growth.

Like business in general the most important element in the quest for greater success is the human element. Your mindset, your values and culture in essence how you behave day-to-day. In this book we will take a look at the kind of actions and behaviours that make a person a true Rainmaker

PART ONE

Bridge the Gap between mediocre and exceptional

Developing your value is based on leaps of faith and trust; it's about many individual skills all merged. It's about taking new knowledge and manipulating it to fit your style and character, as well as the character of your business. It's about your willingness to take heed of others, learn the lessons, use their experiences in conjunction with yours and about learning from your mistakes. Better still learn from other people's mistakes to save time expense and embarrassment. You have no idea how much I wish I had been given this advice when I first started in business.

Most of the content in this book, if applied, can assist you in your business and private life and will, for sure, give you all you need to take on new habits, to leverage your success and position to become a true Rainmaker.

First, I want you to understand how to make yourself more valuable to your business! Developing your value is based on leaps of faith and trust, not succumbing to negative influences from within and from others around you;

In this book we will look at many aspects of creating value most of which will focus on your own personal development and techniques, to assist you in your journey through business, regardless of your level of experience or position.

The difference between exceptional results and mediocre will all come down to your attitude and the people you choose to surround yourself with and how they act. It will also come down to your skill as an entrepreneur and leader. The key, I think is understanding there is only one way to run your career, your business, and that's the right way! There's only one way to treat the people in and around your business and that too is the right way!

Over the years and with a fair share of mistakes, I believe I have got that side of business pegged. I was once told by a mentor of mine, it's far better to learn from other people's mistakes than it is to make them yourself. This is your chance to learn from mine, and if you're really up for it to join the Rainmakers Club too!

I want to help you to bridge the gap between mediocre and exceptional. This gap I talk of is a wide one when looked at from the mediocre side and a narrow one when looked at from the exceptional side. What I mean is, when you're not doing the right things for success and you look out toward those that are already successful the gap between you and them looks like a chasm! When viewed from the other side by those that have already learnt the lessons, or taken the journey the chasm is nothing more than a series of simple changes to bridge a very narrow gap, you just need to know what to do and where to tread to get to the other side. You just need to be a Rainmaker.

If I am making it sound simple, that's because it is. The paradox is it's the simplicity that makes it appear so difficult, difficult to understand how a few simple habits could change your life! We're all looking at it so hard it appears far too simple and therefore is often missed, not taken seriously or ignored. We all look for some great secret or complicated solution or formula that only the brightest and best can understand. That could not be further from the truth, it is in all honesty simple, uncomplicated and logical.

I want to explore the elements, which enhance both personal and corporate success by simply having the right approach and attitude. I use as my reference points my own career, and pivotal moments in my business and life-skills education, a journey that still continues today.

One of the most common tasks performed in my time as a CEO and business adviser was, and is, to assist in the design of business strategies; To give a business the edge over its competition; to enable the business to work towards sustainable results year on year; To develop succession-planning and scalability from within.

The most common failure I come into contact with is that of the disconnection between strategy and execution, owing to the way in which people work together and interact—or should that be owing to the way they fail to work together and interact?

"To make a strategy live, you have to ensure it resonates with the entire team!"

It's an interesting journey I've been on, but then again, all the businesspeople and owners I connect with day on day can and do say the same thing. The more I interact with businesses the more I discover that we all face the same challenges and logjams to sustainable and exceptional results.

The main challenge is that of effective communication, the core to business success is the art of leadership, sales, delegation, people selection, understanding the simplest building blocks of business and the right work and corporate culture to apply. Once you have this right, sustainable exceptional results will follow. As with any journey it is best to start at the beginning. Sometimes it is worth slowing down or stopping and starting again or making a pivot in a different direction. Taking all that into account, it all starts with you and your attitude.

Regardless of your position and responsibilities in the business, good communication is easy to talk about and its importance easy to understand, making it happen is not so easy and needs commitment all the time, from all the people. It's as much about listening as it is about delivering the right message to the right person at the right time.

Regardless of your position and responsibilities in the business, understanding the building blocks for business and how to build the right culture, based on a good solid foundation of values will bring more success to you than you could ever imagine.

I don't pretend to have discovered some magic secret or formula for success I am not promising to tell you something new, there is nothing in this book you don't already know to be true deep down. My purpose is not to teach, but to remind or perhaps coax you into wanting to spend time developing from awareness of the values expressed, into living by them, to improve your position, improve your sales and in turn that of the businesses you're working in or on. If you're the business owner we also want to get you to the point where you work on more than in, that is the road to true freedom and success.

When you achieve this, you'll be able to sit back, watch your value grow, reputation build, and the value of your business, or the business you work for grow! The real deal is not in this book, the real deal is using this and other books to build a foundation of activities that really will work for you, assuming you want to be the best you can be, a Rainmaker!

The power is, has and always will be with you, all you have to do is commit to the activities! Remember this, I may give you this information to remind you, but the power comes from you. The power to succeed, to lead to create success is never given but always taken. It's your turn to take it.

First understand how habits work.

To make the changes you may need to for the advice in this book to work, you will need to commit them to habit—and to help you with this I thought it would help for you to recognise how habits are formed and then commit to unfreezing your current behaviour, adopt the new and then refreeze them into new habits. Sounds easy, it's not! It takes time, effort, commitment and good old-fashioned hard work, like most things in life that are worthwhile!

In short, if you commit to doing something and repeat that action a significant number of times, it will eventually be committed to your subconscious mind and become habit, that must be your aim with all the new habits that will help you either enter into or maintain your position in the world of exceptional results.

These actions will go from being something you do because you are forcing it, to become something you do because you know that you have to; eventually, it will just get done without even thinking about it. It will become habitual.

Habits are formed in this way, and you can improve any aspect of your life, if you understand this, have the strength of mind and the will to see it through. You will need to call on this again many times, to make the tips in this book new habits for you. So, you are going to have to think and work at adopting these tips as habits.

"One of the toughest things you'll ever have to do is change old habits. It takes real commitment and a really positive can-do attitude, all the time."

Perhaps the best way to do this is to take a few at a time and commit them to habit, then add more, but be aware that this could take some time to complete. Once you are there, you will see the difference it will make to you and your business or personal life, no matter what your position in the business.

The following diagram illustrates the dynamics of forming new habits. My advice is to start small and confirm to yourself that this works and then try to build on that with more positive habits. Much, if not all of this will come down to having the right attitude, so important in life and business. Concentrate and have some patience, as I said it won't happen overnight.

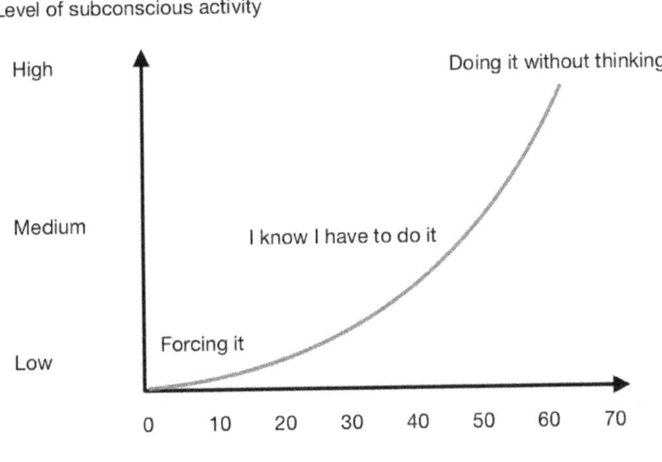

Looking at this from a leadership point of view, knowing how habits are formed can create a revolution in the management of people. Once you understand this you can coach others in your business to change their habits into more productive actions for their own benefit and the benefit for the business overall.

Some years ago, I was put into a position where I was in charge of a sales force of four hundred advisers across the UK. During this period of my career I was involved in developing people on a regular basis. I was not always getting the results I had expected. People weren't responding in a way I had thought they would, and I was uncertain why. This happened on more than one occasion and in the end, I turned to my mentor during that period of my life for the answer.

She helped me to identify that those that were in need of change were not underperforming because they lacked knowledge or training but that they had adopted some very bad habits, many before they even joined our team!

With that in mind she asked me some questions, that in fairness she answered herself immediately for effect. Will extra training work? No. Will discipline work? No. Why? Because in these cases this was not lack of training or knowledge it was the adoption of bad habits over a period of time.

If you as the manager know this, moreover, know that the last thing you should do is manage (rather, you should lead), then you have more than a fair chance to turn this around.

I learnt that the best course of action is to unfreeze the bad habit through coaching, not training, then reintroduce the right actions as a must do, or better still show the individual that this action will enable them to achieve their own personal goals. For that to happen you'll need to have a conversation about personal vision and goals, which is a good practice in any event. Then coach the individual in the specific activities you require, and they should now be motivated to achieve, they will need to create multiple repetitions and slowly but surely build these practices into subconscious routines, the new habit is formed.

If you understand how habits are formed and changed you will change the way you lead your people and how you control and develop your own performance.

"To get the full buy-in from your people, get them to relate directly to your mission with their own personal vision and goals!"

Instead of just talking it through once or twice you need to introduce a system that gets the person thinking about the activity on numerous occasions during their day. Use non-intrusive or offensive methods to unfreeze the old and replace with the new. Make sure this is done on multiple occasions over a period of weeks this will then freeze these new behaviours into the norm.

Of course, rather than understanding how to repair the damage done it is always far better to understand the way to start the journey, which involves smart communication, a two-way street. It would have been far better to start the process with an open discussion about personal aspirations for each individual and work them back to individual actions, which is the Rainmakers way and would ultimately create greater results for all concerned.

Things can still go wrong but at least you know you have the buy-in and now you can help to lead your team members to success, with coaching, flexibility and good communication from all.

The other side of this is your own personal mental attitude, which has a significant affect how you act and perform. I know much has been written about this and some of the finest works date back to the 1930's, my personal favourite being the books of Napoleon Hill.

"I have no doubt in my mind that we influence outcomes, based on what we think and the way we act."

What cannot be argued is we do tend to attract a series of events in our lives that mirror the way we are thinking about ourselves. I have never met a successful person without self-belief. That's not to say we don't all, from time to time, suffer for a lack of confidence. It's more like the prevailing wind. If you can maintain a positive 'can do' attitude for most of the time good things will happen. The people you choose to spend your time with is also an influence over the results you'll experience. Take care with the selection of your people. If you select right, you'll get the right results. The people you select must be of the same mind as you, a subject covered in great detail by Napoleon Hill in his book 'Law of Success.' Too many of us spend too much of our time, with the wrong people, rather than looking to surround ourselves with exceptional people, people who share our vision and values.

Once you understand how to deal with habits you can start to rebuild your own activities into habits of success. The more people around you who know this and want to make the change, the more chance you all have of a successful and happy journey, most of the time.

Don't forget on balance the harder you work the luckier you'll get. Not just hard though, be smart too. Working smart means making time for you personally and your family too. That is the smart way! Sadly, this lesson is all too often learnt the hard way, the key is, to learn from others and avoid the mistake yourself.

Let's bridge that gap!

When I talk about the gap it is simply the gap between average and exceptional performance. For me the start point is not only about having the right mental attitude but also about understanding the kind of things you can do to make yourself more valuable to the business you work in or on. These activities are just significantly more important when it comes to you as the business owner or member of the leadership team. That's because you're the one that will set the tone for how everyone else will behave and perform. If you are in management use the content of this book to build a new training program that promotes these traits and skills, helping you to create an exceptional team an exceptional business, a business of true worth.

No matter how much reading or discussing you do, there is no substitute to learning the lessons, changing the habits and putting these traits into practise. If you find yourself thinking, as you read, I know this, please consider this; you will be remembered and judged not for what you know but for what you do and have done. Knowing is one thing, doing is something else and it is the doing that will bridge the gap between mediocre and exceptional.

Tip 1: Create value for all to see.

This seems so simple and obvious, but you'll be amazed how many businesses I meet where people at all levels can't tell me how they actually create value, how they have direct effect on the profits of the business. In those cases, the chances of finding anyone else in the business who fully understands it is also remote! In the exceptional business you would expect to find the entire workforce being able to answer the value question.

Value can be and should be created by anyone in the business—value means more profit for you and the business, regardless of your position or length of service. You can create more value by adopting the actions and traits in this book; they have been shown to create value many times.

It is also worth pointing out that every point raised in this book comes from my own personal experience, an experience made up, like most in business, of a series of successes and failures and above all lessons learnt.

The failures are more important than the successes where learning is concerned. I would say, despite common beliefs to the contrary, you're much better to learn from other people's mistakes than you having to make them and then having to learn. In my experience doing it yourself can be quite costly! For example, imagine how the divorce rate would fall if we learnt from the mistakes made in relationships from others rather than waiting to make our own!

"Leaning is something we never stop doing and exceptional people crave learning, constantly wanting to improve. It is better to learn from others but to do that you have to keep your ego in check!"

I always find it quite a paradox that of all the creatures on the planet we are gifted with the greatest ability to learn lessons and think for ourselves and yet day-to-day we will all resist the opportunities we get to learn from others; preferring to do it our own way, even when we are knowingly taking a risk by ignoring the experience of those around us. I guess it's because many of us still need to learn how to control our ever-present ego. Academics tell us that what makes a human a human is our ability to learn; we should constantly be exploiting that ability, shouldn't we?

As I said earlier one of the biggest issues, I come across in business is the disconnect between the strategy and the people. All employees should, in some way, be involved in the implementation of the company strategy, as this is the most important and overt way to create value for your business or the business you work in or on.

It will ensure buy-in and generate inspired and motivated people and teams throughout the business. In turn, your reward is the elevated sense of value you gain from those around you and how valuable you become to your business, through your active involvement.

"The first step of creating value for your business is to actively get involved in the strategy of the business and be passionate about the business in all that you do."

Assuming you agree with all of this (and there is no reason why you wouldn't), next understand how you can develop the value, which you add to the business. I believe that this can be done by simply concentrating on the following objectives and making them your new habits, take them on just a few at a time to give you more chance of success.

Understand how your company makes money and where it spends money.

That's obvious, I can hear you say! It is but you'd be amazed at how many people out there working in and on businesses, particularly in sales, can't answer that question in any detail. In fairness most of them will know a little about how the business makes money but have a less than detailed understanding of where the money is spent.

When I started my first software business, which is an interesting story in its own right, I saw a significant change in attitude simply by ensuring all my staff understood where the revenue came from in detail and where it was spent in just as much detail. It didn't take long for the software business to start generating more cash from increased sales and in turn more profit.

Later, I managed to sell the business to a competitor that required me to work with them for a year, so I moved to London and that became the springboard for my first US based CEO appointment. Let's go backwards though to where the software business was just starting to grow.

As my software business started to gain momentum, I had a need to expand the staffing levels to cover all the bases. This brought with it its own set of challenges.

As we grew and started to take on more people I became less and less involved in the selection and recruitment process. As we got bigger, I noted the growth was not as great as it should have been, individual performance was slipping, and this started to concern me. So, my next action was to look into the reason behind this and then do something positive about it.

What I discovered was as we increased the number of people, we had taken our eye off the ball and while we were giving the new intake all the training they needed to do their job, they weren't getting the benefit of full training on the entire business on our foundations, our Vision, Mission and Values, along with an insight into our work culture. Our selection was no longer as good as it needed to be. The result was their mindset was not what we required, and they were just turning up to do a job and that was about it. What I wanted was a team of people who really cared and understood the business, so much so that they treated it as if it were their own.

"When you take on new staff ensure you include in their training a detailed understanding of your business DNA—Vision, Mission & Values. Make sure you induct them into the expected culture of the business."

I set about making sure they all understood the business inside and out. The more they learnt the more responsibility they took. The more they learnt about how and where we made and spent our money and what the impact on them was if we made more profit, the more responsibility and interest they took in their part of the business and also in other areas. Suddenly everyone was interested in performance overall. The result, productivity went up, sales went up, costs reduced as did staff turnover.

When people left the building, they turned machines and lights off and closed windows too! This increased value was reflected in the eventual sale of the business the proceeds of which were shared with everyone not just the shareholders. A tactic I intend to follow again in the future.

Understand how the business creates value for its clients and where you fit into that process.

If you want to be an exceptional businessperson and if you want to be an exceptional asset to your business, then one of the keys to that level of success is to really understand where the value you give to your customers comes from:

- Genuinely care about your customers, all the time.
- Be passionate about the entire business. What you do for the business and its customers?
- Always spend your time wisely and focus on those activities that create value for the business.
- Always look for new things to learn, so that you can develop your skills to add even greater value to the business.
- Think innovation, think about and try out new ideas, which may enhance the business and its value to clients.

Customers are people too.

Take time and make the effort to understand your clients, how they feel and what their expectations are. The more you know and understand about your customers, the better their journey with your business will be.

I believe it's vital for any business to own the entire client experience from first contact right through to use of the product and beyond. If you can do this, you'll find many new, more focused ways of marketing to them at the front end and giving them increasing value at the back end.

Understand where you fit into the customer's journey and how your contribution relates to that customer's experience. Are you active in helping to meet and, we hope, exceed each customer's expectations? Have regard for customers' individuality and, therefore, the way in which they should be treated by you and the business. Understand the moves they are going to make, before they make them and be fully prepared for them ahead of the game.

My top tips to help you really understand your customers and just as important, demonstrate to them your understanding, are as follows:

Understand that people are different.

Make sure that you understand people are different and therefore they need to be communicated with taking these differences into account. Most people are going to fit into one main group. They are either going to be big picture or detail, action people or reflective, they are going to be people that work toward a goal or away from a problem. I feel sure you'll recognise the group you fit into the closest. I say the closest because some of us adapt and so the boundaries become blurred, nonetheless we will all have an underlying emphasis on one or the other.

In most cases a 'Big Picture' person would show the traits of making quick decisions and being action oriented always working toward goals for the future. Whereas those that are very detailed oriented would demonstrate a much slower reflective decision-making characteristic and be motivated by solving current problems more than working toward future goals.

As I have already said the boundaries do become blurred. I have found that many true entrepreneurs learn to adopt the traits of the other side to become a more rounded business leader; they can adopt the opposite but always revert, under pressure, to their original traits.

I want you to consider the power and advantage it will give you in sales and business, if you learn to recognise the kind of person you are talking to and start to communicate with them in the right way. Treating your clients like real people, with real issues and feelings rather than as just someone you have to deal with or just another set of figures on a spreadsheet, can make a significant difference to your business and the way you are treated. Think about the added advantages you can gain just by recognising that people are different and then working in unison with those differences.

"Learn the art of identifying the type of person you are communicating with, speak to them in their language to get the best results."

If you do take time to consider this, then you'll want to acquire the skill of being able to adjust your communication style to suit the person or people you're communicating with. Talk big picture to big picture people and detail to detail people and learn how to be all things to all men when communicating. Learn how to quickly identify the kind of person you're communicating with. One of the many ways you can do this is by simply asking the right open questions to promote a conversation and they will soon give you all you need to understand them and therefore offer greater service.

Know how your customers buy.

There are a number of things you need to know to be able to say you know how your customers buy. In the ideal world you would be able to answer all these questions; when do they buy? Where do they buy? What do they buy? Why do they buy? How do they pay? What do they pay?

Armed with all these answers you are in a much stronger position to fully understand the important how's, where's and why's needed to gain more customer confidence and to illustrate to your market that you really do know them well.

I can remember one of the most successful examples of this exercise and how, as a result of following this particular guide, I was able not just to demonstrate that the business I was working with really cared about their customers. In so doing we were able to create more value. I was also able to design a new business solution for them, which in the fullness of time gave them a significant market differential envied by their competition.

I met this guy and we hit it off on a personal level and within a few short weeks I was not just a buddy but acting as his mentor in his relatively new business venture in the recruitment industry. I have worked in this vertical before some years previously and was feeling that confident about the specific value I could bring to the table because I had operated in this type of business before. So, I turned my attention to some research to bring me up to speed.

The first thing I discovered was that despite the hype most businesses in the sector were all doing the same thing, they all had the same model so there was the first clue, I had to find a differential to give this business a chance to create exceptional results.

Using this model, we were able to discover where how when and why customers bought and what and how they paid. From there it was very easy to discover what their biggest frustrations were. Digging still deeper I looked at the very top end of the market, a place where 'headhunting' was commonplace, and search and selection meant just that. I discovered what it was that made the customers of this type of offering, albeit that it usually entailed a six-figure salary, so happy.

From there the journey was quite predictable. I simply took the positives and made sure we ticked all the boxes from the information I had discovered in the original research and guess what? We ended up with a business proposition that was not just different but was designed with the client's needs in mind, all of them. It was attractive and innovative and demonstrated for all to see that customers were hugely important. Today that business continues to grow and is genuinely engaging with its audience. They continue to innovate and have moved into other areas, again with a new angle and a differential to be envied.

None of that would have taken place and that particular business could well of struggled to survive, if it hadn't been for taking the time to listen to what the customers really wanted, really understanding them at a much deeper level than the competition and design a sales process and marketing material that took into account the different ways in which people communicate, listen and make decisions.

Too many businesses carry on their day-to-day business based on what they think the client wants, rather than taking the time to find out. This has to be one of the biggest and most common errors made by businesses all over the world!

Listen to your customers.

There's nothing worse than talking to someone about something that's important to you only to discover that the person you're talking to isn't really listening to you! How many times has that happened to you and how did it make you feel?

Here's the thing, I think the worst listeners in the world are salespeople who have yet to learn their trade, I mean truly learn their trade. Most, not all, salespeople I meet will tell me they're good at sales, well why wouldn't they, after all they are in sales! The reality is somewhat different. I remember my first sales training course and I can tell you there was nowhere near enough emphasis placed on listening skills!

I know many salespeople who talk too much and then when they stop and the other person gets a chance to talk, the salesperson isn't truly listening, they are simply using the gap to plan what they're going to say next.

There are two things you need to do, the first and most obvious is to really listen and the second, regardless of the fact you are listening, you need to make a show of doing this. This will reassure the other party and make them feel even better about their choice to communicate with you.

Don't fall into the trap of believing that this is only relevant in the sales environment. Listening to your customers also pays great dividends when it comes to being innovative and when you're developing products or services. Not listening to them can be a costly mistake to make. This error has been illustrated by some of the biggest brands in the world.

The most important information about your business, your reputation and your brand will come from the mouths of your customers and the people who take an interest in what you do. Listen to gain valuable opinion, those that took the decision not to do business with you are a great source of knowledge and will often tell you things your customers will not.

Imagine the power of knowing why people don't do business with you and understanding what you could do to change that. From that perspective listening to people will certainly have an impact on your business!

"Listen to those that tell you no as much as you do those that say yes. Listening to people who decline to do business can be difficult. That is a natural reaction. If you can put up with the discomfort you can learn much from those that tell you no!"

Listening and promoting more conversation with well-placed open and closed questions is the key to success. You should use open questions to promote the conversation and closed to control the pace and confirm the detail.

I was working with one particular business owner not so long ago, who was a great example of what you should not do. No matter whom he was talking to he always left them with the feeling that he just wasn't listening to them. The way he created this was quite simple. As you spoke to him, you could see he was waiting for the slightest gap so that he would carry on with his point, with no visible clue that he has any consideration for the other persons point of view! I'm glad to say we worked with him and this is no longer the case. Not only is he better liked by his clients, but his figures are up by a not insignificant amount.

Another interesting fact about the way we communicate is to recognise that there are fundamental differences between men and women when talking together. As a rule of thumb men feel the need, when listening, to come up with solutions to what they are hearing, whereas in most cases women don't want the solution they just want to say it and know someone is listening to them! The moment you understand this you become much better at communication. Men become better at listening to their female colleagues and women can become much better leaders of men in business.

This takes a slight adjustment on both sides and can make life much easier for all concerned. This is just another example to illustrate that people are different, and you need to adjust to fit the individual.

The danger is that you can take this too literally. So do take account of what the other person is saying. If for example you have a boss that is a woman and she is asking for a solution and not just venting, you need to be offering a solution!

Another important part of really understanding your customer is finding out what motivates the client to take action. Different people will react to different motivations. A good example of this is the difference in motivation between those people who constantly strive to work toward future goals compared to those who gain their motivation by navigating away from problems, rather than toward goals.

Make sure that you know your space.

Ensure that you know, not just what you do, but the entire industry and the position of your company in the bigger picture! For me, the best way to do this is to take time every day, or at least every week, to review the trade press and news channels and most importantly of all, the web, I use my iPad™ for all my research in the evenings or early mornings, with a hot drink in an easy chair. I am looking for trends and opinions, I also check out the global picture too, as trends tend to travel.

All of these will have an impact on your business. Spend time listening to what your clients have to say, as I've already said your customers are a fantastic source of intelligence to be used in the development of your business.

"Build a reputation of always looking for new information to share across the entire business. Use the vast resources on the web to achieve this."

This knowledge of your space is not just for business owners and leaders it's for all that work in and on your business. As a boss you should invest time in developing a culture where the entire team have an intimate understanding of the marketplace, not just for their own use but also to disseminate to others who will find use for it. This is a great way of creating value and creating a great reputation, personally and for the business as a whole.

If you can do this you don't just bridge the gap between mediocre and exceptional you'll create a greater gap between you and the competition, one that is difficult to close, as it is based on culture and attitude founded on responsibility and accountability, some very underused and undervalued attributes in the SME sector in particular.

The challenge is how you go about making sure that all in your business really know the space. Start this process by making sure you know it first, then create the desire in all others to know as much as you do. Create in them the desire to continue to learn about the space day-on-day, week-on-week, month-on-month and year-on-year. Be warned this is never going to happen unless your team is as passionate about the business and its success as you are.

Here's how to start the process, the sooner you start this the sooner people will understand the benefits and copy you. Before long this will become the normal behaviour, and everyone will start to join in the process. It will become commonplace and part of the rhythm and culture of the business, here's what to do. If you see an article or hear something from a client which is of interest to you or the business, copy it, or document it, and send it to others in your business who you think could use it. Include a note explaining why you've sent it. This will increase your value to the business and you, and your activity will soon be noticed and copied throughout the business.

By doing this you will expand your knowledge and your experience. As a result, you will be able to react faster and make better decisions, which will benefit the business and all those around you. Which after all is the job of a Rainmaker.

"Building a new culture in your business will always start from you. Don't lose faith it will take time, but it is time well spent and can inspire significant gains personally and for the entire business."

One of the most efficient ways of doing this is simply to set up a range of 'Google Alerts' based around key search terms you might use to discover more information online. I use these to follow individuals in business, the competition and general trends in areas of business that I have a particular interest in, and I urge you to do the same.

Use Google Alerts for other things relating to your business, including keeping up to date with the competition, new entrants and your key customers. If you've never used these alerts before, simply go to Google™ and follow their instructions.

I also use my iPad™ to subscribe to appropriate news and magazine feeds that keep me in the loop. I go further than just sharing the information with my own business, I share relevant and interesting information with my clients to enhance our reputation and their journey with us. I think that is a really great way to instil the right culture and to win 'hearts and minds.' The mantra of my business the Rainmakers Club, is in fact Learn, Share and Develop.

Understand the language of money.

You must take time to understand the technical language of money. For many businesses, financial understanding is one of their weakest areas. In most cases having this kind of understanding will increase your value to the business! No matter where you are in the business, this is a good idea. If you're not the owner operator, consider starting this process by knowing the financial profile of the section of the business in which you work.

To do this, find out who in the company is the best person to talk to, able to walk you through those areas you don't understand. You should aspire to understand and be able to interpret financial information.

Make sure that you can read a balance sheet and understand its content and meaning. You might even want to help others to develop similar skills from within your team. More than just understanding, it is good if you also understand the implications to the business. If you're a member of the Rainmakers Club, we can help you with this, if you're not maybe we should talk? https://www.rainmakersclub.co.uk

I also feel that it's a good idea to know the profit margins for products. The profit margin is net income as a percentage of sales or revenue. Then, to be really smart, find out how your team might increase or threaten that margin. I hope you agree this should be a fundamental for all businesses and how it could have a very positive affect on the business overall.

Can you imagine how great your business would or could be if everyone was aware of the money and worked toward making it healthier and took a real interest in the financial wellbeing of the business? As with understanding the business and sharing quality information, which we covered earlier, you need to work on getting this attitude towards financial awareness and responsibility, embedded into the culture of the business.

This is something I wished I had taken time to do in the early years. When I look back, I find it quite embarrassing that I went into business with so little knowledge and understanding of the world of financial control and accounting. This lack of understanding was destined to catch me out and it certainly did. Learn from me don't wait to make your own mistake. Take some time to learn about business finance and financial control and make sure you understand the language of money.

Here's a good way to start that process, I used this in a previous business after I got my fingers burned! Once you've got it right you can get your staff into the right culture of asking questions, wanting to know the financial profile of the business and the subunits, as well as taking full responsibility for their areas of the business.

I made sure I started most meetings with a financial update about monthly business results and how the people in the room can have a positive effect on those results (note this was not just restricted to those in the finance departments but all areas of the business). I then briefed and coached others in the business who would be required to run meetings to copy that style and include it into as many of their meetings as was appropriate and practical.

When I was doing this, I would also then close the circle at the end of the meeting by bringing it back to financial performance and how the meeting conclusions can have an impact on that performance. I think it is also important to ensure that each member of the team understands his or her role and effect on the financial performance of the company.

"This is not an opportunity to show off your knowledge. That will not win you any friends. Wherever you can use plain English, avoid the use of jargon. Know your subject and keep it simple."

Don't assume that everyone you talk to understands the jargon. If you use technical speak, define it in plain English, to enhance everyone's knowledge. Similarly, never pretend to understand something you don't. Ask questions and ask for definitions as often as it takes to learn what you need to know. This one point is at the epicentre of the culture behind the Rainmakers Club. Ask questions and learn, share and develop. It's what being a Rainmaker is all about.

I believe, like many others, that asking is a sign of confidence, rather than weakness. Understand numbers and make yourself part of the financial health of the business or, at the very least, understand the financial health of the team or division that you belong to.

I can remember being at a conference not so long ago, where the speaker was talking at a technical level. It was a subject I was very confident in and I got a great deal from the session. At the end we, the audience, had the opportunity to do some networking.

I was standing in a group of about five local businesspeople, I joined them after the conversation had already started and they were unsurprisingly discussing the content of the presentation they had just sat through. It quickly became apparent that none of the people in the group had understood some key parts of the presentation. I was very interested in finding out why, when given the opportunity to ask questions, they didn't seek clarification?

The best way, I thought, was to simply ask why they hadn't sought that clarification. It created a silence as none of the people in the circle wanted to admit to not feeling comfortable at the time admitting that they didn't understand! Asking questions to gain understanding is not a sign of weakness and not something to be avoided, how else can we learn from each other?

If I were a betting man, I would put money on the fact that each time you don't understand something and want to resist asking for more, others in the room will be going through the same thing. Don't wait, raise your arm, ask and be the one who helped all the others, by asking what they wanted to ask but were too shy to do! Don't be afraid to raise questions to really refine your understanding of money and business! Questions like these perhaps:

- What are COGS?
- What are Sunk Costs?
- How do you read a Balancer Sheet?
- What does Burn Rate mean?
- What are Current Assets?

I like to think I put my money where my mouth is and so if you have just read the phrases above and don't understand them ask me and I will give you the answer with pleasure, chris@rainmakersclub.co.uk

Have a visible sense of urgency, in all you do!

Always work hard, work fast and do as much as you can do each day. Having said this, it's not about churning out high volumes of work just for the pleasure of crossing it off your list; quality and accuracy are, and always will be, key! Your sense of urgency should come from your passion for the business. Have a true desire to do the best you can for the business which you are working in or on, through creating value for the customer and, therefore, the business.

"If you don't feel pride in your work, if you don't believe in what you're doing, you're probably on the wrong bus!"

You should have great pride in your work and therefore want to get it right. You will soon find that working in this way will give energy to those around you—and you will all finish the day with a feeling of accomplishment. That is a great thing to be able to say—and so few people can consistently claim that. This is because they are influenced by the activities and moods of others around them; where these are negative, they erode value and create office politics! The opposite is true—so being positive is essential.

I'm sure you will all have experienced the way in which moods can travel between people and not just in an office environment. This is also true of activities, if you start working at a particular pace those around you will automatically mirror your pace within a surprisingly short space of time.

So, having a visible sense of urgency in all that you do can pay dividends, enhancing performance throughout your business. There is of course a real need to be cautious as you really don't want to replace quality with urgency, rather strike a balance where greater quality is always sought but the sense of urgency is ever present.

It makes a significant difference to the way customers feel about your service levels if they are constantly presented with an attitude of urgency to their requirements. This making them feel like the most important person. This can still be achieved even if you're unable to react immediately, simply agree a very doable time scale to create a more than acceptable expectation and then deliver on, or better still, before time.

We've all heard it many times before, you should never over promise and under deliver, far better to under promise and over deliver, don't you think?

Always aim high, set the bar higher and higher.

If you work in a business, never make yourself indispensable; instead, help to develop those around you to do your job, while learning how to do the job above you, but never do this to the detriment of performing your duties. This is a balancing act of great difficulty, although if you put your heart and soul into it, you'll amaze yourself at what can be achieved. Focus on the benefits and you will give yourself the ability to achieve great things and even greater value for your business.

As a business leader your role should be to encourage this as a standard culture throughout your business and this should start at the selection process and continue right through the journey you create for your business and your team. After all you want an exceptional business and so should promote exceptional rather than mediocre! I often hear people in business saying you have to dare to be different if you really want to make an impact.

The interesting thing is that so few practice this, preferring to be a creature of habit and following the masses and yet history is littered with examples of business leaders who have done amazing things against the odds, just by not following the mainstream. Think about it, if you look to the masses, you'll find mediocre and average, look toward the few and you'll find exceptional, now that must be a clue, right?

Dare to be different, think about the journey you want, the future you really want for you, your business and your team. This is a behaviour that helps to create the right attitude and a positive outlook no matter what happens. It's that constant positive attitude that will attract good things and more opportunities for you. Don't accept today as being all there is. Set your personal bar higher and higher, accept the challenge and push yourself constantly.

I am often asked how can I go further, higher, find more success? I say, follow my lead, I just never know when to stop raising the bar, there is always more to do, more to learn, more to achieve! I think I have always thought that way from the moment I joined the army, but particularly when I entered the world of business.

In business from the very beginning I used the same tactics that had worked so well for me in the Army. I constantly looked up for the next level and at the same time around me for people who might be perfect to replace me to help me continue my journey upwards!

"Take more control of your destiny, build succession into your plans and at the same time learn new skills. Take some time to help others too."

I did this because I wanted to be at the top of my game all the time and needed to get as high as I could. I realised that to make this possible I would need to demonstrate I could do the job and at the same time give those above me the vision to see that moving me up would not create a gap, even back in my Army days I was bridging the gap!

I started early in my career and to be frank have used the same tactics often and still use those tactics today. It's never too late to start working and thinking in this way no matter who you are and at what stage of development you're at. Making rain is the duty of all true Rainmakers.

I joined the world of business as a financial adviser and during the first few months balanced my activity between generating new business, which is how I got paid, as I was commission only, and developing an improved business model for the original founders of the business.

I spent quite a bit of time learning about the back-office functions and the accounting of the business and spent increasing amounts of time each week on helping the admin team with some of their reporting. This gave me enough experience and information to be able to work on some improvements on the operational side of the business.

It took a while but eventually all the effort was worth it, and I was invited to take a position on the board heading up the compliance team to manage all the new regulations. Once in the chair I set my sites on the next level and the journey continued.

Eventually I became the Managing Director and from there we developed the business to a point of exit. This then became the springboard for my next exciting position. All of this came about by me working hard for the business in the job I had been given, as well as demonstrating the possible capabilities of more senior or challenging roles.

I spent time delivering as much value to the business as I could, coupled with learning new skills and making sure that I constantly demonstrated what it was I was delivering to the business. As a result, I began a journey that still continues today. It has its ups and downs but usually results in bigger, better business opportunities.

Each turn I make; I try to ensure I follow the same principles, which, historically, always resulted in me taking on roles more significant than the previous ones.

I was hired by a Norfolk based business to assist with some sales development training. Originally it was just going to be a few days' work, using this same approach I was soon hired to head up sales and marketing and then from there I became the CEO of the business during a period of significant change and development!

On another occasion I was hired to develop the UK sales of an up and coming Heavy Lifting Company. Within a few months I went from Head of sales to head of global sales and then from there to CEO of the US business and the business in the Middle East. Always using the same principles of creating value, raising the bar and being demonstrable.

There is nothing at all stopping you from doing the same in your career and journey through business. You simply need to act and work like a Rainmaker.

Have your own performance standards.

You should create your own thumbnail sketch of performance, so that you can see how you are doing against your own targets, don't just turn up, turn up to win. Start by having clear goals with clear timelines and then a means for measuring them, so that you can speed up and slow down, as you need to. There is nothing wrong with mistakes, as long as you don't keep repeating them, and nothing wrong with the odd change of direction to achieve goals. Remember the plan can change the mission always stays the same.

Not all of your goals will be visible to those around you, so, you should share an overview of your results with others, not to beat them over the heads with your good work but so they can see where you are, where you have been and where you are going. Importantly, your boss, if you have one, will also be able to see what help you might need too. If you are the boss, the same rules apply you might want to share your results with your mentor instead.

Sharing the results is a positive step and helps to keep you focused on the mission, the more you support the business the more support you should get from the business.

"Mimic those that have already achieved exceptional results. Share your results to gain more empowerment and recognise the importance of mentors and advisers."

Make the effort to understand the goals of those around you too, so that you can help them to achieve theirs. Think about sharing your goals with those around you because they can help you, that is what teams are all about, mutual support. This is where good strong leadership skills are a necessity for all levels of the business. It will also get you noticed for promotion, perhaps! Connect with others outside the business to help you too. Use **Rainmakers Club** to connect with new people and invite your existing connections too. The bigger your support network the better!

In the businesses that I have worked in and on, I always make sure there's a relationship between my personal goals and the vision of the business; I believe this to be an essential relationship. What is more, I personally believe, if you're to achieve your goals you need to have consistency of activity and work ethic to keep that part of the balancing act that is business, on course. You need to have those all-important performance standards in place and work to them consistently.

Oh, sure sometimes, like the rest of the world, I wake not feeling great about everything. We all do that from time to time. The secret is not to let that drag you down, take a long deep breath and a long look at yourself in the bathroom mirror and remember why you're doing this. Also remember all the others that felt the same way and let their inner doubter sell them on 'NO' instead of **'YES.'** Make sure you create the difference and be one of the successful ones by buying into **'YES'**, even when things are tough, scrub that I should say particularly when things are tough.

The difference, my friends, between the truly successful and all the rest, really does come down to your positive attitude and understanding you have to get up one more time than you're knocked down to make this life work for you. Just get up and do it. Have performance standards that you can stick to, helping you on this journey, hang on tight;

the pole we are climbing is a greasy one. Keep the faith, keep your powder dry and keep the activity high, make high performance standards part of your personal values and part of the overall culture of the business you're working in or on!

Be organized—have an action plan!

Create an action plan for each year, taking account of your goals. Keep to your plan, but only while it remains relevant, and understand what it is you need to do each month to accomplish the items on the plan. Set milestones and, where it will involve others, make sure that they are aware, so that they can build the actions into their own plans. Working to your action plans takes self-discipline, from discipline comes greater performance and greater freedom, which is something we all strive for in business and in life or at least that's what I do.

Prioritize and then schedule, so that the work required gets done and monitored—put it in your diary or Smart Phone, or any other device you're using. Do all the important, urgent stuff and delegate the other stuff. This is a simple, effective time-management technique. The ability to be effective in prioritising and delegating will be the difference between mediocre and exceptional, being successful and just turning up!

I have used this system of priority and delegation myself on many occasions and still stick to those principles today. The simple but effective system I am using is worth a brief summary, I use letters to prioritise as follows:

'A'—These are the top priority and if I do nothing else during the day, I must get my 'A' task(s) completed.

'B'—These are the tasks that are important and have to be done but it won't cause issues if they are not completed today. At some point the 'B' task will become the 'A.' therefore if you can get them done all the better.

'C'—Tasks with this designation are not that important although it might be good to get them done at some point. A task with this grade is unlikely to get upgraded but could well be downgraded to the next two levels of the system.

'D'—D is for delegate this is a task that needs to be done but can be done by someone else and will be one of their 'A' or 'B' tasks.

'E'—E is for erase this is a task that was a 'C' perhaps and has no importance and does not need to be considered due to lack of importance, relevance or time.

Just try this system for a few weeks and see what a difference it can make to the way you approach all those tasks you have to do each week.

When I first tried this system, I thought it was a bit of a gimmick but maybe worth giving a go. What I discovered was a real eye opener. I discovered that I often took my time during the day doing those tasks that were the easy ones to complete. I also discovered that in many if not most cases the easy jobs were either 'D' or 'E's.' Once I discovered this, I was suddenly able to delegate or bin them and spend much more time doing the things that would get me the true results I was looking for.

This change took nothing more than delegation and not spending time on tasks that didn't get me further toward my ultimate goal.

"Before you try a new system for time management and priority of tasks. Do a survey on your time for a few weeks. Are you happy with the amount of time you spend on your goals? Do you need to re-think your current system?"

Complete at least one important thing every day.

We have all had days where we do nothing but firefight or sort out minor issues. This can be a major drain on morale and can affect performance. Therefore, make sure (by the end of each day) that you accomplish at least one really important task. If you need to bring in others in your team to accomplish this, make sure that you e-mail or text them and thank them, for their help, that too is important, as it will motivate them by creating empowerment. Thank you is far more powerful than you give it credit for. If you want to be really different send a handwritten note, it will be greatly valued!

Knowing that you have done something important will give you a great feeling of accomplishment and the fuel to keep going and going, adding value to you and the business. I have already talked about the importance of maintaining a positive mental attitude and this tip will go a long way toward helping you achieve this. Please don't underestimate the importance and power of this in maintaining the edge, which you need, to be a winner and of course you need to bridge that gap between mediocre and exceptional.

I can think of a great example of how this worked for me, albeit slightly off the business track. I was doing one important thing each day, out of hours and really important to me rather than the business I was working for at the time. Please note out of hours, this meant that it had no negative affect on the business. It did however result in a really positive outcome for both the business and me, let me explain what happened:

In 2002 the most important thing for me on a personal level, excluding my family and friends, was my desire to finish the book I was writing and get it published. With work I had complete control of things. Everything was going as expected, both in the US and UK businesses I was running at the time. However, when I got home, I was not feeling accomplished despite maintaining a good level of activity.

The reason for this was simply that by the end of the day I was going home and not spending any time on the book that meant so much to me. This caused me frustration and so following my own advice I decided to make room for writing every day of the week. To me it was important I could do this without interfering with work or my private life.

That way it would make me feel a whole lot better. So that's what I did. Instead of finding endless reasons why I couldn't do this I looked for smart ideas to help me achieve that aim.

I can't take credit for the idea; I borrowed it from one of my US mentors. I remember he told me that it was possible to create a 13-month year just by getting up 30 minutes earlier than planned and going to bed just 30 minutes later each day. He maintained that would give you another month of waking hours in the year to do something constructive.

So, my constructive activity became writing the book for a minimum of one hour a day every day, without using work time. The truth is that at weekends I did significantly more than that. I ended each day with another few pages, sometimes much more, towards the book and a real feeling of satisfaction that at last I was doing that one personally important thing each day in addition to at least one important thing each day at work!

I still work on the same basis today only this time it is more like 2 hours a day and some of it is spent reading and learning, as well as the writing, for books, web articles and Rainmakers Club content too.

What it gave me, that I wasn't expecting, was a renewed passion and direction at work to get those all-important tasks done so that I could get that buzz from a job well done, twice a day instead of just the once.

The reason I can still do the same today, top and tail each day with some kind of writing or reading is simple, it has now become a very important habit for me. Getting as much of the important stuff done at work and in my own time each day, gives me a tremendous feeling of accomplishment and helps maintain a positive outlook, oh, and I never get bored, life is too short and there is far too much that needs doing!

The 6 P's.

We've all heard this before, probably hundreds of times but that makes no less important to a Rainmaker, who understands this is not just a saying, it is a way of working that attracts success. The 6 P's stand for; **P**rior **p**lanning and **p**reparation **p**revent **p**oor **p**erformance.

The version I was taught had an extra 'P' in it, but I was in the Army and you expected that most things would include some good old-fashioned 'Anglo-Saxon!' This saying is so very true, so very obvious. I use it a lot, I wouldn't want to count the number of times the saying is met with a rolling of the eyes from the recipient, who, in fairness, is only hearing from me because they clearly didn't prepare or plan!

Knowing the saying is one thing; acting on it is an entirely different and quite a rare thing. 'Doing' makes the difference between mediocre and exceptional results; doing helps you bridge the gap between those two states of performance!

"The difference between successful and unsuccessful? It is oh so obvious, it's the difference between thinking about it and doing it."

If you wing it, you may get away with it once or twice, but the more you wing it, the more likely you are to fail. The more you prepare, the more effective and successful you become.

Last minute cramming is too high a risk and does not substitute for quality preparation time. Please remember this. It is of course particularly true when we talk about presenting and public speaking too.

So, whatever it is that you are planning to do, think about ranges of questions and different outcomes which could be asked or take place and then think about a range of solutions. Make sure that you plan every aspect which can be planned and communicate with others who can help to achieve the plan, whatever the subject matter might be. This is how we make rain.

Preparation takes hard work, that is why so few do it well, but think about it this way—how many people can you name who have made a significant success of themselves without doing more than those around them? You can always find the most successful people have put in significantly more effort than the unsuccessful, who appear to prefer to moan about stuff, a poor substitute for planning preparation and hard work. I can't think of one negative person I have known who has ever spent the day complaining about their situation, their job, and their boss. Who then sits down in the evening and reflects on a great day, a job well done! Those people are far more likely to take the moans and groans home with them and infect their families too.

On more than one occasion I have been approached by a member of the audience after I have given a presentation, who compliments me on what they describe as my easy natural style. Many will go on to say it's clear I have great confidence when speaking and have all the bases covered.

Well, they're nearly right, I do have my bases covered, that's because I spend so much time preparing. I don't think I've ever done a presentation without feeling like running in the opposite direction just before its time to face the audience.

The hours of practise I put in hides the nerves and build's my confidence. The more I know about my subject the greater my confidence. Like most people I do suffer from time to time with confidence issues. The secret is no secret at all in reality, it's this simple, the more you prepare and practise the better you get at it. The audience be it one person or hundreds get to see the swan above the water, they don't see the frantic activity going on below the surface!

When I run my workshops, I like to keep them interactive. I start by asking people in the audience what they would like to take away with them. I then write this onto a flip chart, white or smart board and tell the audience if I don't cover all those points, that have come from them, I will consider the session to be a failure. People tell me that takes great confidence to pull off and I tell them it really doesn't. The reality is it takes no more than a few hours of preparation. Being prepared for all eventualities, knowing my subject as well and usually better than the rest of the people in the room gives me the confidence to deliver on the day.

"Knowing your subject is key but just because you know the subject it does not mean you don't have to prepare and plan before the meeting, the interview or the presentation. Preparation is all important, preparation is King."

Flexibility.

Now, more than ever before, we need to show increased flexibility in business. Gone are the days when you could write a business plan to cover a five-year period and stick to it. Things now move at a great pace and most businesses keep Internet hours (24/7). So, one of the new elements to success is that of greater flexibility and the ability to handle and manage change and move quickly.

The subject of change management is an entire book in itself. However, the key is to embrace change, accept that it happens and grasp all the opportunities for development and broadening of experience, which come out of this flexibility.

The key is very much to accept that despite your priorities and plans, you will, from time to time, be pulled off course. You need to rise to the challenge and have a balance of planning and flexibility.

Stick to the task in hand and if something comes from left field, roll with it. If circumstances or your boss gives you a new task and you have not completed your priority, then simply tell him or her you have not finished a higher priority. If your boss or circumstances dictate that you must go with the new priority, then go with it and give it your best shot.

Remember there is nothing wrong with changing direction, slowing down, speeding up as long as you stick to the mission. Your mission can be achieved in more than one way and there is nothing wrong with change to gain the advantage and achieve the mission.

"The mission is always the mission, but the plan will have to change to adapt to the inevitable counter moves that will be made by the opposing forces—Infantry battle rule 101."

I should go further and say that I can't remember one occasion in business, or the armed forces, where to achieve the stated mission the plan did not have to be adapted during the execution to take account of the ever-changing circumstances. Flexibility and the ability to embrace change is therefore paramount to success, don't gripe about it just do it, is my mantra! If I could give you one piece of advice about dealing with change it would be this:

Don't fight it, get in your 'corporate helicopter' and hover above the issue and view it from all angles looking beyond the field you're in, over the hedgerow and toward the horizon.

Where other people are involved you need to handle their natural responses to change. This is a 'must have' skill if you're a business or team leader moreover it's essential if you have ambition to break into leadership as part of your career journeys. This skill will also help you no end in your personal development. So, take some time to learn how to handle change yourself and manage the emotions it will bring to the surface in others.

Use your empathy and do all you can to truly understand why people feel the way they do about change. Once you understand the emotional process you can start to manage it with very positive results. I think the best illustration of what we all go through, with what we have to deal with, and what we might feel during significant change is best described by Elizabeth Kuber-Ross with her generally accepted grief cycle.

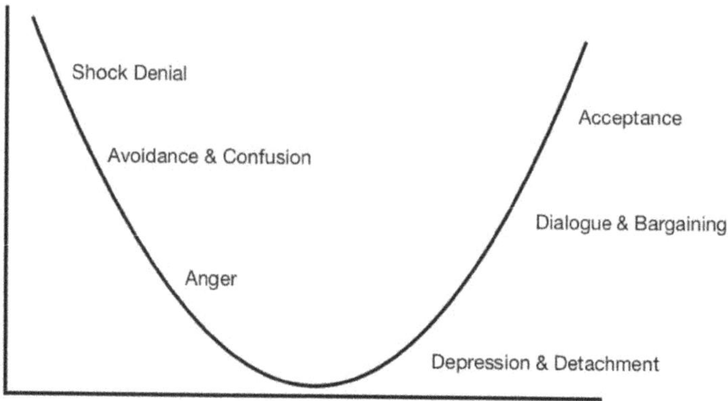

Do you recognise this cycle in yourself? When confronted with a change that has been imposed on you without your full involvement? The initial feeling of shock and denial about the change and the reasons for it, followed by confusion and avoiding adopting the change, by ignoring it or deliberately avoiding engagement in the actions that endorse it. Followed by a feeling of anger, then depression or detachment from the team. Finally, you open lines of communication and try to bargain, perhaps illustrating why you should not be included in the change or maybe offering a diluted version more in tune of the old way. Finally, you begin to accept the change and work with it and things go back to how they were, with your attitude and emotional stability. You may even start to think to yourself, 'why didn't we always do it this way!'

I wonder how many of you reading this will recognise yourselves in that description at some time in the past. As a leader you'll never be able to avoid this natural tendency but there are things you can do to make it an easier journey for you and everyone else in your team, department or business.

I remember when I took over a business a few years ago; I used my knowledge of this natural cycle of emotions to ease into the change the staff were facing. It worked so well for us all that I have used the same process each time I am in a position of leading any change in business, which is often! This is how I managed the change, a process I would urge you to adopt practise and make your own:

I was looking to merge one business I had just acquired with another business that I had identified as being a great opportunity to create a new income stream and leverage their product to create a significant differential for the other business. This was going to create much change for all the people in both businesses including a change of top table leadership. I took full responsibility for the leadership of this change and started work on winning the hearts and minds of all those concerned. Winning the hearts and minds should never be underestimated and should always be on the top of your priority list, when starting this process.

The first step I took was simply to have a detailed plan, which also included contingency for those unexpected developments and challenges. As a footnote to this you should have contingency plans in place for all aspects of your business. The best way to think them through is to ask 'what if' questions.

Next I took some time to understand all the personalities involved. I spent far more time on those that were new to me, as the existing team were already well known, I had a good picture of their character traits. All involved needed to be treated equally so my knowledge of the new people was key.

Getting to know all the people involved was time very well spent and I was able to determine generally how the main individuals would react to the changes that would need to be made if the mission was to be accomplished.

When it came time to make those important changes the first thing I did, was get closer to those I would call the chaos makers. These were the people, or in this case the one person I knew would be the greatest challenge to win over. This person would rebel the most against the change and would encourage others to follow as they were well thought of and a centre of influence. Some members of staff were known to be loyal to this individual and would surely join the rebellion if the situation was not controlled in the right way.

I was told early on by one of my American mentors that people wanted to be led and a real leader takes control early, but that control doesn't have to mean dictatorship. Good leadership is smart and takes into account the people, good leadership, like good sales, is all about the people and great communication!

I set out to arrange a meeting with my chaos maker, before there was any talk about potential changes. I already knew what needed to be done to get the business performing in the way I had planned, and I also knew there was room for other viable alternate tactics to achieve the same aim.

I knew this because I had done all my preparation work and research previously. Not just research however, I had also gone through the various 'what if' scenarios to ensure I considered all the features, advantages, benefits, disadvantages and risks each potential course of action would bring with it.

The meeting with the chaos maker went something like this. I started off by explaining why I had asked for the meeting. It was important to be sincere and at the same time achieve the ultimate aim of the meeting, which was to make this chaos maker my biggest advocate of the change I was suggesting.

I seem to remember telling him that I had asked for the meeting because I was facing a challenge and many people in the business valued his opinion and involvement in projects that had been executed in the past, this was true albeit only part of the story. I went on to say that sort of involvement was exactly what I was looking for and what the business needed and so invited him to become part of the planning team.

With my chaos maker now lowering his weapon I continued the offensive by sharing with him my desire to seek his advice and help in planning the solution to the challenge ahead. This of course, was making him feel very comfortable and to be frank quite important. The truth is I did want him by my side feeling comfortable and I did see him as very important to the success of the project.

Then again, all chaos makers are important as they all have the power to have significant effect on any change. Your role as a leader is to ensure the impact is always a positive one and to remember, their actions are natural and instinctive based on the well-documented theories of Kuber-Ross.

I then introduced him to the challenge and told him I would like him to work with the team I was putting together to design and implement the solution. I told him I had been thinking long and hard about the situation and the best options I had come up with were. I then asked him the killer question, I said, "What is it that you would do if you were me?" From that moment onwards in this project at least I had a willing participant.

This guy was a thinker and that gave me a win, win situation. If he did come up with a better plan, then that was good and if he agreed with mine that too was good. If he didn't fully agree but had no ideas, no problem, we would discuss and end up back at my solution with complete buy-in. If he had an idea that I thought wouldn't work, we would discuss it and slowly redirect to a solution that would work.

In this particular example the latter was indeed the direction the conversation went in. He expressed no real love of my carefully thought through solution and instead came up with his own version. A discussion continued and the result was my plan, with a few valuable additions, was adopted with of course his complete buy-in. I gave him the job of communicating the messages to the team, job done!

I used him to communicate the message because those that knew his chaos making would be even more certain this was the right thing to do because of his buy-in and those that followed his lead would continue to do so.

Just one more thing on this, it wasn't all about what I said, much of it was about how it was said. For example, if I had strong feelings against what he was saying, I didn't say that. Instead I would say, "I can see why you're saying that, if I were in your position, I would probably say the same, but I see it slightly differently, can I explain?" Using this approach ruffles no feathers and treads on no toes. It's all about hearts and minds, always was and always will be!

Flexibility is, has and always will be one of the defining differentials between good and exceptional leadership, which leads to exceptional and sustainable results for the business and for you, just another way to bridge that gap!

Timing, it's all about timing.

Just as in Rugby (I could have used football but it's the wrong shaped ball!) the timing of that run by the winger is vital, so too is timing key in business. Don't let your competitor get the better of you. If your client requires a call back, do it—don't wait. Remember, that if you're not meeting their expectations, then they will walk! If you are not talking to your clients, then your competitors will do that for you, and we don't want that!

If you don't follow up a call, you will lose your advantage. If you don't respond to the team in time, you will lose your advantage. Timing is everything in business, a lesson worth remembering. There are other aspects of timing we need to consider if we are to bridge the gap created between good and exceptional businesses and results.

Another important aspect of getting the timing right is to employ timing and control to your change management projects. Most businesses need to embrace change and new opportunities if they are to develop and achieve their specific mission and vision. This means they need to be constantly looking for the next big thing for their business and control their use of time.

During your career in business you may well, like me, embark on many projects before you get one that results in something that really works for you. This is where timing becomes even more important. In essence when trying something new you need to be able to discover if the project is going to be successful or fail as quickly as you can. If it's to fail, you want it to fail quickly to reduce the risks you take and the potential loss of investment. On the other hand, you will also want to see success quickly to demonstrate there is a real opportunity for an ROI (Return On Investment). Timing is key!

We all understand that it's not possible to get things right all the time, it is well worth trying to ensure you use time efficiently and understand the importance of good timing for you and your business. Allocate time carefully to all your activities and create a business that is known to have expert timing.

Enhance your timing by investing in your own development and training as well as the rest of your team. This personal development is one of the key purposes of the Rainmakers Club. The better you get the more effective you become with time. Also spend time on research. Find out what's happening around you and in the sector where you operate. Find out what's happening elsewhere as there are many examples of new entrants coming into an industry and stealing the advantage from the 'dyed in the wool' businesses already operating the sector, with their eye slightly off the ball. In business there is no time to relax, things are moving at pace even while you are reading this!

The more time you spend on these types of activity the more you learn, the more you innovate and the better your timing becomes. The other great thing is the smaller the gap becomes between you and the best of breed in your sector, which can only be a good thing, for you and the rest of the team. A really good example of this in recent years has been the way brands like Amazon™ and Google™ have made an impact in so many new verticals and why their timing looks so good. They use their time wisely; they make time and then they drive the agenda to further increase their success. There is no reason and no real barrier for the start-up, micro or small business to operate in the same way. The Rainmakers way.

Avoid the blame game!

To achieve avoiding the blame game, you will need to lead from the front and take responsibility rather than looking for others to blame. Make taking responsibility and being accountable as part of the culture of your business or department. You may delegate parts of a task to other people, but, when the deadline comes, you still need to take responsibility. Don't just delegate and then wait. Don't micro-manage but don't leave things to reach the deadline before taking action.

Take action in advance of deadlines and ensure that the others are doing the job, give even the smallest task a timeline that is realistic and agreed and use that as the goal. Make sure that they know how important it is and do some floor walking, visit the trenches, not just e-mail, face-to-face is better, where possible. You need to own the project and take full responsibility for the task you have delegated. Taking this approach is also healthy for the business and promotes succession from within the ranks.

"Smart communication is the answer to all your questions. When giving or receiving a task both parties should be asking these questions; have I been given enough information to carry out this task? Have I given enough information to allow this person to do this task effectively?"

If you're running a team or indeed part of a team you may experience the individual who needs to constantly check every move they make with the boss. This is often to do with a lack of confidence and a need to cover this lack of confidence by creating a closer relationship with the boss. If this sounds like someone you know, what they won't see is the long-term damage this can cause to their personal progression.

As the boss you should discourage this kind of reporting, after all you're trying to build a great team that doesn't disappear down the gap between mediocre and exceptional.

This sort of behaviour often leads to the blame game so often played by people in business. This is where if something goes wrong the immediate action is to look for someone to blame. Getting rid of the culture of blame is essential if your business is to develop into something special with longevity. As I have already mentioned the best way to approach this is to set a good example for all others to follow.

So rather than concentrating on the autopsy, concentrate on the solution and maintain the forward momentum of the business, rather than wasting precious time on who's to blame.

A good leader, a good manager will understand that when things go wrong, the natural instincts of most will be to look for someone to blame. The natural instinct of most, when things go well is to congratulate themselves on a job well done.

Here's what I believe you should be doing overtly in your business when things go well or not. Don't just think about doing it you need to force the activity to make it a habit. It will not take too long before your teams start to copy your actions and before long, you'll have a culture that encourages performance and lacks blame, concentrating instead on innovative solutions and self-development. Here's how you get the ball rolling:

Learn the difference between 'Windows and Mirrors.' When things go good or bad resist the temptation and natural instincts. When things go bad, take a look in the mirror and take full responsibility for the actions of your team. When things go well, look out the window for someone to share the victory and congratulate, not the other way around no mirror for self-congratulations and no windows for finding people to blame!

Get everyone to treat the business as their own.

Imagine how great your business could be if your entire team treated the business as if it were their own, as if it were their own money they were spending! People who own businesses should always have a view of the big picture, but, because it is their business, they also worry about every little thing. They need to know what is going on in every aspect of their business. They should focus particularly on aspects, which relate to the customer. They should build strong teams and constantly review the impact of actions on the customers. Imagine if everyone in the business thought that way within their respective teams.

To grow truly successful people for your business, you need to create a culture that sees them act and think as if it is their business. Imagine the value it would create if your people were to run and work in their unit as if it were a business in its own right. Take its success personally. Think and act like an owner.

How you get people to think and act in this way is, of course, the challenge we all face each day in our respective businesses. I have faced the same challenge myself on many occasions in the businesses I have started or been involved with over the years. You'll never get an existing team to think and act in this way if they don't have good role models to follow, and don't have incentives to adopt the approach. Of course, they also need to want to make the changes. Life becomes so much easier if you think about these characteristics when designing the values and culture of your business, and also introduce the identification of these values in your selection process.

Ongoing success in this area will come down to the way in which you recruit and induct your teams. It all comes down to that. Your people need to really believe in the product, the company the clients and the people in the business, without this, I feel it would be almost impossible to achieve.

"Teaching skill is far simpler than teaching attitude & passion. I would always hire a person willing to learn with aptitude and passion over the expert with no passion!"

When you recruit, make sure you do it not just based on their ability to fulfil the practical parts of the job, you need to hire based on their emotional and motivational fit to you and your business. I would rather hire a person with lesser practical skills but great motivational and emotional fit than a highly skilled person with little or limited passion for the job. You can teach skills; you can't teach passion. In the early years of business, I had little success finding good people even with the help of some quite expensive search and selection specialists. In the end I had a major stroke of luck and did some consultancy work for a London based head-hunting business. They only dealt with 'C Suite' candidates and I was able to not only help them with their expansion but also learnt much about the art of selection and onboarding.

Later my knowledge and experience were to improve still further during a project that saw me assist in the setup of a local Search & Selection business delivering a comprehensive selection model, perfect for the small business!

If you hire the right people, by testing them first, and make it clear what you expect and how you need them to act, assuming you've done your homework during selection, they will already have the attributes you're looking for. It then becomes only a short step to get them to treat their part of the ship as a business in its own right. Taking direct responsibility and interest in the bigger picture and the detail, just like a business owner or director. Someone who has such a valuable and attractive trait; would never be out of work with that attitude. Imagine the power of a team where all the individuals thought that way, wow!

Know the burn rates.

Burn rate is an expression used to describe how quickly you use up resources and in particular cash, within the business and its departments.

I believe that as a leader, a Rainmaker, it's essential you know what the various 'burn rates' are within your entire business. If you work for a business as a manager or even if you aspire to become a manager, you should be aware of what your own department's burn rate is, so that you can help with developments and innovative ideas to increase revenue and reduce the burn rates.

This kind of attention and activity by a leader is or should be a given in your ideal business! Your ideal business should be the one you are working on or in right now and if it's not you need to consider a change, don't sell yourself short, invest in you and do what you're most passionate about, what you believe in the most. If more people did this, there would be more happiness, more productivity, better relationships and better results.

If you aspire to be a leader, manager and want to be noticed, having an intimate knowledge of burn rates is a great way of pinning your colours to the mast. If you're unsure how to go about gaining this information, probably the best way to find out is to talk to those who run the finances of the business; they will be able to calculate these important figures, if they have not already done so. If you're the boss and your finance team doesn't know the answer to this, you might want to make them aware of the value of that exercise. If you do it yourself then invest the time to make the calculations. It will pay you to do so.

Think of it as a petrol tank—and every time you use any of your resources, you burn the fuel. You need to know how much has been used, just like you have a reasonable idea of how many miles you get to the gallon in your car and how full your tank is!

For example, do you know how much it costs your department or the business to have a meeting? Do you know how much it costs if you are late for a meeting? It's not difficult to do, but I tell you what, it really is an eye-opener, and you will soon see how much of the company's money you are responsible for burning. Imagine how this is compounded, if you keep others waiting too!

Imagine if you were 15 minutes late for a meeting with ten others and you all had meetings afterwards. Because you were late the entire meeting finishes late making all eleven of you late for the next meeting. How much money is being wasted? Now multiply that by the number of meetings you attend where people are late, wow!"

The way to create value is to know this and to use as little petrol as possible to achieve all of your targets or, if you prefer, get more miles out of each handful of cash your department spends.

This is something I have always been aware of. Well, to be accurate it's something I became aware of after I started my first ever business and was ignorant of the importance of such metrics. The result was predictable. I completely underestimated the amount of cash needed to start the business and underestimated the amount of time it would take to get the sales up to a level that would make the business self-sufficient. I also spent more time procrastinating rather than sitting in front of customers selling. If I had known my 'burn rates' I would have been able to predict the outcome and change the tactics accordingly to ensure the early success of the business.

I made that mistake and learnt the lesson and have never done that again. I have, however seen many other businesses make the same mistake and some of them, I am sad to say, were businesses that I was helping! That old saying still holds true, you can lead a horse to water, but you can't make it drink! It's always a frustration that people are often unwilling to take advice and learn from mistakes others have made. Preferring to make their own instead! A very costly trait! Save some time, save some money and save some face and learn from my howlers!

Stop bleeding money.

Is your business losing money? I'm not talking about running at a loss overall, although that too is or should be all the motivation you need not to waste your cash, I am referring to the amount of money most businesses bleed without even knowing it.

"We all know many businesses burn money on big things that are either not planned correctly or executed well. However, the real significant wastage goes largely unnoticed because it just drips out between the cracks!"

Most businesses are bleeding money and don't even know it! Cash may be slipping out between the cracks and not be noticed. A classic and common way in which money is lost is in the area of staff turnover. Another is the cost of getting new clients, as against keeping existing ones.

Think about the cost of bringing a new person to the business and then the investment in both time and money to train him or her to the standard required. It will cost any business significantly more to replace than it does to keep. Therefore, retention is a key element to financial success. This is without even considering the effect on staff morale, customer satisfaction and productivity, all of which use money and all of which are affected by the turnover of staff.

I would rather take time to hire the right person than to hire whoever turns up and then pay the price. I will share my thoughts on the right way to recruit later in the book under the title 'Step 5 The Right People Mean Business.'

Other areas in which you waste money are in the use or misuse of assets and not working them to full capacity all the time. Think about the person who is brought into the business to produce sales and now think about how much of his or her working day, week or month is spent in front of clients, which is where the money comes from. Every minute away from activity that involves the client is money leaking.

Okay, we all agree that they have to spend some time in preparation and administration, but I have seen advisers or salespeople who have spent less than one day a week with clients. Only spending 20% of your time with clients, when you are in, or need sales, is a criminal waste of time and money and yet most small businesses watch it happen and do nothing!

Another big area is that of rework, where work delegated is not done to the required standard and is therefore done again or reworked by another. So, you should consider all of these elements in the management of the business at all levels—and it should be the concern of everyone in the business, not just the bosses. Rainmakers can be found at every levels of business, just like making rain can be done by everyone.

If this is not the case, then you are employing people who just don't care, why would you do that? Quick, stop the bus and let them off!

Let's look at these common ways to bleed money in a little more detail and even look at some ways that might help plug those cracks.

The first is probably the most common, staff turnover. What this problem usually consists of is a number of people being hired over a short space of time and sometimes within weeks discovering that they were not what you expected or needed, or perhaps they make the decision as your business was not what they expected or wanted. On many occasions this is due to incorrect recruitment techniques. Although I cover this later it is worth a mention here, it's that important to your business success!

Here's what I think on the matter, the smarter you work on your team selection and the more support you render in the early months the greater your success in establishing and maintaining the right team to help you achieve the quest of exceptional and sustainable performance for you and your business.

I also believe the more layers you use in your selection the better your chances of success. This, as a strategy, is not for the faint hearted. I know from my own experience how frustrating it can be to see a multitude of people without finding the right person. I also know from my own experience the frustration of hiring in haste and wasting all that time and resource. With most things in business it is too easy to fall off the wagon, being lured by the promise of a quick win!

"Be tough in your selection. Don't just sell the position, don't get sold to. Take your time and test everything, ask or support from Rainmakers Club!"

The real key to this is to grasp the nettle and not be tempted by the quick win. The only exception to this is if you are head hunting an individual who has been known to you for some time and you know, I mean really know, they have what it takes, they have what you're looking for and there is a motivational and emotional connection to you and your business.

This idea of having many layers to the selection process has been proven, in my eyes, many times to be the smart way forward. Stop using recruitment as a two-way sales process where you sell the position and the candidate sells themselves. We all know a sale will result, but will the match be the right one or will you both regret it within weeks? My experience tells me that in majority of cases it will be the latter, if you fail to take your time and be really selective.

We need to employ a little common sense here and not have layers for the sake of it, they should all have a purpose and all help in finding that ideal person for your team but multiple layers to the process, in my view are necessity, rather than a nice to have. If you'd like more on this ask. We have a bunch of tools we can send you to help build a robust and successful process, ideal for the growing business about to take on staff or partners.

Work smarter, not just harder.

This is not something which is just the concern of those at the top of the business—it is a concern for everyone, or at least, should be! The best way to deal with this is to look at the jobs you do daily and make a list of those tasks which bring the greatest value to the business. Then, look at what gets in the way of you doing these valuable tasks? Where are the barriers to these tasks? How can you remove these barriers or at the very least reduce them to increase your progress?

Business today moves and develops very quickly, particularly in those businesses promoting innovative thinking throughout the enterprise. Guess what though, many businesses forget about the back-office systems and the workflow process and just add new stuff on top of the existing, without getting rid of the old obsolete systems that become redundant with the introduction of all the new systems and procedures.

This can create in extreme cases contribute to local or business-wide failure of new and old systems and complete confusion throughout your business. All staff should be encouraged to think about systems and processes, which are redundant, or perhaps nearing redundancy and all should be encouraged to think about how they can smarten things up. Smarter—and harder, creates success! Then, write it down with a calculation of what it will save the business; you could get help from the financial people in the business for this too, if needed.

In my early business life, I joined forces with three other financial advisers, this was a no brainer for us, we all shared similar visions and were individually on a journey toward the same end game. The industry was going through significant change and regulation was and still is increasing the burden on the smaller businesses in the independent sector.

We had all come from the same background and had the significant advantage of the infrastructure and support of major international life companies. Also, we all suffered from the same disadvantage of only having one provider's products for our clients. We all desired to gain the advantage of independence and the wider range of products. We all understood it would be easier to be successful if we banded together in mutual support as well as significantly reducing the fees and operating costs, one set of membership fees rather than four and one central compliance control mechanism.

We got things together, found office space, worked on the business plan and started to trade as an independent financial adviser. I soon became frustrated at the lack of technology in the independent sector. That is when I built my first database, this took time and was a leap of faith, but it gave us the edge and gave us more time in front of clients, which was smart!

I was eventually approached by a major software house in the sector and after some serious talks the software part of the business was sold to them. Part of the deal included me working with them for a while and that short stint with them introduced me to one of the best mentors I have met and got me noticed for my first CEO position in the US. Working smart and hard really does get you noticed and creates exceptional results!

Bring your mission to life.

Too many people in business, including many bosses, which is astounding, treat their company mission statement as something to put on a plaque on the wall and that it is just so much rhetoric. This sort of attitude and thinking creates a barrier to leadership in the business. The mission needs to be a living part of the enterprise and all should have buy-in. If they don't live the mission, then I'm afraid there is no place for them in the business in my view! Now that may sound harsh but trust me if your people don't have the buy-in you'll never bridge that gap between mediocre to exceptional.

Like the vision and values, your mission statement is part of the DNA of your business and should help you in making important business decisions. Buy-in is essential; belief in it is everything. Are you on the bus or off the bus? This particular bus should have all the seats taken by people who are overtly living the mission and values of the business!

All good businesses start, or should start, with a strong foundation and the foundation comes from a balanced combination of the ultimate vision of the business it's mission and those all-important values, your left and right boundaries beyond which you'll not venture in terms of behaviour.

"When you hire people, find out about their own personal vision and demonstrate how your corporate vision, if they work to it, will help them achieve their own. This is a sure way to gain complete buy-in!"

The way you use these elements, the DNA of your venture will have a direct effect on the development of your business and the success it experiences. Let me share with you one of the examples of the difference this can make from one of my recent projects.

I was heading up a business a few years back that had a great product and a reasonably good team too. The leadership was dynamic and ambitious. On the face of it the business had all the elements to make it as a top player in its marketplace. The problem was that the business, like a marathon runner, had hit the wall and was finding it difficult to make it to the next level. I was called into the business to lend a hand. This came from a recommendation from another business I had done some work for on a similar project.

I met with the board and we talked through all the issues they were facing while trying to get the business to the next level. It soon became apparent that the real issue was one that I have seen in businesses on many occasions. There was a disconnect between the strategy in place and the staff. We needed, I concluded, to work on the level of buy-in from the entire team and on getting them all onto the same page so that all were pulling together for the greater good of the business.

So together with the leadership team we embarked on a project to get the entire business onside with the strategies by getting their complete buy-in to their vision, mission and values.

My first step was to make sure I fully understood the vision for the business from the founders and their own personal vision too. Once I had this, I did the same with all the key staff. The reason for this part of the exercise was to ensure that we communicated the main vision in a way that each of the key people in the business could relate to because they could see how achieving that vision would in turn achieve their personal vision too. This first step required a slight rewording of the corporate vision, not a fundamental change just a change in the way it was communicated to make it more attractive to all.

With the original vision rewritten to be more understandable to the entire team the next step was to put together a presentation and workshop for a full staff meeting. This was designed to be fully interactive and educational giving value to all present.

"I believe in sharing the knowledge, educate your entire team on the true purpose and power of the Vision, Mission and Values of your business."

The presentation started with the 'top soldier' presenting to the staff the newly revised corporate vision and then straight into the objectives of the day. These objectives were to design a new mission statement and core values for the business going forward, explaining how important it was to the founders that the entire team were involved in the design and execution process.

The first exercise of the day was to ensure that everyone in the room fully understood the vision. That done, the team were given some time to write their own personal vision relating to their position in the business and in their own lives. With that exercise complete each person, in turn was given the opportunity to present their vision to the room. After each statement we were then able to demonstrate how this fitted in with the companies own corporate vision, so ensuring a closer connection between the team and the company.

The next phase was to educate the room on the purpose of the vision in real terms and why businesses that wanted to develop and progress to exceptional and sustainable results needed to have clear mission and values to guide them on the journey and the importance of the active involvement of everyone in the business.

Now that all in the room understood the real purpose of the vision, mission and values moreover understood what a good set of these corner stones looked like, by giving some high-profile examples we were able to begin the design process.

All in the room were asked to write down phrases and single words that they thought described the business and what it was all about. These were then distributed, and discussions encouraged to refine add, subtract and to gain a consensus on those words and phrases that best suited. From here we were able to come up with a simple and quite brief statement of intent that was to become the new mission statement for the business. Everyone in the business had contributed to its design and as such had far greater buy-in for the future.

The final step was to go through a similar exercise only this time it was to discuss those characteristics of the way we did business, the way we treated our own people, customers and the external community.

We discussed how we wanted to be viewed by the outside world. This of course was done in conjunction with the now accepted vision and mission in mind. The result was a set of core values that the entire team bought into and all agreed could, should and would be abided by in their day-to-day dealings both in and outside the business.

With further coaching on the subject from time to time and the inclusion of these vital components into the performance review process we ended up with a mission and values that really worked for the business and started to change the culture.

What is more important, within a few short months the business was through the wall and developing at speed towards its goal's. Last time I checked they were still going great guns and had a very happy and engaged team all pulling together for the common goal. Their mission had come to life!

The story does not end there. To keep the vision mission and values alive in the business we appointed a staff run committee to meet twice a year and review the core values and departmental missions, to then make recommendations to the senior management team on possible amendments, subtractions and additions to the values and code of conduct.

Don't be shy, invite feedback and value it.

Most people will shy away from external opinion, and many will even get incredibly defensive and feel the need to retaliate and often lose control at the same time! A point to make here is that a little controlled anger is not **always** a bad thing, but losing control is!

You should welcome opinion, as it gives you a chance to develop, improve and see how you are viewed by those around you.

So, what I am saying is, you should encourage opinion and give it freely. Receive it without getting defensive and without feeling uncomfortable, deliver it without taking cheap shots and encouraging negative or retaliatory moves from the recipient. Opinion should be viewed as an opportunity to develop by all, sadly this is not the case and therefore we need to learn how to react in the right way.

"The main reason people get prickly when receiving opinions about their work or ideas is usually due to a combination of the way it is delivered and their ego. Learn to control your ego and communicate with respect. Consider the feelings of the recipient."

This is one of those things that we all know and understand but equally we all fall off the wagon from time to time and react badly to what might be very constructive observations on how we might improve our performance and or personal brand.

The best way to give opinion is with sincerity and candour—and the best way to receive it is to maintain eye contact, so they know that you are listening, and then thank them for the feedback. Don't say I disagree, say thank you for pointing that out; I am going to think about it, and then do just that, think about it, and try to avoid the knee jerk reaction. Take a deep breath and see it for what it really is, an opportunity to develop or an opportunity to adapt your style for that particular person.

In my own case I have, at times, found it difficult to give and receive feedback from people I work with and know. On the other hand, when I have taken the time to give and receive honest and well-motivated feedback, I have always felt the benefit of the exercise, maybe not right away but once the ego was back under control and I was not feeling sensitive. With my ego under control the feedback always seems to work to my advantage. I guess part of that is because I am a firm believer that we never stop learning and through learning we become stronger and more effective.

I, like many others, do fall of the wagon and sometimes resist providing feedback because I am not willing to deal with the negative way the observations are received. Sometimes I avoid asking for feedback on my own performance because my ego takes over and the last thing, I want to hear are a few home truths! If you work at it though you can control the ego and see through the mist of anger to gain a constructive outcome.

Rewind the action of today & visualise the future.

It is good to review things in your mind, which have been said and done, after the event; it's something you should do every day; make it a habit. Review the decisions you have made and the conversations you have had and think about what you could have done or said which was different and learn about yourself and those around you.

I try to do this every day, usually just before I sleep. Replaying the highlights of the day to look for future improvements. I also like to visualise the day ahead or important events that will be taking place in the next few days. I certainly always use this technique when preparing for any of my speaking engagements and always did it when I was playing rugby.

Our minds are far more powerful tools than we give them credit for, and it is very true that we end up being what we think about. If you think about nothing other than failing all the time, you're more likely to fail than you are to succeed. There are so many examples of this in practise that we should all take it very seriously. If you spend your time thinking in a positive light about the future and the successes you're going to have, it will change the way you act and this in turn will attract positive outcomes and greater success will be just around the corner.

When I say I do this each day after I have finished work and constantly use the technique of visualisation to help me to improve my personal performance, you can take it from me that this is true. Not a single day goes by without me doing this and I can tell you first-hand that it really does work for me and countless other people including most topflight sports personalities.

You'll hear many professional sports people and teams talk about the power of visualisation before the race or big game, you'll also hear about as many who also play back the race or game in their minds after the event to try to improve their future performance by learning from mistakes during the game.

In business I have learnt the power of visualisation, I wish I had maintained the habit throughout my entire business career. The sad fact is that after leaving the Army I did let that slip for a year or two, I really did see the difference once I started it again a few years later and now it's a constant part of my daily ritual.

At the end of my business day I will sit somewhere quiet and contemplate the day I have just had and replay all the important parts of the day to review my performance and the results and how I could have done better. Each meeting each decision taken will be reviewed, constantly looking for mistakes, lessons and improvements.

For me this is a great way of keeping my ego in check and making sure I never start to take myself too seriously, for in those thoughts lies certain corruption and failure. I have let my ego get the better of me far too many times in the past.

The other side of this hugely valuable habit is my constant visualisation before the event. I really do get great benefits from doing this and not a day goes by without me going through the process of visualising the events of the future that I know are going to take place. This is an important part of my ritual of preparation for my business development, my meetings, presentations, and workshops and for that matter anything else I am getting involved in.

This method of visualisation and replay is in my view a vital planning tool. I would urge you to use these techniques as part of your daily routine too. Repeat the exercise a number of times and then take actions based on the outcome. In addition, don't underestimate the psychological affect this can have on you, your mental attitude and ability to adapt, think on your feet and remain positive. You'll begin to attract more positive outcomes for you and your business.

"Make visualisation and replay part of your daily routine. Use it for all your important meetings and presentations and use it to find ways to improve your performance."

Invest in yourself.

This really is a key factor in your future, I can't emphasis enough how important it is to invest some of your time in you; the greatest asset you have to contribute to your happiness and success! Invest in different ways and play to your own strengths when it comes to absorbing more or new information to help you on your journey, what I mean by this is use a multiple of different media to suit your preferences and lifestyle.

Personally, I use a combination of a couple of mentors with whom I meet online at **Rainmakers Club** and chat, read books interspersed with occasional face-to-face meetings. I do also from time to time use audio podcasts and listen to them while traveling, squeezing as much value from each minute of the day. There is no downtime during my normal working hours. To avoid burning out it is also important to get the work\life integration right. Something I have had problems with in the past and continues to be a constant challenge.

My advice to you is to take regular exercise, training and make coaching goals for yourself and review progress. Finding a person in or outside the business with the skills you are seeking is a great idea, ask that person to help you to develop those skills. Be willing to do the same for others, where you may have a skill they are seeking. This has the added benefit of building your reputation and the quality of your business network of contacts.

As a rule of thumb, spend 80% of your training investment on the subjects you are weak in or don't know and only 20% on keeping up to date with subjects that are your strengths! Don't wait to be told by your mentor, adviser or coach, what skills you need—go out and get them yourself. Have fun doing it, though. Business and learning about essential business skills should be great fun, otherwise what's the point of all that effort?

I really do strongly advocate using mentors to assist in your personal development, however, take time to select the right ones for you. I think it's a good tactic to find people who have recently experienced what you're going through not those that may have the same experiences but from years ago. I say this because the best mentors will be those that have recent experience similar to yours and still remember vividly what it feels like to be where you are. They will also have up to date experience that you can take advantage of right now. I do not believe you can be a mentor just by reading a book. You have to have real life experience. This is where the Rainmakers Club comes into its own.

I also think it's better to have a range of opinion and possible solutions and so it's worth looking at alternate methods rather than just one, this will in time pay dividends and prepare you to be open to alternate options or, at the very least willing to consider them when choosing the best possible outcome for you, the business, your team.

"rainmkersclub.co.uk is a great platform for building your professional business contacts and giving and receiving the kind of mentoring and business intelligence I am talking about."

Tip 2: Three Sixty Communication.

What is true communication? That may seem to be a strange question to ask but I have my reasons. Communication is often misunderstood in the high-tech world we live in. Executives and other staff in many organisations make the mistake of thinking that the transportation of data from one electronic device to another is communication! They think that sending out a series of e-mails is a substitute for face-to-face human contact and dialogue. Trust me on this—it is not, relationships will soon die if all there is to show for it is email contact. People still want to do business with people, that is why social media is so successful it is using new technologies but also has that all important human touch.

Important messages should be sent to the recipient in several ways, and the message should be repeated to be effective. If the message is important, it should not be left to just e-mail, which has its place and is woven into the fabric of all our lives along with mobile technology.

"Use Social Media platforms to maintain the human element when using technology to communicate and build relationships. It will take more than email!"

Many businesses could significantly improve their communication by using a combination of the most up to date technology and the good old-fashioned face-to-face interaction. if you have doubt about this let me give you something to think about. Assuming you're like me and are a bit of a gadget freak would you consider buying a new gadget that did this?

New B2B Communication Technology, a necessity for all businesses:

- *Unlimited connections.*
- *Get instant responses, no delays.*
- *Full audio-visual and touch capabilities.*
- *Mood interpretation.*
- *Full physical contact stimulation.*
- *No batteries.*
- *No wires or carry case to worry about.*
- *Unlimited usage.*
- *No billing.*
- *Fully programmable.*

- *Unlimited memory.*
- *Multiple covers available.*

Sounds good! Of course, we are talking about the most sophisticated technology on the planet, people! Great communication in business is a combination of the old and the new. It is possible to build and maintain relationships using a range of electronic gadgets but that only works if there is an existing relationship with emphasis on the human elements of personality, compassion and curiosity. These can be achieved both face to face and through well thought out social media strategies.

Communication is, or should be, a two-way thing and is as much about receiving as it is transmitting the message, you can't really experience active listening when the communication is all electronic. That is why I say great communication is a mixture of new media techniques and the good old fashioned but effective face-to-face talking. I think this is why people who join the various B2B online networks and platforms organise physical events with their local connections.

Good communication is also about understanding the impact you're having on others, when you are communicating. It is all about human interaction and, as such, is a very complex thing prone to misunderstandings and conflict, if not done well. The easiest way to create sure misunderstanding is to communicate only by using email, text or other electronic means. I have experienced this myself on many occasions.

It is all too easy for the person receiving that text or email to get the wrong end of the stick for a variety of reasons, for example; they can't hear the inflection of your voice, they can't see the expression on your face or the tone of your voice, they can't witness your body language and so they fill in the gaps. When we do this, we can be influenced to fill them in with significant bias, based on how we are feeling at the time we read the message. That is why we started using shorthand in our electronic communications, such as emoticons to place emphasis on the mood or intention of the communication.

My personal preference, when it comes to communication is to use more than one method to get the message across and the more important the message the greater the need to find more than one way to transmit it to the people who need to hear it.

Communication—the rhythm of business.

You may read about how a business can suffer because of too many meetings and that you should avoid holding meetings, where possible. I do agree with that point of view, but it is a balance and there is, for sure, a need for regular meetings in departments and other units within a business, any business! These meetings should be used to ensure that the message is getting around the business and that these vital communications are getting the right reaction throughout the enterprise. Frequent meetings should be held with clear objectives, they should be used to maintain the rhythm of the business.

Concentrate on never having a meeting just for the sake of it, each meeting should have an agenda, all present at the meeting should have sight of the agenda before the event so that they can prepare. Each meeting should finish on time with positive and defined outcomes.

I remember when I acquired a telecoms business a few years back we had quite a large management team and there was a need for regular meetings. The business was in quite an early stage of its development and the economy was suffering from a downturn that was affecting people's confidence. With that environment marketing, to generate leads, was at the forefront of everyone's minds and of course the conversion of those leads into sales.

I was quite passive, relating to the administration of the meetings for the first few I attended, as the new boss I didn't want to come on too strong too early. I was less passive with the actual content and like many new CEO's I was keen to set the right tone for the business very quickly, without upsetting the existing team too much.

Although the meetings were needed, they were far from efficient and so I stepped in and introduced a new procedure for all future meetings. The changes I made were simple and effective and from the date of implementation you could see the difference. Each person had a much more effective contribution to the meeting and improved results soon followed.

"Making sure that everyone attending the meeting has enough information to prepare for their contribution will save time and make for a more focused and responsive meeting."

All it took was to get each person to write a short review of what they were doing with observations and agenda items including supporting information. These were then collated centrally and redistributed so that each participant could see the full picture and prepare for the meeting. This simple act contributed to the rhythm of the business and significantly improved communication and the all-round performance of the group, bridging the gap from average to exceptional.

Is it important? Then say it twice, with feeling!

When you want to communicate, make sure that you do it with feeling and say it more than once. We suggest that, for key communications, you should use various methods and get in the habit of cascading the message too. So, for example, tell them in a meeting, then send them an e-mail to confirm; then, cascade the message through their immediate manager. If it's important, say it twice with feeling. Passion—remember, it's catching and that is what you want, a message delivered more than once with passion will be remembered more than any other!

"Say it with passion. Your passion is infectious. Then visit the trenches to deliver the message directly to your community and or team!"

I can't put enough emphasis on the importance of showing physical passion and belief in your communications to your people. You see, people listen to your communication with more than their ears; they also absorb information from their other senses. If you don't use physical communication as well as doing it using electronic devises, they will simply replace the other elements they could be observing or hearing with their own feelings at the time of receiving the communication and therefore you lose some control over how the message is interpreted.

I can remember when I was in the Army and heading up a group of men, it was always important to me and to the team, that I went and visited each two man trench with my message, even though I had already spoken to the section commanders with the same message. That way they would hear it twice, plus they would understand both how important the message was and evidence that I cared because I had taken the time to see them individually. I always thought visiting the trenches was a very important part of my leadership. I took this technique into business with me and have always made the effort to find the time to visit the team individually at their version of the trench (usually the workstation).

A word of warning though, if I gave the message to my section commanders and then visited the trenches with the same message word for word, I would achieve my aim of getting the message out there but at the same time I am running the risk of undermining the authority given to the section commander. So, there is a right way to do this to enhance the relationship rather than make it worse. I would simply ensure the section commander was approached first and permission gained, I would then top and tail the same message with my own personality and knowledge of the individuals being visited.

The visit to the trenches was then executed as a hearts and minds exercise with each individual and at the end of the brief conversation just a test to their understanding of the key message I wanted to emphasise. Done well and done with care this method works perfectly and I continue to use it today in all the businesses I meet, it's still as effective today as it was all those years ago in the Army.

It wasn't just me that did it and I was merely copying the actions that I had witnessed myself on my journey through the ranks. I remember the first time I saw the technique employed by my own section commander and great friend George Thomas, I guess he was my first ever mentor, many of the lessons he taught me I still use to this day.

In one of my businesses I had about 35 staff working from my office and a further 400 self-employed sales advisers across the UK and USA I made it a point each day to visit all the 35 just to connect to them and let them know how important they were to the overall success, giving them key messages that were delivered to and by their managers too.

I made sure that each manager was aware of these actions and happy for me to continue. Not only did this make sure the messages were passed on but also that they were given the right level of importance and urgency, it did much to maintain the morale of the team overall as well as maintaining relationships with me that in turn created more performance. I would also try to get to see all the advisers at least twice a year at national conferences.

Employ active listening.

Active listening means making sure that the person talking knows, without doubt, that you are listening, I mean really listening. How? That's simple, look at them, while they are talking; maintain eye contact; show them that you are interested. Think like a business-owner or a CEO and that means, when listening—ask questions to learn more. Learning more is good and saying that you don't understand or need more information is a good thing and should be encouraged. Ask questions to ensure that you have the meaning right and to illustrate that they really do have your attention.

"You can show active listening on Social Media sites too, by contributing to the content and asking the authors and commentators questions. You can also use emoticons and symbols to reflect your mood. This done well will get you noticed and build your network of valued connections."

These are all very important aspects of listening. Also try this and see how much it improves your communication and get others to do it too. If you're giving information to a member of your team or if you're receiving information from a member of your team, when the information has been passed you should, as the communicator ask yourself if you've given the recipient enough information to carry out the task and deliver the result you're looking for. As the recipient you need to be asking yourself if you've been given enough information to carry out the task. If the answer is no, you simply need to give more information or ask for more information. It really is that simple and can make a significant difference to the results the business generates.

Listen to yourself too!

You need to know what you are saying; this is as important as knowing what others are saying. You must never be on autopilot—it will stand out a mile and you will consequently lose the support of those around you. It is vital that you sound, and indeed are, sincere in what you are saying, making it real, passionate and interesting; then, your message will be heard and acted on.

This is never truer than when you are involved in group presentations. Never underestimate the importance of thinking before you talk. As my father always used to tell me when I was a child: "engage brain before opening mouth!" Great advice albeit advice as a young teenager I didn't heed or fully understand the importance of. I do now! Pausing before you answer is good for two reasons. It lets the other people know you are a thoughtful person and gives you a chance to construct the best possible response.

Consider the impact you have.

Another vital component of communication is to understand that what you say will and does have an impact on the people you are talking to. What you need to know is, regardless of the message, that your attitude and mood will be transmitted in not just your words and your voice, but also in those subconscious signals which you send out.

"Everything you say and do has an impact on others, calculate the impact before you say anything"

Be positive and sincere and, above all, be passionate in all that you say. Regardless of the message, show passion and sincerity and always be aware of your mood and ensure that it is appropriate—then, you will find that your message will travel far more efficiently and, what is more; your reputation will grow too.

Fight selectively.

If you get involved in every fight going and always have something to say on every issue, you will give completely the wrong impression. Far better to pick your fights carefully and, in this way, when you do decide to go into battle, people around you will think, you must really believe in this and will rally around such an important cause; this is as opposed to thinking, oh, it's him or her again, causing more trouble. You will be no more than just a background noise and a centre of ridicule if you're picking fights all the time. Most important of all, it is vital to be aware of relationships, particularly the long-standing ones. Ensure that you argue your case professionally and with consideration, never taking the 'no prisoners' approach.

I can remember a time in business when I was working with a person who did just this. There was always something to fight about; there was always an issue that she wanted to have a fight about. Her reaction and passion for the beliefs she had become no more than white noise to those around her. The sad thing is that on one occasion that I can remember she was right to stand up and fight for something but sadly nobody listened because the attitude was; oh, it's her again waving her latest protest banner!

Avoid the surprise.

Encourage a culture where people openly communicate when things don't go to plan. Don't be the last to hear about issues. Get your team to have the confidence to talk to you. If something is not working out or if they have made an error, then they should say it loud and say it first. You want to discourage the practiced of keeping quite so that you ned up finding out too late or find out from someone else; this will damage the culprits reputation and your relationship far more than if they come to you direct, telling you they think there is a problem or that they have made an error! Ensure that your team understands that you expect the same from all of them, all of the time.

When I first started out, I had a few confidence issues and like most of us I still do from time to time. When I was working for the Bank, despite my success with sales, I did make a few errors now and again. Because my confidence was still a little on the low side, I was very nervous about admitting to the occasional mistake. When they happened, they always got found out and I would face the consequences. After the event I always felt some relief that it was out in the open and dealt with.

Later I was to discover that I would feel even better if when errors were made, I communicated them first. What surprised me though were the other benefits I gained by doing this. My boss seemed to be more understanding and actually thanked me for the heads up. I also gained coaching to avoid repeating the mistake. The lesson was learnt, if you make a mistake, don't let people find out from anyone but you and you'll gain respect and support.

"Mistakes are good because they give you the chance to learn. Show me someone who makes no mistakes and I will show you a person who isn't doing enough!"

Later, when I started my own businesses, I found the value in sharing some of your mistakes with your team. Showing your human side and some vulnerability is a good thing. I saw the same benefits as the boss in communicating mistakes, more respect and tips on how to improve my own performance. For me this was easy because as I always try to surround myself with people that are better than me at all those day-to-day tasks, so I am always learning.

The power of thank you!

Don't be insincere, if you're going to say thanks then mean it. When something goes well, send thank you notes; if you get a referral or someone agrees to a meeting, send a thank you note; for me, it is far better to do this with a handwritten note and so much more personal. At the very least, top and tail the note with a handwritten salutation and sign off. You will find that this one gesture will go far. When doing it by electronic means use informal but easy to read fonts, make it personal.

Money is an important driver in our lives, and everyone wants to earn a good wage for the effort they put in and get other rewards too that will give them a feeling of wellbeing.

I used to run 360-degree review process for my head office team and the messages I got from those being reviewed on a consistent basis was the value they placed on knowing that they were valued and that they were doing a great job for the business. That in itself is not that surprising. What is more interesting is the importance to them of the simple act of verbal recognition for a job well done. Even the coolest person will melt when confronted with a warm well-timed and sincere thank you.

When you reward with your thank you, do it with consideration and do not use it as a tool to put others under pressure. For example, in my sales team they were all working hard and trying to get the results. One person was doing a fantastic job and I decided a public vote of thanks was needed. I singled them out for their thanks but also gave full recognition to the entire team. Later I would take aside the person or persons (individually) who were not doing quite so well and have a motivational coaching talk and a pat on the back for their continued efforts. Actions like this make a significant difference to performance and show good leadership skills too.

Always answer your mail and calls quickly.

If you get a message and you are not going to deal with it yourself, ensure that you let callers know, by telling them in a message or (if you can't talk to them) by e-mail. Say thanks, tell them that your colleague will be getting back to them and will deal with the query.

If you are not going to be in the office, make sure that your voice mail message is accurate and that you have a means of reviewing. If you are unable to respond in person, send e-mail. Try not to wait for more than 24 hours to respond.

I think the key is to remember your business is all about people and not just the people that are your customers, they are not the only ones that are going to talk about you, your business and affect your reputation and in turn your sales. So, make sure you treat everyone you meet in any medium, with the right levels of respect. Remember the old saying; treat people the way you would want to be treated!

Don't just share the good stuff.

Too many managers and business leaders concentrate on telling their team only the positive things that are going on. While this is a good thing to share and creates a positive attitude throughout the business, people are not stupid. If things are not working to plan, they will get wind of it.

This being the case, not telling them what they may already suspect does nothing to help you and can damage not only your reputation but also any trust, which you may have built.

"When you're honest with your team and tell them the bad news too. You will be amazed at the extra effort they will put into their jobs to help resolve the issues—keeping them in dark will only serve to undermine your relationship with the team."

People love to hear the good news, and it will act to inspire them and create corporate pride. However, they will not take kindly to being left out of the loop when things are not so good. Tell them and they may not feel so positive, but they will certainly risc to the challenge and you will see thcir trust in you grow. Integrity is key; value your people, as they are the greatest expense when they don't feel like you are telling them everything and keeping them in the dark. Show them you trust them and that they are part of the team by keeping them in the loop! If you really feel this is something you can't do, then perhaps you have got the wrong person or people on the bus with you; or maybe, just maybe your ego is getting a bit too big for its boots!

Make yours the no-spin zone.

Cut to the chase; don't say in 30 minutes what could be said in 30 seconds; get to the point and say it loud and clear. Don't ask the people to whom you are talking to interpret what it is you are asking of them. Just ask—keep it brief and accurate. The higher up the food chain you go, the more important this practise becomes.

"The rule always was and always will be, keep it simple. The only reason to make it complicated is to confuse or to demonstrate a higher level of knowledge. The first you should never do and the second is just a question of ego!"

As with many things in this life, the skill of direct and respectful communication is a bit of a balancing act, so while it is important to get to the point it is equally important to leave nothing unsaid that needs to be said, for the right reasons. When you are communicating try to balance brevity with no spin and respect.

Spin has its place, mainly with those that want to hide the truth and those in politics! Some would say these are the same! You will find however that those in business that tend to gain the most respect are those who keep it short, keep it sweet and leave nothing to chance by saying all that needs to be said. Work on gaining the reputation of a person who says exactly what needs to be said but treats all with respect and empathy.

What does your team think?

Ask your team what they think about the things you are working on, particularly the new ideas and projects. Don't leave them out. Make sure they are involved. They will have an interesting viewpoint and will see things from angles you may not have considered. It's worth the effort and helps to build the strength of the team and individual self-worth.

As a business leader one of the things you should be concentrating on is decision making based on a range of possible solutions, with a range of possible futures. One of the ways you can do this is by seeking opinion and alternate views. Here are just a few of the times you should include their views:

- Identification of new opportunities.

- New policies or the review of existing policies.

- New technologies.
- Development and training.
- Cuts and expansions.

Be open-minded.

This is so easy to say and so difficult to achieve, when lurking in us all is our nemesis, our ego! However, if you remain open-minded to other people's point of view, you may learn something. So, next time you are in discussions or just general conversation and a person has a different viewpoint, try to avoid saying that you disagree which, to them, implies that they are wrong.

Instead, say: "I see what you are saying, but I see it slightly differently." This allows you to have your say moreover does not offend; you never can tell—they may be right and, if they are, your new approach will not leave you with egg on your face. The ability to be open-minded is a vital trait in leadership, but it's not good enough just to say the words, you have to live them too. Many a great opportunity can and will be lost with a mind that is closed to other people's opinions, ideas and knowledge.

Be the King or Queen of feedback.

Make giving your opinion to others commonplace to your business routine. It's not so difficult to do, and the rewards are great. Be warned, though, not all people can take the opinions of others and some will let their ego get in the way. For those who fit into this category, don't be too concerned; their days are numbered, as there is no place for outsize ego in business, not in the long-term! I learnt this to my cost a few years ago when I started to show the signs of letting the power I had corrupt my personal values. I paid a heavy price for this and trust me it took much time to get back on track!

Opinion is a great way to let your colleagues know what it is you are seeking, but it has to be delivered well and with empathy. Always begin and end with the positive, this will keep the players onside. Make sure that you welcome opinion and that you give it regularly.

"Power can corrupt. Make sure you keep control of your ego and bring your team into the loop to ensure you gain a full range of possible solutions and maintain full buy-in."

You might even want to have a set time during the week (maybe at an end of the week-review meeting) when feedback is given, so that it becomes an accepted business routine.

When giving opinion, try to give some coaching points with the opinion, so that the recipient has an idea of what actions they may need to take; this can turn the feedback, even when negative, into a positive experience.

"Create the expectation that feedback will be sought and given. Create and promote the trait of positive reaction to all opinions!"

Let the people know that you are happy to receive feedback and, when you do get it, make sure that you listen and think about what you need to do to improve. Thank them and then let them see the actions you take as a result of their opinion. Try to create, within the business, the expectation that opinion will be given. You could even make it a habit, by making it a regular occurrence. There are great motivational qualities in giving opinion and then seeing it makes a difference, with people really developing as a result of your contribution and the contribution of others.

Have difficult conversations.

Too many people in business and in their private life avoid having difficult conversations, preferring instead to ignore the issues and, in some cases, causing more issues by not talking than if they were to face it head on. This is as true in private life as well as in business.

In leadership, this can be devastating to the entire business, as the leader can lose, through inaction, all credibility and staff loyalty. Leaders are expected to have difficult conversations and to make tough decisions, rather than seek popularity.

"As a leader you will earn more respect and popularity by doing the right thing and having those difficult conversations than you will by trying to be a friend to everyone!"

If you never hide behind others, you take the responsibility, remember that regardless of how difficult the conversation may be and how sensitive the content, respect those to whom you are talking and keep calm. Speak with integrity and, where appropriate, with passion and sincerity you will win respect and the reputation of being a good leader and listener.

As a leader your role is not to gain popularity by making friends with as many people as possible it is to gain the respect through good decision-making. I remember learning this lesson quite early on in my career in business. One of my original managers was very popular with many members of the sales team and would often take members of the team out for drinks and even meet with them at weekends.

The lesson was learnt when things started to get a bit tough in the market and in turn the pressure was passed onto the sales teams. As the difficulties continued this manager continued to maintain his close personal relationships with many of the team. Some members of the team that he was friendly with were not fairing so well and their performance was slipping. Extra training and coaching was given to them and the rest of the team and it was clear they would not make minimum target.

The situation got worse when rather than make the right, albeit hard, decision to reduce team numbers as it was clear improvement was not going to happen and the lack of performance was affecting the bonuses for the entire team, the manager failed to act. He was trying to protect his friendships over doing his job.

It wasn't long before the team, all the team, even those who he spent time with were talking about him behind closed doors, saying that he was letting them down. In a few short weeks he lost their respect and the team started to fragment.

All he had to do from the start was concentrate on being a good leader not a friend. It is quite possible the team would have still been performing to target during the difficult times and in any event the team would have been stronger as a result of his correct leadership and ability to have tough but fair conversations and make those sometimes-difficult decisions.

Candour has value.

Candour is one of the rarest of qualities in business and in life. It is so rare that it is highly valued. The art of speaking your mind and being honest, without hurting, is not easy, but is one of the traits, which will define the difference between good and exceptional people—and not least true natural leaders.

If I could change one thing about people generally, it would be to give them the ability to use candour every day and to be able to accept the views of others, without offense. It's worth noting that the biggest enemy of candour, in both its delivery and receipt, is ego. Trust me on this; there is no room for ego, leave it outside. Instead develop the reputation of being someone who will give an honest answer, with respect.

Start the process by thinking before you speak, as I said earlier, and find ways of saying what you want to say without having to revert to cheap shots or offensive language. Earlier I suggested it was a good idea to calculate the impact of what you are saying; that is a real art and one that needs to be practised. When you have that skill pegged you could even think further and start to assess how what you say may ripple to reach others like the ripples when you throw a stone into a pond.

Hostile environments and change require more communication not less.

When in what might appear to be a hostile situation, do not let your imagination take control; ensure that you are actively employing more communication, not less, jumping to conclusions can change what could still be a positive outcome. The key is to not let your imagination run away with itself. Think things through make sensible assessments and seek evidence to support your assessment.

When you let your imagination take control and interpret circumstances it is all too easy to come up with the wrong interpretation and therefore solution. So, take a breath look at the facts and make an informed decision. Let me give you an anecdotal example of how the imagination can throw us a curve ball:

Imagine that you had to work late, it's dark and the streets are all but empty. You have to walk down a lonely back street to get to your car, and the streetlights are not working. The situation reminds you of an article you read in the local press about an assault and mugging that took place not too far from where you are right now.

You are a little nervous, and your imagination starts to work overtime! Then, it happens, you hear footsteps behind you, and your concern increases; you speed up, in an attempt to get to your car quickly. As your pace increases, so, too, do the steps behind you.

You now feel under direct threat, and your imagination starts to paint pictures of mugging and worse. Your pace quickens, again, and you increase your grip on your papers and brief case and hope that you can get to the car in time.

You dig deep into your pocket to retrieve your keys to save time. Your worst nightmare happens; the pace of the assailant has just increased and now you fear the worst—what to do, flee or fight? Should you break into a run and risk escalating the chase or do you turn and face the threat and risk a full-on confrontation?

Then, it's too late, while you were fumbling for your keys you feel the person right behind you and there is no option but to prepare for the worst! You half turn, but (before you have had a chance to complete the turn) you hear your colleague's voice saying: "I thought I was the only person left in the office, can I give you a lift or do you have your car here today?" The moment has passed—and the fear of not knowing which had taken over your brain and had created a whole new reality for you, based on fear and suspicion has gone! A simple act of communication and all is well again.

This happens all the time in business, maybe not quite as dramatic as that; the fear or uncertainty of the unknown, the new boss, the new initiative—without the full story, you create an alternative situation which gets a life of its own.

If the environment is hostile, things are changing—which, to survive, they have to. More communication is the key, not less. Say it, and say it more than once, using more than one medium to get the message across. The more important the message, the more you should communicate it. Remember, communication is not just for good news!

I am not saying ignore your gut instincts, I value those instincts in myself highly and they are often proved to be correct. Just control the feelings, build a plan of action and gather evidence rather than letting your imagination run riot.

Express anger constructively.

We all experience anger, from time-to-time, in our business and personal life. The secret is to be constructive in the expression of such anger and not to lose control. Losing control will give you a feeling of temporary power, but that is about all. The damage it does is far more wide-ranging than a simple short-lived feeling of power. Add to that the effect which it has on your standing; you will see that you lose a good reputation and, worse still, those around you may start to see you as a tyrannical leader!

"Express your anger but do it with control and do it constructively to get positive results!"

People never respond to intimidation, so stay focused on expressing your frustration in a constructive manner, which promotes better performance from the people with whom you work. Isolate the core issues and then start constructive dialogue.

The thing to remember is that an angry outburst will make those around you take a defensive stance. Constructively expressing your concerns lets others stay open to learning and improvement.

Resist dependency on the opinion of others.

The office is (and should be) a competitive environment, focused on getting the right results. When you are sick, you might take your temperature to confirm your illness, but if you take it every five minutes, people will say that you are overreacting. In the office, avoid checking with others every five minutes for approval; take responsibility and work independently, but alongside and in conjunction with the team.

Share key decisions with your team throughout the process in short e-mails which highlight the information required. If you are managing high-stake projects and you need assistance or guidance, in those circumstances it is a good idea to talk to your team, but don't become dependent on them for every decision made.

Tip 3: Know how to deliver results.

Getting results is about knowing what you need to achieve and then doing it in the most effective way possible—always within the values of the business and your own personal values, which should be in line with the business, or you could well be on the wrong bus!

Don't throw spaghetti against the wall.

If you want to check to see whether your spaghetti is cooked, throw it at the wall—well, that's what my mum told me. The trouble is if it is not cooked, you can lose your spaghetti and, in any event, it is quite a wasteful way to judge, I'm guessing she didn't mean the whole pan!

This is not the approach, which should be used in business, as it proves far too costly. Make sure that you test everything before you commit to spending your cash!

Get the discipline of planning and preparation. Have a method for judging success and monitoring your progress. Use the items on the list below, to help you avoid waste:

- Understand the objectives.
- Create a way of reporting success measures.
- Understand the people resources you have available.
- Research the relevant facts.

- Make sure communication lines are open.
- Write a plan.
- Have a schedule.
- Hold a planning meeting.

This will make life so much easier and will give you a much better chance of success, when working on projects for the business.

Data does not equal knowledge.

Now more than ever before, we are bombarded with data which is often mistaken for knowledge. The true value of data is understanding that only a small percentage has value to you—and then only after it has been converted from what we call raw data to valuable information, through a process of collation and dissemination.

"Data is not knowledge; it is the raw material which should then be refined into knowledge!"

Before sharing data, you should ask a few questions:

- How will the data be used?
- What is relevant?
- What's new about it?
- How much do we really need it?

- How much do we really need it?

You also need to think about the best way to format the data and highlight it, so that the significance is clear to those using it?

Our development and the development of the businesses that we are connected to are reliant upon data that we collate and use correctly. The reason I include a little on data is because I firmly believe the majority of people in business either don't bother to collate data that is relevant to their success or in some ways worse still go through the motions of collecting the data but then don't bother to use it correctly or worse still not at all!

Those businesses that we look at and would call exceptional, those people we look at and would call exceptional all have one thing in common. It's the amount of effort they put into the journey they're on and their attention to what might first appear to be minor details. Data is often seen as one of those minor details that suffer when time or money is short.

My advice where this is concerned is to make the effort to really understand what data you need and then collate and use it. Examples would be the data relating to performance. If you don't regularly collect metrics on the performance of your business, then you should start today. If you don't regularly collect data relating to your competition, then you need to start today. Start-collecting data on what is going on in your market and parallel markets too. Once you start, you'll quickly experience the benefits.

Accountability begins at the beginning.

People cannot be held accountable after the event, unless they know from the start what the expectation is and what they are required to do! So, provide clear expectations before the work is started, so that they know (from the very start) that they are accountable, for and what your expectations are.

This will then encourage them to take responsibility and be accountable. It will also make them think more seriously about the task in hand and, if things are not working to plan, they will be more likely to resolve problems and ask for help, when needed.

If you are responsible for a task and are going to be held accountable you need to make sure you are at the centre of the journey, even if the execution of the task is done by someone else. As a CEO you learn this very early. I cannot emphasis enough the importance of this point.

"Delegation is a powerful tool in business. Just because you have delegated it does not mean you wash your hands of it, stay in the loop but do not micromanage every detail, let your people perform!"

Delegation does not absolve you of the responsibility of the task you were given. This is another reason why data is so important in the execution of your duties. With the right data at the right time being used correctly you can second-guess what is going to happen and react promptly, which in some cases can save significant cash and even careers!

Be realistic.

When you are working on an assignment, ask yourself if you have given enough information on what the goals are and how success will be measured. Then, bring together the people who will be involved in the process and ensure they not only have, but understand the information. Work together to determine how the task will be carried out, detail specific tasks and milestones so that the entire team understands exactly what is required and are able to deliver.

Agree on start and finish dates and other items such as people, technology and space. Make sure that the right skills are at your disposal and that the right people are doing the right job. Be creative and be aggressive. If the task does not seem possible, in some way, though, for example time lines—be realistic and go back to the original plan give a well organised account of why and always look for alternative tactics and a range of possible solutions to offer the team as a way forward that will work for them.

Let your people perform.

In most cases, people will push themselves harder than they will let others push them. So, give your team the information required to determine how they will contribute and then let them do it. It is an error which many managers make; they manage too much and lead too little—don't do it, be a leader. Let your people perform and coach them when they need it, promote a coaching culture throughout the business!

"Don't manage them too much, lead them instead, coach don't manage, it will create more value in the long run."

This is an issue with many business leaders just starting out in their business career, it's a combination of power drunk ego and a lack of confidence that leads to the boss who starts to believe that they are the only person who can do the job well. You need to let go and let the people around you perform. Give them the space to try things, make mistakes from time to time, and learn from those mistakes, making them a much better person for any business going forward.

If you know they are simply not capable rather than it being you not able to let go, then I suggest you still have the responsibility. After all, why would you hire a person who was not capable of doing the job? Your recruitment and training processes are key to the success of your business. Take your time and only hire exceptional people. Hire based on their passion and attitude, skills can be taught, the right attitude cannot! This is where search & selection businesses offer greater value than standard recruitment agencies.

Establish an agenda.

Too many times, I have witnessed meetings taking place without an agenda. A well-thought-out agenda can save time and increase the value of every meeting, but only if those attending are given notice, time to review the agenda and the scope to prepare.

"One of the greatest wastes of time and valuable resource is meetings for the sake of it. Any meeting that does not result in a positive action is simply burning your time and money."

Meetings without preparation are a waste of time and burn cash—don't do it! As a guide, the agenda should include standard items, such as:

- Start and end times.
- Purpose.
- Participants.
- Location.
- Order of items.
- Decisions to be made.
- Expectation (participants).
- Name and contact info of person chairing meeting.

I am finding it difficult not to break into one of my rants about meetings. I shall resist the temptation save to say that if you have a meeting with no outcome then all you are doing is burning time and money on a pointless exercise.

If you're not ready for the meeting then don't have it, if you're not ready to make a decision then there is no point in having the meeting at all. Only meet if you're ready for an outcome, only meet if you're going to act on the outcome!

Keep meetings focused.

The agenda will not only make it clear what the purpose is but also assist in keeping the meeting focused. However, it is obvious that the agenda alone will not keep the meeting on track, unless all participants keep to the agenda and have been given the opportunity to prepare for the meeting.

Too much valuable time is wasted with meetings, which are not organised correctly; this retards the ability of the participants to add value to the various subjects being discussed. It also lengthens the decision-making process, while preventing, in some cases, informed and well-thought-out alternatives and arguments from being aired.

Infuse meetings with energy.

Never, and that means never, enter a meeting with a negative attitude. Always ensure that you can be seen to be attentive and listening to all that is being said. Congratulate people for a job well done. When it's time to come up with ideas, give it your best and make sure that you contribute to the meeting, listen to others' ideas and never just shoot them down, but comment constructively and with candour. Never underestimate the power of a positive attitude, not just on others, but also on your own development and wellbeing.

Having the right attitude at all the meetings you hold, or attend will have a far reaching and positive affect on your career and the ultimate success of your team and business. When run well and then acted upon, meetings can be one of the greatest assets in the development of your business. Of course, the opposite is also true. Run badly with no decisions being made will simply frustrate and retard development for the individuals and the business.

"Your positive attitude not only brings energy to meetings but will elevate the mood of all those working in or on your business."

Go for the buy-in.

Getting buy-in requires more than just telling people what it is you want them to do! You also need to let them know what the outcome is going to be. If they have no idea what outcome you are seeking, you will also not gain the benefit from their contribution, which could be most valuable to the mission.

This process starts with you ensuring that you are talking to the right people and getting the right contributions and opinion. It is good practise to speak to them all individually and ensure that they all know what it is you're trying to accomplish, asking them all for feedback.

You can then potentially use their ideas to improve your plan. In some cases, you may even have to revisit your plan to incorporate the good ideas, which fit with the mission. If you trust their opinion, you can be in a position where you will have the very best plan and get the best results; that is what makes buy-in so important!

Overcome resistance to change.

Change is something, which is part of life and part of all businesses. It is essential that change take place in the business; otherwise, it gets left behind and begins to struggle to make its targets or even to make profit, we have seen some really high-profile examples of this over the last few years with some major brands falling foul of complacency and resistance to change.

This essential change has a natural enemy—and that's the human element. In every company, there will be those who will really rebel against any form of change and resist it with every fibre of their body. These people can create chaos and often do.

The reason for this is simply that they are afraid of the change and what it means to them. They do not want to be taken out of their comfort zone and will try anything to remain with the status quo.

If this is you, then don't think that you are alone! Change affects us all and we all go through the same feelings and process. Take time to understand what it is that makes you feel this way and do the best you can to see things from all angles. I have no doubt that, if you do this, you may find that the fear of change turns into excitement and vision for the future.

If you know a person like this in your business and you are involved in the management or implementation of change, then these next points may help you to help them and, in turn, your business.

- Recognise that the chaos maker's resistance to change can and does come from the misinformation used by the dissenters. You can remove this power by simply using frequent communication with the individuals and the entire team.

- Give them a voice and let them communicate but avoid letting them dominate the conversation. You must let them have their say and get their opinion across, to move on.

- Use information and any other supporting evidence, including, perhaps, any statistical information, to counter any of the baseless claims, which are made to discredit the change. The delivery of this type of supporting information will help to take away emotion and erase the fear, which they have of change.

- Always, and this means **always**, keep the entire team in the communication loop, so that they are not left outside with the chaos-makers and start to believe the rumours.

- Be aware that the naysayer may let slip work or targets and tasks, which form part of the change initiative, just to try to prove that the change strategy will not work. You must not let this happen—the best way to achieve this is to ensure that you make everyone accountable for his or her actions and performance, ensuring that this accountability is clear and obvious, before the tasks are undertaken. Don't make people accountable after the event.

- Spend as much time as you can on creating and communicating the mission and the positive vision for the future. You really cannot do this too much: the vision needs buy-in and needs to be constantly reinforced.

"Without change we would still be in the trees or living in a cave!"

Ok, I want to emphasise that these people are not bad people and we all, to a certain extent, get discomfort from change. They are not bad; they are just afraid, so remove the fear and let them see how they can benefit as a result of the change. This will let them rise to the occasion and build up their confidence for the future.

Don't under-deliver on promises.

Never over-promise and, just as important, do not under-deliver. Owing to the desire to offer too much and not being able to fulfil that obligation or promise, under-delivery is the most common result. Instead, be honest and offer only that which you know you can give.

Try making notes of what it is you are saying yes to and at least, then, you are not going to forget what it is you have promised. I would recommend having a list on your phone, tablet or at the back of your diary or notebook listing all the things which you have promised and then track them. Once you have done this, you must make time for yourself to do the tasks, which relate to the promises made. Employ time-management techniques, listing the tasks and then allocating a timeline and keeping to it. By doing this, you will be equipped to deliver on your promises. Later you may want to invest in technologies that help you to project manage.

If you don't deliver on the promise, your reputation will be damaged, with those affected unlikely to forget! Sadly, people always tend to remember the negative much longer then the positive!

"Some find it hard to say no and that can have a negative effect on everyone. Rather than being a positive this is negative. Learn how to say no when you need to and say yes when you can deliver or over deliver on the promise."

Behaviour speaks out loud and clear and has an impact.

You can gain great insight into people by observing the way they behave. Get into the habit in your daily dealings of considering two things. First, remember that people will be watching you and second, you can get a great indication about how people feel within the first moments of meeting or observing them. Always take time to consider how the person is acting and what affect that kind of behaviour may have on the business or your team.

Another thing to consider is that your mood and behaviour will have a huge effect on those around you. Fact—the higher up the leadership chain you go, the greater the impact it has. So, think about what affect your mood and behaviour will have on others around you and consider how you can improve.

Always use the actions, moods and behaviours of those around you as indicators of how they are going to act in any given situation in your business. Forewarned is forearmed.

Understand your budget.

Most people in business are required to work to a specified target or goal and, under most circumstances; this also requires them to use other resources of the company too. Giving them information that allows them to understand the budget they are working to, not just in cash, but other materials and resources, is a great way of getting them to understand the full effect of the actions they are going to have to take, as well as a more accurate means of monitoring their own performance against the true performance targets.

I think it is far more useful, exciting and interesting for your team to have a greater understanding of the full budget connected to what the business is doing, rather than just having a bland target, for example the number of sales you have to complete.

"The more you understand about the budget, the more life you can bring to the target you are working toward."

Not all bosses have thought of, or agree with, this way of expressing missions and targets for individuals and departments, but this has two very positive effects on the business overall. First, it gives you much more understanding of the business and a greater feel for what affect you have. Second, the process of doing this gives the boss a greater feel, as he will have to be more detailed in his understanding of the true cost of goods sold; this, in itself, is a very positive exercise for any business, which wishes to either establish or maintain exceptional and sustainable results.

Take time to understand financial reports relating to you.

Like understanding the full budget, I consider it a great idea for key people in a business, not just the directors and the financial team, to have a fundamental understanding of the financial reports produced by the company, I covered this earlier in the book but it is certainly worth mentioning again.

It would be so powerful, if all managers and department heads with responsibilities to direct reports knew how to read and understand the fundamentals of reports related to parts of the business in which they had responsibilities.

If you're not already doing this then ask either your financial people, or if you're a Rainmakers Club member, ask us for some coaching on what to look for and how to read or interpret figures for the business or at least your part of the business. If you have a financial team, they should be really happy to help you because if you are successful—they are too. It goes without saying, we will be very happy to help as it is our reason for being in business, to help you achieve exceptional and sustainable results.

Be aware of every penny as if it were your own cash.

Every penny, which leaves your business, is a penny, which is not going toward your salary, commission or bonus, so it makes sense to treat each penny, which leaves the building as if it were your own.

If you are in a sales role, think about how you can be the most efficient, regarding travel and incidental expenses. For example, booking meetings in geographic areas, which require logical travel, rather than being disorganised; employ time-management techniques.

There is, of course, the really obvious stuff, like turning your PC monitor or printer off; if you are the last to leave, turn off the lights, it all counts, every penny counts! Did you know if you leave a computer on standby when you leave the office it will be using the same amount of electric as if it were being used! Switch off, it's good for the environment and as I have said every penny counts.

Risks are OK, as long as they are managed.

The most effective way to achieve this is to maintain high levels of communication, to ensure that the project on which you're working is in line with expectations. You also need to be sure that the actions you're taking are within the budget and that you are aware of the point at which you should cut your losses and run. It is for this reason also that it is so important to ensure that you have good lines of all-round communication.

"A key skill to have in business is to know when to quit and mitigate the risk. Sometimes your ideas or projects just won't work so get out before they burn even more cash!"

If you are working on a project, which requires you to innovate, or even invent, or you are working on tactical or strategic issues relating to the business, take time to test the model and get others to test the assumptions, which you are making. This action will also act as a control for the risks you are taking. Taking risk is not the issues, what's important is the amount of effort you put into calculating the risk and mitigating it as far as is possible. Remember all business is risk.

Mistakes are OK, as long as you learn.

For me, the pet hate is seeing people in business who have never made a mistake! You show me a person who has not made a mistake and I will show you a person who has done nothing of note! The thing about business is that you do have to take risk and you do need to put your head above the parapet, from time to time. This means that you are going to make the odd mistake. Here is the message—mistakes are fine, as long as you take action and learn.

Here are some good pointers on what you can do to not only learn from your mistakes, but also handle errors in a professional manner:

- Control the situation and try to limit the damage caused.
- If the mistake is your responsibility, then own up.
- Communicate openly, if you have a boss make sure they hear it from you, rather than second-hand.
- When communicating, make sure you have some ideas for solutions to the problem.
- Make sure you talk to the people affected by the error and explain the actions you are going to take.
- Work out what needs to happen to ensure there is no repeat, for example:
- Identify what the true cause was—system or individual?
- Could it happen again; how can you avoid it?
- How can systems and process be improved to prevent a repeat?

- Is there a training need and will training help in the process of prevention for the future?

- Could communication be improved to help to prevent the same thing from happening again?

It is also really important to continue with the communication right the way through to the end, making sure that all involved know what has happened and the result too.

Be nice—it's more powerful than you think.

Too few people understand the power behind being nice; it will cost you nothing but will get you so far in your business and life. Make a point of noticing people and wishing them a good morning; when you leave the office, say goodbye.

When you pass people in the halls, say hello and smile at them, ask how they are, ask about the weekend, the family. Be sincere and take a real interest in what they have to say.

By doing this, you will create positive goodwill around yourself and this will always come in handy when things get tough. So, get the goodwill building up and bank it. I promise you that this is underrated and, if done with feeling and sincerity, will improve your well-being and position in the business.

"Open your goodwill account today and start saving; avoid the overdraft!"

Tip 4: Conduct yourself with integrity.

Consider yourself to be a brand and think about the message, you send to others. If your brand is not giving a consistent message or style. Start to ensure that you are consistent in your actions, your attitude, work, in all things act with integrity and a positive attitude. Make your brand a leader.

Self-confidence.

Self-confidence is so powerful and makes you more effective and more dynamic. It will help you to be open to new ideas and learning. The best way to develop your self-confidence, other than believing in yourself, is to start (and continue) acting in keeping with your own personal values and those of the business. Working to these will have a very positive effect on you and those around you.

Warning; if you work against your personal values, this will start to erode your positive attitude and confidence, so quite simply don't do it!

Respect yourself first.

Before you worry about others, you need to respect yourself—only then can you show respect to others and have a positive effect. If you don't respect yourself, how can you expect others to respect you?

Don't let people take you for granted and don't let them undermine you. Keep them in check but do it by being fair and polite. Don't lose your temper be firm, but friendly— try it, it works.

Now respect others.

If you show someone no respect and give that person a task to do, will he or she do a better job than if you showed respect and asked that person to do the same task? The answer is too obvious! However, take a look around at the number of managers and bosses in business, who show little or no respect to others. I know I mentioned ego before a few times but in most cases, it is out of control ego that causes this lack of respect. Rainmakers know how to control their ego.

"Managers and leaders who don't show respect to their teams and others they meet never last too long!"

Most people in business you talk to will know that it's obvious, but they just don't think. They are in the habit and there is nobody willing to tell them where they are going wrong, for fear of getting their head bitten off. Everyone starts out deserving respect. Next time you have to talk to someone, take a moment to ensure that you are about to do it with respect. Here are some things you can do to show respect:

- Be on time & be prepared.
- Listen actively and avoid interrupting.
- Avoid wasting other people's time—prepare first.
- Avoid being distracted when you are being spoken to.
- Always acknowledge people you know.
- Always acknowledge people you don't yet know.

Having respect is all about value. You need to value yourself and then others—value their views, their ideas and their time, you'll find they will start to do then same for you.

Ethics only.

We all believe, or want others to believe, that we are ethical. The fact is, though, that not all of us are. To ensure that you act to the highest possible standards, you need to understand that those around you will have an influence over you. If you surround yourself with the wrong type of people, they will erode your standards, if theirs are lower.

"Select those that influence you with great care."

If you are surrounded by people who engage in gossip, which is damaging and not ethical, you will be dragged down to that level too. So, remove yourself from harm's way and surround yourself with people who share your values. If you want to elevate your game, associate with those whom you look up to. Have great standards and stick to them, but do not become critical of others and do not become self-righteous.

Set a good example.

Telling people what to do and then not doing it yourself does not work. There is only one right way and that is to practise what you preach, so set a great example for others and stick to it. Your values and approach will be infectious, and your game raised, as will the game of those around you. Doing this will make you even more valuable to the business you work in or on!

Always be discreet.

Never get involved in office gossip and speculation about your colleagues and their private life. Gossip is destructive and should be avoided. Always avoid passing judgment on leadership and policies to others in your team.

If you are given information in confidence, at all costs make sure that it stays that way. Discretion is, and should be, highly valued in both private and business life. If you are approached by people who announce that they want to tell you something in confidence, you should make a judgment call and use your discretion. Do you want to hear what they have to say, or do you decline? Your decision should be based on their position and values. Don't listen for the sake of gossip. Just say: "I would rather not know thanks."

It's got to be more than a job!

It's all about value, and there are many people out there who just turn up and do a job. Make it your personal mission to create more value and inspire those around you to give their best too.

Avoid adopting the attitude that you have been with the job so long that nobody else could do it. Instead, concentrate on being the best you can be and always work on stretching yourself and going that extra mile. That action alone can create greater value for you and the business. Don't let complacency affect your performance; always look to improve your performance and your position.

"Challenge yourself, push and push, then push some more and watch your position improve!"

Tip 5: Take time to invest in your relationships.

It's a clear fact that success in business is based on the strength of your relationships, and so you should actively seek to invest in them, and improve them, at every opportunity. Not one person attains success on his or her own and so the only sure way to be a true success is to take time and make the effort to invest and build on your relationships. Choose your connections with great care.

Set up a 'network database.'

Salespeople do this, or they should do, and so should everyone else. Business is all about networking and surrounding yourself with the right people. The reality is regardless of your position, we all sell. Each time you talk to someone to ask for some kind of outcome that is a sale. Selling is influenced significantly by who you know and who knows you. With that in mind you should constantly be building your database of contacts. I would go further and say you should do this as a matter of good practise! Every business owner, entrepreneur and enterprising person in the land should be a salesperson if they are to fulfil their role well.

I have always maintained that if you show me a great business leader, I will show you a great salesperson who is always building their contacts. These are the most successful and you can clearly see this if you take some time to look around. Sales and selling at any level is not so much about process but about trust, friendship and creating an environment where people want to buy and these people will come from your contact database.

So, when you meet someone, record that person's details in your Smart Phone, Tablet, CRM or book and make notes. Share information build a rapport and work on building a relationship. We can't like all the people we meet; so, if you are not getting on, let them go, but maintain balance and respect all the time. Use social media to do this too, join **Rainmakers Club** and start connecting with new people to create new opportunities, new learning and new relationships.

Once you have this set up, make contact by any means and, for the more important contacts, make effort to set aside face-to-face time now and again. Use e-mail, use Social Media, use the phone, use handwritten notes and remember birthdays and other memorable dates.

What goes around comes around.

This is said often, and most often when things are not working so well—and the blame is on the shoulders of another. We have often heard the phrase 'what goes around comes around'!

It works the other way too and so when building your network, remember these pointers as they will help, particularly if your primary role is in sales, which as a business owner it probably should be it also applies to anyone in a leadership or management role!

- On your first meeting, give value first; don't wait for the other person to give you something.
- Always concentrate on the small details like birthdays, anniversaries and the names of children or a favourite sport and team.
- Make a special effort and go that extra mile, on special occasions.

Just remember, people do business with their friends. To be friends, you have to take care of them, earn their trust, maintain contact and remember the small details.

Try to have a breakfast meeting.

Lunch is good, but it can drag on a bit and can make you feel a bit sluggish. So, from time to time, have a breakfast meeting with people from your network database. These meals are usually shorter, more focused and set you up for the day. So, do breakfast and build relationships at the same time.

Get in front of people—it counts.

Don't get lazy or complacent. Take the time to see people face to face. When I was CEO of my last few businesses, I made a point each day (and sometimes more than once in a day, in difficult times) to visit each workstation and spend a few seconds talking to each person in the team and thanking them for their efforts. Actions like this will, and I mean **will**, strengthen your relationships and build on the loyalty of those around you, providing you're getting everything else right too.

"Build loyalty and maintain relationships by visiting the trenches often, in person, by email and Social Media."

The wrong team can kill a business.

Kill a business with the wrong team—it sounds bad: it is bad. Getting the right team around you is essential and I am afraid to say that too few businesses understand the importance of selecting and getting the right people on the bus and, once they are on the bus, getting them or keeping them in the right seats!

Now, this is a difficult task at the best of times, and some businesses do nothing to increase their chances of success by failing to take advantage of all the resources at their disposal, to ensure that they get the right people on the bus—and in the right seats! Remember, as people develop, a new seat might be needed!

You can significantly increase the chances of success for each of the following protocols, which you use in the selection process:

- Prepare a profile for the job, based on performance of others who have done well and their traits.
- Use the profile to ask searching questions of the candidate during an initial telephone interview.
- Don't believe all you read on the CV—question everything!
- Use a testing pre-interview and use industrial psychology, where possible.
- Match true character traits to the job, based on those in your industry who excel at the task.

Be a team player: help your team get ahead.

If you help your direct reports and other connected people to get on in the business, you will become known as the right person to associate with, and people whom you help will do better and may even get promotions, based partly on your efforts.

A team player brings value to the business every day, with those around them sensing that value. Doing this is infectious—and this attitude of team orientation can turn the fortunes of a business and, on a personal level, can be very fulfilling, so why wouldn't you be that person? Sometimes, people will fail in your team or business. Do the right thing and let them go, give them a chance to succeed outside of your business.

"Appreciate your people. Sometimes this means letting them go to be better elsewhere."

So, be encouraging and offer congratulations for a job well done; offer advice and ask questions; above all, treat all your people as people and appreciate them. This approach will always serve you well.

Be a coach to your people every day.

The act of coaching team members will benefit you in three ways, it will improve their performance, it will give you greater learning and understanding; it should have an impact on the profitability of the business. These are good enough reasons to start now!

"When coaching, be smart and concentrate on those who respond. Don't waste time on those that refuse to change."

It is a good idea to try to initiate a coaching relationship with all of those who report directly to you. You do have to get smart, though, and concentrate on those who respond. There is no point in wasting time on those who do not listen or have no desire to use their own powers and skills, with guidance from you, to improve their position. All the others are certainly worth the effort, and you will both benefit from the experience.

Try to remember the difference among training, coaching and giving opinion. For sure, coaching does involve both giving and receiving opinion, but that is not all it's about—and it is certainly not training. Coaching is about bringing out the knowledge which your people already have and getting them to mix it with their personality traits and imagination, to become better at what it is they are doing and more aware of its effect on themselves and others. Coaching is about development and expansion.

Coaching does not have to happen in a formal session, although it often does work out that way. It can also be done on a one-to-one basis and given during normal routine and conversation.

Some people just don't want to be or can't be coached. These are normally those who reject change constantly and cling on to the old ways. It's a shame, but it's just not worth spending the time on these people! I am not saying don't try, I am saying if they don't respond cut your losses and concentrate on those that do.

A great way to start this process is to get team members to write a list of what they do well and what they would like to do better. Once coaching has started, remember to look out for changes, so that you can offer congratulations; this, in turn, incites further positive actions. You will know when you are winning, as people will come to you to ask for coaching, rather than your having to offer.

Boredom kills innovation and morale.

A person's mind is kind of like a muscle—just like any other muscle, it needs exercise. It is so important that you be challenged and pushed to perform. If there is a lack of challenge, it does not matter how motivated you may start out being, you will find that your motivation will wane and with it your ability and desire to be innovative. Your morale will slip to a low.

"Keep your brain well exercised and active.
Challenge it every chance you get!"

Motivation needs to be bespoke, as what motivates one may not motivate that person's team-mate—so you need to be selective. Challenge, but don't overwhelm, as this has the same effect as boredom, insofar as it will demotivate. It's all about balance—and remember, the top performers in the business will always be hungry for new experiences. In all of my businesses I have always worked to achieve a culture of coaching and innovative thinking to keep the entire team involved and motivated.

Recognise others' work.

This may come as a surprise, but (in a survey conducted for several employers in the US about their employees and what motivated them) there is a mismatch between what employers thought the main motivator was and what the employees said the main motivator was. The employers assumed that the number-one motivator would be money earned. In reality, this ranked only fifth in the survey, with the number-one being having work appreciated by managers!

So, you need to make the effort to recognise the work of your colleagues and show appreciation often and in public. At the same time, though, don't oversell it—keep it simple. Tell people what you want more of, relating to work or attitude. Oh, if you're reading this and you have a boss then please don't forget the boss—they like recognition too!

It's a simple formula, SE = LC = BP.

This is so simple and yet ignored by many businesses and the people in them: SE (satisfied employees) = LC (loyal clients) = BP (bigger profits)! As with so many things this appears to be so simple. I think that might be the problem, it's so simple we forget about the relationships that really work for all business.

If the people that work for you are happy and motivated their interactions with your clients will be that much better and so in return, they will demonstrate their loyalty which will lead to more sales, more referrals and bigger profits. That's it, what more do I need to add?

True leaders let others perform, to become stars.

Some leaders forget to give space to their teams, so that they can perform; this is such a fundamental mistake to make and just decreases the effectiveness of the team and the morale of individuals. On top of that, the leader will start to lose any respect.

*"Not giving your team space to perform is a mistake.
Let them perform, they will surprise you!"*

Good leaders let their people perform; they lead the people; they don't stifle them and take away their responsibilities. If you take away responsibilities or, worse, don't give them responsibilities to start with, you will not create a team. You will not develop your leadership skills. You will simply create incompetence and ineffective groups of people.

You can be replaced.

When leading, don't let your stars get away with things, for fear that they are too important to the business! The rest of the team will see it and you will lose respect and morale. Let people know that you value them, but do not be held hostage. If needs be, you will have to get rid of them. Anyone, and I mean anyone, can be replaced!

When building effective teams in your business it is so important that all your team regardless of their performance get treated in the same way. If I do something wrong and I am the top performer I expect to receive the same punishment as everyone else. If you do succumb to the temptation of treating people differently for the same set of circumstances, you will start to see the loyalty to your leadership decrease and the team begin to fragment in confusion.

"To build a truly coherent team you need to have consistency in hiring, firing and reward, across the business."

If a person doesn't want to be productive, you can't change that.

Despite our best efforts and intentions sometimes we won't be able to get the best from some people, they just won't fit. So, the message to management is—don't waste your time on the timewasters. You will not get people to perform, unless they want to, if they don't want to, get rid of them. It really is that simple! You will need to follow the HR rules and that is why it is so important to build in accountability at the beginning. Make sure the team understands what happens when people don't want to perform, so that there are no shocks, when it happens!

The real secret of course is to take more care in your search and selection of people. Make sure they have a detailed induction and are given all the early support needed to grow into an exceptional person, who will help you and your business to bridge that gap between mediocre and exceptional.

Seek the positive and avoid the negative.

If you surround yourself with positive people, you will enhance performance all round. If, however, you are with negative people, you can almost feel the motivation being sucked out of you.

Therefore, in team selection and recruitment, ensure that you are able to identify the true person and his or her traits, rather than the possible false persona created for the interview or selection process. This is why I say it is so important to have multiple layers to your search and selection processes. Watch out for the indications of a negative attitude!

Gatekeepers are people too.

Gone are the days when the gatekeeper to the CEO or MD was just a tea-maker and general dogsbody. In today's business environment, they are highly skilled and valued by their CEO. If you want to get to see the top soldier in any business, then you need to treat the gatekeeper with respect and not fall into the trap of thinking that they are not the person you want to talk to. To run the life of a CEO, you have to be very smart and so deserve respect!

Of course, you will encounter gatekeepers at all levels in business and the same rules apply. Treat them well and treat them with sincerity and they will help you. Don't push too hard for your end game take a time out to get to know them. Not only can they get you in front of the right people, but they are also a great source of valuable information.

Tip 6: Take time to look at the bigger picture.

Looking at the bigger picture is a really important part of being a leader in business. The best way to do this is to take a break and look down on your work from the high ground where, rather than looking at the individual blades of grass, you can see the entire field, as well as those to the north, south, east and west.

Without this ability, you are simply going to disappear in a mist of stress and lose direction, eventually letting people down and missing targets. Have a good understanding of what lies beyond the horizon and encourage others to look too so that you can use your collective intellect to innovate and prepare for a range of possible futures that you would not see if you were to fail to look up from your work occasionally. This is all about finding the balance between working in and on your business.

"To gain exceptional performance and to develop you and your business you have to find time to work on not just in the business, department or team!"

Know what you need to do to get there.

To get to where you want to be, both in business and in your personal life, you need to be clear about what it is that you need to do. There has been much written about the importance of goal setting. It is a good idea to write down what it is you want to achieve in a given period—say in the next three to five years. I go for the shorter period, as things have a tendency to change rapidly, with the smaller chunks of time easier to visualise, which I am a great fan of.

Regardless of the timeline, it is a good idea to take some time to think about where you want to be and then to think about the best way to get there. This will form a series of goals, which will propel you towards where you want to be. It is these, which should be written down and reviewed against your activities regularly, to ensure that you are working towards them. Every step you take should take you a step closer to those goals you work so hard to achieve.

Get strength from experience and error.

Have you ever taken time to think about what you have to do to become a millionaire in business? Have you ever stopped to look at the trend in business, which clearly shows that, on one-to-one comparisons millionaires are more flexible, decisive and do not fear mistakes? Money may breed confidence that can explain this. However, if you take the time to research the self-made millionaires in business, you'll find they have always had those traits.

Let me help you: successful people, by default, have to be more flexible, but remain single-minded when it comes to the mission. They don't tend to get hung up on status and fear making mistakes. Don't get me wrong this is more of a statistical trend than a given. The message here is simple: if this sounds like you stop protecting your position and do not avoid doing the things in your business you know to be right. It is better to make a decision than to do nothing.

"Be flexible and stop protecting your status. Concentrate on doing your job to the best of your ability."

If you get it wrong, simply learn. It's not your status that makes you, it's who you are as a person and how you learn and adapt which matters. Don't try to be the best at everything; try to be the best at getting things done using your skills and others' skills, surround yourself with the best and you will all succeed, don't be threatened by their success.

Leave the ego outside and work with your team.

Your individual success is a combination of effort from several people; this, if you think about it, is how it has been all of your life! The point is that you have never done it alone—and nothing has changed: you still need people around you to succeed.

"Submit to your ego and watch the support you have walk out the door!"

The support you get from those around you can and will be eroded if you submit to your ego. To avoid this, do not try to protect your status, forget title and understand that all good leaders who achieve success do it by surrounding themselves with those who are better at something than they are. So, leave your ego outside and concentrate on your people, then watch your success grow! Power has a great knack of corrupting us and so be aware all the time and keep the ego in check.

It's okay not knowing.

Stop trying to be the best at everything; stop trying to create the impression that you know it all. It's okay not knowing. Everyone has different talents and areas of expertise— learn to influence and use their skills, rather than trying to do it yourself. Copy the great leaders who do this well. The great leaders openly admit their weaknesses but have people around them able to compensate for the weaknesses.

Sometimes, it's good to slow down or stop.

Have you ever had one of those days when nothing is going well, and you feel like you just want to go home or kick the job into touch? Most people will have feelings like this, from time to time. The best thing to do, in this case, is rise to the high ground and take stock. See the bigger picture and, if you are heading in the wrong direction, take a deep breath, slow down or stop and change direction.

"If it's not working slow down and change direction!"

Whatever it is you do, never make a decision when you are in this frame of mind, slow down, think it through and then decide. Remember the difference between good and bad:

- **Bad—Look to shift blame when it's not working—congratulate you when it goes well!**

- **Good—Look to you and take responsibility when it goes wrong—congratulate others when it goes well!**

Never jump before slowing down to consider the impact. What seems big today is no more than a heartbeat in your life, so take your time and do it well and for the right reasons.

Get some balance.

Much of what is being said in these pages is about investing in the people and teams within the business. However, you also need to invest in yourself and take time to recharge your batteries, to allow yourself to continue with the good fight!

Do this by taking time out for yourself and do the things you like doing; spend time with family, in the garden, walking the dogs, reading, whatever it is that you do to relax—and do it regularly. By doing this, you will avoid exhaustion and maintain a fresh approach to your work. This, in turn, will contribute to your success

Don't avoid the grey and get help.

In business, things are constantly moving and changing; the higher up you go, the more this is the case. Things become less and less black and white and greyer. The greyer, the more difficult the answers become.

"Ask for help and never avoid making hard decisions."

Do not avoid asking for help; recognise that not knowing the answer is common. Use those around you to assist in the process. Learn to ask for help, use all the information you can get your hands on and then use your best judgment to take things forward. Most importantly, though, ask for help and do not avoid the decision! It was this point that became one of the main motivations for including unlimited support and advice for members of the Rainmakers Club.

The steps that make a business work.

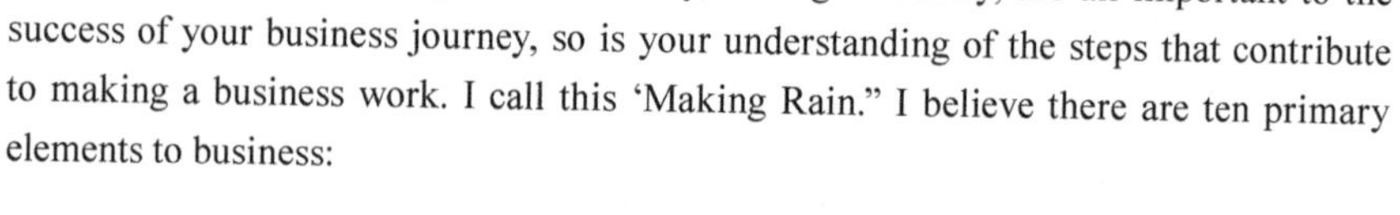

While culture, values and personal activity, the right activity, are all important to the success of your business journey, so is your understanding of the steps that contribute to making a business work. I call this 'Making Rain." I believe there are ten primary elements to business:

1. Vision, Mission and Values.
2. Strategy.
3. Business Plan.
4. Marketing.
5. Sales.
6. Financial Control.
7. Operations.
8. HR & Selection.
9. Coaching.
10. Innovation.

I maintain that if you have any of these ten elements missing the business will have no longevity. If you have all ten in place you have a fair chance of survival. The real skill is having them in balance.

This all important balance will need to be adjusted as things around you change and develop, without the skill and understanding of how to get the balance right and then maintain it through repeated changes you'll always be in the mediocre camp and never get to where you'll find exceptional and sustainable results, which should be what we all want.

No matter how good you think you are without these elements a business is just not going to work that well. The first step is to build a strong foundation on which to build your business. This foundation will come from the following basic business steps. The interesting point for me is that the same rules and activities work for individual improvement and performance. Treat yourself like a business and see what a difference that can make to your results. You can start that journey by considering the following steps.

Step 1: Why are you in business?

No matter who you are, where you are and what business you're in, you need to have a defined purpose, a primary purpose if you will. Without this primary purpose being ever present in all you do in your business life, success and I mean real success, will elude you for sure. Oh, you may have the occasional victory but if you're serious this is not going to be enough for you. You want to be a Rainmaker!

Assuming you have a primary purpose for being in business; the next challenge is not to just have this as a slogan on your desktop but to live it. Live it every day and in everything that you do, each communication, each element of your day and each interaction with prospects, clients, suppliers, consumers and for that matter all your stakeholders.

Your primary purpose must be to have a product that is so desirable that you never need to worry about not having more customers to buy from you. You do this by having the highest levels of service, design and value. Your target market should see you as the expert and want to seek from you, information, advice and the product you're in business to provide. If you want to know more on how to demonstrate your expertise, then join our program in the Rainmakers Club.

The key to a primary purpose, that helps you on your journey to exceptional success, is to live it for the right reasons. Not just because of you but also because of them; your customers, care about them, show them you care through your activities and make sure these activities are aligned to your primary purpose. Above all, be sincere in your actions and words, for if you're not sincere you will be found out and again true success will elude you!

"Make sure your primary purpose is based on the people that will make up your market and not your product."

With your reputation of treating your customers right, their well-being graphically illustrated as being at the forefront of your mind; along with the quality and value built into your offering, people will come to you, 'If you build it, they will come!" Not just because of your sales activity but because people buy from people. People talk to people and you're clear and visible purpose will get them talking about you. It always was and always will be about them not you or your product. Most people don't buy the drill because they want the drill; they want the holes it will make.

Step 2: Don't show me the money, show me the passion!

The next step, and one I think is misunderstood in so many cases is that of passion. What is the point of having a prime purpose if you have no real passion for it? If you want to achieve true unbridled success then you need to be doing what you really care about, it really is as simple as that.

Try this basic but very effective self-assessment test, the key is total honesty. You can use this test when thinking about your business and its primary purpose too! I call it "The three circles test." Members of the Rainmakers Club will be very familiar with this; I won't take credit of it as many people before me have also used it. Like so many things in business it's already out there but in my view woefully underused as an effective planning tool for the individual.

We only live once and the time we are given passes all too quickly, therefore we should spend as much time as we possibly can doing the things that mean the most to us, don't you think? That is why I feel doing this really simple exercise is so important, we don't get many chances to get it right so grasp every chance that is presented to you!

All you need to do is ask three very simple but key questions of yourself, or for that matter your business. If you've got it right the answers should be such that they all complement each other and place you or your business right in the centre of the Venn diagram where all three circles interlink, if not then I urge you to think again and do all you can to get yourself into the centre.

These questions are important and will guide you into making the right decisions for the longer term. I have used this model myself since I left the Army and have rarely deviated outside of the centre of the Venn.

The three circles Venn planning tool

Sometimes that has meant my financial position has not been as good as it could have been. I know however that money isn't everything and I have always made enough to get by; but what is more important, I have always been happy with what it is I've been doing. It has also been a challenge, from time to time, as others around me find it difficult or even impossible to understand why I would take such risks or make such sacrifices, while pursuing my dream, when instead I could have just taken a job, any job.

Sure, I take risks and have held out for the business of my dreams, but the rewards are there and I enjoy the chase and the thrill of this never dull journey I am on. I guess it's in my blood. After all those years in the Army I was bound to want to find another way to get the adrenaline rush!

Over time in my 'three circles' the answers have changed, as I have gained experience and completed significant steps in my journey. While the content may have changed the principles have not. I am doing what I am most passionate about and what I can be best at and it does fit with my current economic drivers. I wish you'd embark on that journey too, if you haven't already done so!

Quite simply if you're not passionate, I mean really passionate, about what you do, true success will always be just out of reach for you and that is a gap that you'll never be able to bridge without genuine passion for what it is you're doing.

Be passionate about what you do for the client not passionate about the money. There's nothing wrong with wanting money, there's nothing wrong with wanting personal success but these should not be the primary reason, these should not be the main passion, they are the icing on the cake, a welcome by-product of your passion and purpose!

"To get the very best results be passionate and more concerned for the customer than cash you earn."

If you truly believe in your product and give or strive to give great value and really care about your customers, I mean really care, the result will be greater success and with that comes financial reward. So, concentrate your passion on the right things, not the money. Use your talent to concentrate on the right things, the things you can be truly passionate about.

The other interesting thing about true, sincere, clear and present passion is, it is completely infectious, and that one characteristic can make an incredible difference to the success of your business. Simply speaking your passion will act like a magnet to others and will attract more people with a similar outlook and so the passion, motivation, excitement and success spreads throughout the business including those all-important customers and prospects.

Step 3: Master or Salve, you decide?

You must quickly ensure you do not become the slave and the business or job your master. This happens more often than you might think in business, particularly in the start-up and small business arena.

It's confession time, when I talk about this it's worth knowing that on more than one occasion I have fallen into this trap. I'm pleased to tell you however the lesson was learnt and never repeated, much! The hardest time to avoid this is when you first start out with a new business; particularly if you are not awash with funding! **The Rainmakers Club** was such an example where initially I was spending most if not all of my time working in rather than on!

Long before that, I can remember working at the bank selling four to five contracts each and every day, working from about 0830 to 2100 five days a week. At weekends I would create my call plans and put together the reports needed for the management and later on Sunday I would even make a few calls to the manager to brief him on the week ahead, which as you can imagine didn't go down too well with the family! I was a slave to the bank.

I was straight out of the Army and into a sales career with no experience and only two weeks residential training. At the end of the course I was given a certificate and the keys to a brand-new Ford, with a boot full of application forms and a list of people who lived on my route home! The idea being I call on them on my way back from the course, ah the good old days!

My first few calls were a complete disaster, the real thing was so much harder than it was in the classroom, I was soon to learn that is always the case! The truly successful people are those that put the extra effort into the real thing and get up one more time than they are knocked down.

For the next 12 months it was like a war of attrition, endless hours of planning and execution followed by more planning and still more execution. By the time I had got to the end of the week all I was capable of was gaining as much sleep as I could. Before sleep I would have to write my reports and prepare for the next week, I was nothing more than a slave, or at least that's how it felt.

At the end of my first year I was in a good position, all the effort I had put into my sales and planning were paying off. I had achieved about 140% of target, which put me in the top performers in the company and was giving me a modest bonus.

With the year done and all the figures in front of me I did some calculations and decided I was probably better off and maybe have more time if I were to do this for myself instead of the bank! It looked doable and quite easy on paper all I had to do was keep up the levels of activity I had done at the bank. This was my first demonstration of how naive I was at this early stage of my business career. My thought process was far from complete missing out some important facts, for example where was the raw material (The People) going to come from without the bank? Later I was to pay the price for that lack of experience and thought.

The next lesson on my journey in business was a really important one; If you're going to go into business for yourself, make the decision but take your time with the research and development of your plan before you decide to start in earnest. Don't pay lip service to the research and planning, it is crucial to the success of the project. Then when you start it is still not a given, so make sure you find the weak points early and put them right.

As my mentor once said to me when you start something if you're going to fail you need to fail quickly, that way it won't cost you so much. Cost in this instance is not just about money, it's about reputation and opportunity!

"Make sure you do your research before you start and plan everything. Start the journey with the mindset of being the master not the slave to the business!"

Start the journey as you intend to continue, be the master not the slave. If by going into business, all you're doing is creating a job you'll be better off not bothering with the business and just go find someone to work for as it will amount to the same thing at the end of the day!

Most of us wouldn't embark on such a journey if we thought this was all that would happen, the problem is it is through our own actions that this becomes the slave. Take my story as an example and learn from my mistakes to avoid them yourself.

After the first year, as I've said I already I had done quite well as a Financial Adviser for the bank and took the decision that I should go it alone. I set up my first business and spent the first few weeks planning and putting in place all the tools I thought I would need to get it off the ground.

The day came for the official launch and that entire week was spent meeting with providers to get the best deal I could from them. In those days Financial Advisers were still able to negotiate commission rates and the more you could get the more you could then sacrifice to reduce charges or pay professional introducers, or at least that is how I saw it.

I was already thinking of ways to effectively compete with the other local advisers. Many of those local advisers would not work in that way, preferring to pocket the uplift in commission, I saw this as a great way to compete and create a differential, for me it wasn't all about the money.

Once all the meetings were completed and rates agreed the business was ready to start trading, now was my chance to do a better job than the bank. Yes, I really was that arrogant, or perhaps confident, or both!

I lacked experience in those days and despite all those years in the Army I hadn't thought things through in as much detail as I should have. This resulted in my typical working day looking something like this:

06:00—Up shower, dress and prepare applications and other papers for day ahead.
07:00—Either start the day in home office with correspondence and prospecting for likely candidates to sell to or take the short drive to the office to start the same activity.

This was the lifeblood of my business as it was new and I was subject to restrictions for the first year by the bank, I guess they were concerned I could do a better job too! Without prospects to sell to you could say my business had no prospects. These activities would last for a few hours each day. If I had meetings to go to, I would still find time after hours to do this important work.

10:00—I would either be in the office calling prospects for appointments later in the week or on the road visiting clients. Clearly the best and only way to make a living is to be selling to the prospects and so most of my time day on day was spent on these two activities. On average I would do five meetings a day with clients. By day, I mean during the day and early evening up to about 21:00.

12:00—No sign of lunch here! I was usually working too hard seeing people who only had their lunch break as a time to talk to me about their financial planning needs. The meetings would then continue for the rest of the day all being well, if not it was back to the prospecting or perhaps more meetings with product providers to give me an update on what was available to present to my clients.

20:00—On most days I would start my last client meeting of the day at about this time, this would mean as a rule I was getting home around about 22:00. I quick drink or something to eat, while checking for last minute admin to do and then off to bed, before starting the cycle all again.

I was doing that day on day and the reality was I was earning a little more but was working harder and at full speed and all I had done was create for myself the same job I was doing before, it was just longer hours and harder to keep the extra balls of running the business in the air at the same time. Despite earning a little more money, I was also now looking after my own expenses and so in reality I was worse off!

All I had done so far was create an identical job to the one I had just given up; this was not a business this was just another job and I was a slave to it!

When most of us start out in business we are probably underfunded and under the wrong impression about the role we have to fulfil. Get these two right and your journey can be completely different, let me explain.

If you start a business and it's underfunded the first thing you need to do is bring in the sales to fund the initial development of the business. This will immediately force you into the habit of spending the majority if not all your time doing the day job, working in the business, just like a regular job! The problem is we are all creatures of habit and this **will** become a habit, making it increasingly difficult for you to do what your business needs most if it is to grow, which is you working on its development not just bringing in the sales.

This is why it's so important to do your homework and plan the business well, plan it to succeed with you having the right balance initially, a balance of working on and in, not just in. It is true that initially the weighting will be more in than on, but your goal should be to turn this the other way as quickly as you can and eventually only work on and let others do the in!

Another bit of advice is to work lean, your product does not have to be perfect, get it out there and concentrate on selling, the right way and concurrent to that develop the product based on feedback and needs. Working lean is smart!

"Find the right balance from the beginning working both in and on the business. Your mission to work on and get others to work in!"

The other issue is the temptation to believe that you are the only or best person to undertake the tasks in hand. The sooner you recognise the importance of letting others take on some of those tasks, leaving you free to spend more time on the business the better.

You may think you can do all the jobs that need doing in your business day-to-day and perhaps you're right. Regardless of this the challenge is to surround yourself with people that can do the work leaving you free to work on the business rather than in the business. You may have to grow people to manage this but nonetheless it is an essential part of your growth.

Your ultimate aim should be to replace yourself in the business as quickly as you're able and surround yourself with people who can do the day jobs better than you. Don't feel threatened by this, feel relieved. All you need to do is concentrate on being the best leader you can and give your team the space to perform. Act as their coach, their mentor, their rally point and their moral compass, using the values of the business as your guide.

Be the master of your business not a slave to it. Make the changes you need to make in your business now! When you've got it right watch that business or career soar and with it your success.

The best tip I can give you at this point is to tell you to find yourself a mentor and then lean on them and use them as a valued second opinion and sounding board. If you can't find someone to do that role in your business then give me a call, really, call me. I can help, and if I can't someone on the **Rainmakersclub.co.uk** site can!

Step 4: Replace yourself ASAP.

This step is a direct follow-on from step 3. In my first few years in business I was told to do just this, replace myself; but I didn't really understand what I was being told and continued to work in the business becoming more embedded in the day to day activities, as a consequence the strategy and ability to compete was eroded and changes that were happening around me on the outside of the business went unnoticed.

The risk is this weakens the position of the business. Take a look around and you can see businesses all over the place suffering from the same issues. Look deeper and you'll see businesses failing because of this preoccupation with internal daily routine. Having strong business leadership is as important to development and survival as sales!

Here's a good way to begin this process in your business: The first thing you need to do is make a list of all the things you do day-to-day in your business. Make the list as comprehensive as you can, forget nothing.

When I did this exercise the first time, which was during the development of my software business, just after I sold my financial services business some years ago. I went all out to make sure I missed nothing. I did this by keeping a diary of all the tasks I undertook during an entire month, including weekends.

Once the list was completed, I simply went through each entry one by one and determined which tasks I was doing that could or should be done by someone else. This included many, if not all, of the administration tasks, accounting, marketing and other tasks. It would be no exaggeration to tell you that in those early days of my business life I discovered nearly 80% of the activities I undertook during that month were tasks that could have been left, ignored or should have been done by others. I had been using the same patterns for many months at the time of the review.

Imagine how much better developed my business could have been had I delegated just half of those tasks and replaced them with strategic, planning, sales and leadership activities!

I do still, from time to time, find myself doing things that others could do but this is just me falling off the wagon and letting my ego take control. It happens less and less frequently as you replace the old way of working with the new, and I spend more time working at a strategic level and concentrating on leadership rather than doing the things others can do better than I.

The specific things I spend my time working on these days is leadership, strategy, innovations and high-level sales and marketing planning and execution. Getting the job done day-to-day is the domain of others much better suited to those vital tasks than me. I see myself as the custodian of the original vision and the core values of the business. Each action I take day-on-day must be toward the published mission and results that progress me toward the fulfilment of the vision.

So, on the journey to a better business, a better you, make the effort to replace yourself from all those tasks you don't need to be doing, freeing up segments of time so you can focus on strategic activities, then watch your business grow. Just as important watch your people grow too, and they will because you're trusting them with more!

Step 5: The right people mean business.

Your ultimate aim as a business leader, owner or manager is to build a team that is made up of people who are more capable of doing the day job than you are; leaving you free to concentrate on other things like; leadership, motivation, inspiration and planning.

One of the things I hear quite often is the defensive stance of "I've tried to hire people better than I, but they just aren't out there."

The reality is they are out there you just need to look harder and understand that sometimes you have to grow these people too. Take your time and invest time in the search then you need to take the people you've selected on the right journey, a journey that will inspire and motivate them to want to be the best they can be for you and for themselves. One thing we should never do is restrict their growth knowingly or otherwise.

Most, if not all people would agree with this sentiment and yet in application this seems to be forgotten. In the worst examples I have seen poor leadership take a superstar and turn them into a shadow of their former self, simply by not leading, not inspiring, training and motivating. In many cases the superstar is never given the space to perform by the boss. If you take a person on to fulfil a task the very least you should do is let them run with the task. Give them the space and time to get the job done.

Let's take a look at finding the right people in a little more detail because it's so important to the success of any business.

Advertise for superstars.

To attract the superstar, you need to think specifically about what your version of a superstar looks like. If you're not specific about what you're looking for you'll just be attracting everyone. Finding a superstar is all about quality over quantity. The more demanding you make the advert for the position the lower your responses will be but conversely the higher the standard of the people who respond. Recruiting superstars does take longer but is worth it in the long run because you significantly improve your chances of finding that special person who will be with you for a much longer period. My advice is using the services of a search and selection specialist to work with you exclusively is the way forward but remember the rule select with care those that will operate as your agent, or if you have the skill and the time, do it yourself.

"Hiring on first impressions is not a good idea. Take time and select with care. Recruiting the wrong people can kill your business!"

If your need is too great to wait, then you should be willing to accept that the people you hire may not fit the bill for too long. It really has to be a balance because hiring, training and then losing people is a dangerous and expensive game to play. In the past I have used wording that clearly shows we are looking for the best, here's an example of the kind of words I have used in advertising for my superstars in the past:

Superstar Salesperson Wanted for busy Business

Basic wage plus a very generous performance pay. Featuring no ceiling potential and an on target earning of £60k.

Fast growing Sales Business is looking for a smart Salesperson who loves to sell, loves people and takes pride in doing a superstar job. Superb training and support provided.

You will take ownership of your job and be generously rewarded for your quality and reliability of work. Call or email your interest and tell me why I would be mad not to take you on for this position.

Contact details . . .

I know you won't all agree with my wording, but this is the sort of advert that really can work, feel free to adapt it to suit your own particular needs. I would probably go further than this and offer specific contact times by phone. I would do this because it helps manage your valuable time and second you can find out how well the candidate follows instructions and call within specified times. If they can't even do that, why would you want to hire them?

Start tough.

I can't count the number of times I have witnessed interviews taking place, where the employer spends all their time selling the position and the person, they are in front of spend all their time selling themselves, you just know a sale will be made. Turn the clock forward a few months and already the cracks are starting to show!

I would always maintain a minimum of three interviews before you make a decision and I would always make the first interview a tough one. Tough means not sugar-coating things, just tell them what you expect from them if they are to fill the position.

Remember your aim here is not to make a friend, not yet, you just want to know if this person has the right stuff! If they're not get rid when you've found out, there's no point in wasting their time and yours, which is already at a premium.

Remember, you can always teach skills to someone who has the capacity and willingness to learn but you can't make them willing or likable if they aren't already that way. You can't make them believe if they don't feel it and you can't make a person that feels no passion be passionate. That's a big clue, right?

In some cases, no matter how willing the person is you'll not be able to make them into a superstar. These are cases where there needs to be a degree of natural talent to start with and no matter how hard you try, if they don't have the natural talent, you'll never get them to the level you require. An example of this is sales; if they don't have a natural talent at communication it's doubtful, they would ever be your superstar salesperson.

I believe you can't just train anyone to be a sales superstar any more than you can train a poor soccer player into a world-class player. They have to start off with a high level of natural talent.

Back to the first interview, you want to find out about their ethical match too. Do they have similar personal values that will complement the values of the business they may end up working for, if successful? Are they going to get on with you and you them? Are they hungry to progress and do they have the right stuff?

You need to ask questions that will draw out information to show you what they are really like, what they will be like if they end up working for your business. I would say it's worth using some of the basic principles we use in marketing in the recruitment process. When we market to potential new clients, we focus our attention on those in our target market, those that are most likely to buy. If we don't do that, we end up wasting far too much money on marketing that ends up being fruitless. If I did that, I wouldn't expect to keep my job for long!

So, when marketing the position, you want to fill I would suggest using the same principles. In other words, concentrate your attentions on those who fit your requirements, have the skills and experience you're really looking for.

I believe one of the key things you should be looking for has to be their levels of natural passion for life and signs of creativity in their thinking. I would go as far as saying if you don't see signs of this then you probably should not be considering hiring them.

I believe the more stages and the greater mix of tests pre-hire the greater your chances of success. I do understand this can make the process longer and maybe even cost a little more, but I am sure this up-front investment will give you better success in your hiring and in the long run cost you less. The model I use in my business, comes from a system I designed when I was hired to set up a Search & Selection business. It has a series of stages all designed to be challenging and fully test the potential recruit.

The first part, which I call the 'Talent Footprint,' is a pen picture of the key traits and attitudes you are looking for. These are based on questions asked of people that are either already in the business and performing above average or people undertaking a similar role where they have the attitude and traits you are looking for. Candidates are then assessed in a comparison of answers given. The questions are based on a combination of the job description for the vacancy you're filling and a pen profile of a person in your business or a business you know who has all the traits and values you're looking for in the ideal world.

From this you design a series of questions, which your sample of exceptional people are required to answer. The system I use would then collate all the answers and merge them to one version that covers all the important points. This then becomes the ideal answer you are looking for.

I like to run telephone interviews as the first part of the assessment process. Each applicant is asked to send their CV, if not already in my possession. I don't prejudge the content or assess based on the content; I will however use the CV as a source of questions to ask later in the process. I never put too much value on the CV at this stage as anyone can say anything in a CV and their value at this point is questionable, in my view. I say this because evidence suggests a very high proportion of people put things in their CV that are not strictly true or accurate!

I ask the candidates to call me at a given time for a short telephone interview. During the call the questions designed during the 'footprint' exercise, are used and the answers recorded on a spreadsheet and scored against the ideal standard I am looking for. I usually set a standard and anyone that meets or exceeds that standard score will be invited to the next phase, those that don't are removed from the process.

"You'll learn much from your candidates if you put them in the same room and ask them to perform a joint test under pressure. They will show you sides of them that would never be seen in a traditional interview!"

Assuming the next interview goes well the candidate progresses to the selection day, which is a series of exercises, a combination of individual and group tests, for example it could look like this:

- Icebreaker, all the candidates stand and present themselves to the room, each person getting a few minutes to break the ice, where they will be judged on their communication skills and confidence.

- I usually split the group now and some go for a one to one interview and the others a one to one role-play based on the role we are looking to fill. When the entire subgroup has been through the exercise, they swap; so, all candidates complete the entire exercise.

- The final part of the selection day is also a group exercise, during this we are looking for other natural traits that it's difficult to hide when working in a group. This is a real window into the personality of the short list candidates. You'll discover things about their character that won't come out in the normal course of traditional interviews. Things like, leadership skills, interpersonal skills and much more.

- As a result, I end up with one or two people I would like to hire and they are put through one final check, a final interview prior to offers being made.

This system does, however all come down to a detailed and effective 'footprint' and the ability to interpret what's been placed in front of you.

Recruiting the right people is something that should be invested in and should never be done in a rush. Sadly, the mainstream recruitment industry does not always promote this as they are in too much competition with each other and often the first to the post gets the fee. That is another compelling reason for search and selection over traditional recruitment models. After all you would not buy a technology specifically for one particular job when it is installed with the wrong chip!

Given the choice to hire someone I will always go for the one with real passion and mission orientation over a textbook expert in their field. The exceptional result we are all looking for, is finding that all too rare beast that has both in equal share!

Step 6: Balance performance and pay.

If you pay in peanuts don't be surprised if you end up with monkeys! There is so much truth in that saying but here's another thing for you to consider; If you pay too low you may find performance is a constant challenge. Pay too much and you could struggle to achieve a healthy per head margin.

Many businesses base their sales packages on the majority of their pay being delivered as a basic salary with a smaller amount as a bonus based on performance. Many people live on the basic salary with no need for the bonus to get by. Tell me how this creates exceptional sales performance? I truly believe that an exceptional salesperson will prefer a smaller basic and higher bonus. That was certainly the case for me personally.

How about considering using a model that has always worked for the most successful businesses, it's simply based on the reverse of the norm. Try paying a lower basic but very lucrative bonuses and watch performance soar, assuming you've hired people with the right software installed, they are on the right bus and in the right seat!

Although not always true, I do hold the opinion that if you have the right people this will be people who you know can do the job in hand and not just get by. These kinds of people will understand the bigger performance related deal is much better for them. It is however true that the more financial pressure your people are under the less attractive the lower basic becomes, particularly those that fain confidence or have a crisis of confidence based on their own past performance!

I truly believe that if you reward in this way and operate the business as a series of teams who are directly responsible for elements of the business and rewarded on their performance you will see improved results and will start to bridge that gap between mediocre and sustainable exceptional performance that we should all desire. This does rely on a strong financial model to work to.

I also like to reward on overall company performance and individual attitude and alignment to the Vision, Mission and Values of the business. Exceptional businesses should promote and reward exceptional performance.

Finally, I like to pay my additional bonuses at points in the year that mean the most to the team. Traditionally this would be June and December, in time for the summer vacation and the Christmas break.

"Reward your people for their own performance, their overall team performance and the company as a whole and watch the culture of coaching and cooperation take over!"

Step 7: Make day one count.

First impressions are very important and the first impression your new superstar is going to get will be based on what happens on day one or perhaps the first two or three days of their time with you. For this reason, it's important that you make sure the first few days give them all that they need to hit the ground running and have complete confidence in you and the business. A lack of preparation can damage their success from day one. So put the hours in and get it right, remember preparation and planning is king or Queen or both!

The best way for this to be done is to have a formal induction program that covers all the bases. For me this must include some really key touch points with the business that will set the tone for journey ahead. Concentrate on the culture and values the business expects its team to adopt and live by, both in and out of working hours. In my view your team members should be ambassadors for the business 24/7, if you're to build a really great reputation, brand and be taken seriously by all.

When I take people on, I run induction that will last between two and five weeks, depending on the function and how complex it might be. Regardless of that all new people received identical sessions to start the process.

Week 1 Induction must have—A session on the Vision, Mission and Values of the business, this is after all the DNA of the business If we don't get this right then we will be building our house on a weak foundation giving it no longevity.

Within this first week I would also make sure my new superstar understood all the things I have written about in this book before starting the other important subject of their specific job in or on the business. Each point in this book is a trait that will bring significant value to the business and the individual.

Step 8: Train constantly.

Businesses that stand still and don't improve and change along with their surroundings will eventually die. Recent history is littered with examples of businesses that have suffered in this way. Guess what? People, like businesses, shouldn't stand still either. Good people want to be developed and constantly improve. The best way to achieve this is to constantly train them, giving them the opportunity to develop still further. In this way your people will be constantly improving and working to the highest possible standards. Customers will get higher level of satisfaction too as by default the service they receive will also be of the highest level. That is one of the founding principles behind my personal journey and now my business the Rainmakers Club, which is directly linked to the principles of Learn, Share and Develop.

"You'll never know it all and so should be constantly seeking new experiences and knowledge. Training in business should be treated as seriously as training in professional sport. Adopt a culture that embraces training for all!"

Step 9: Responsibility & Accountability.

I can remember one of the main reasons I started my journey in business was because I wanted to work with a degree of freedom and be responsible for my actions and the results those actions would generate. I wanted to design solutions for the areas I am most passionate about in business and truly make a difference to as many small businesses as I can. That still remains the same today and is just as fresh as it was when I started. I'm guessing that some of these will be resonating with you as they probably do for most entrepreneurs in business.

I believe it is this freedom that makes for some of the great results gained in business. That being the case we should ensure we give the same benefits and opportunities to all.

The reality is often different to this and instead of giving our people the space to perform, we operate under the misapprehension that we can do it better and therefore do it instead, undermining their development, loyalty and confidence!

In some cases, it could be that you can do it better but how are your people ever going to develop if you don't give them the time and space to learn and improve?

"Start to delegate but don't leave your team to flounder. Show them how, get them to copy and then coach to improve the outcome, creating a culture of coaching and training throughout the business!"

Encourage your people to take responsibility and to be fully accountable; in so doing you'll be far more likely to progress into a business that is capable of generating exceptional and sustainable results and that is a great place to be, for any business.

Step 10: Performance & Reward.

The first thing I want to say about this is you'd be wrong to assume that reward means cash, surveys undertaken by Harvard University have proven that remuneration is not the only motivation that inspires people to perform in business. Sometimes it's as simple as acknowledgement of a job well done. It is the responsibility of the managers to ensure the best performance from all the team, to ensure that as individuals and as a team they are getting the very best results they can and then to reward them accordingly.

As a manager the role must include the development of performance and the reward of performance too. Business should be concentrating its efforts on motivating controlling, congratulating and rewarding performance at every level in that business.

Don't underestimate the power of open and public recognition of a job well done. A genuine and sincere recognition of good performance from managers and owners of the business means more to the individual than you might first appreciate.

If you do use this and it fails to get the performance you're looking for from an individual, then you need to recognise that you've probably hired the wrong person for this particular role. That being the case, you need to take responsibility for the failure, after all it was your business that made the hiring error. The business should always take the responsibility and learn from the mistakes made.

Just because this person is not performing for you, it doesn't mean they can't be successful for some other organisation fulfilling a different, more suitable role. Assuming you have adopted the right core values, you'll now help them to find a new position that is more in keeping with their skills and personality.

Step 11: Work on your mindset.

In my life, to date, I think the two most important lessons I have learned and the two pieces of advice I would suggest would always be relevant are:

- If you need more money for your business, then you need to sell more!

- You will become what you think about most, so make sure your attitude is right, think about the right things!

  The part that I want to concentrate on is the second, having the right mindset is vital to success in business in general. You really can change the way things turn out simply by concentrating on having the right mental attitude. If you think positive thoughts, positive things will happen. It's also your role to promote the ongoing positive outlook of the entire team.

  We all fall off the wagon from time to time, it's human nature to have doubt and sometimes be a little negative about things. What we should all be working on is to maintain the positive thinking, the positive outlook for as much of your time as we can. The more we think and act positive the better things will turn out for us.

  Have you ever noticed that people with this attitude seem to have more than their fair share of things going their way? The opposite is also true, so decide which side of that fence you want to be on! Here are a few tips that might help you to maintain that all important positive outlook:

- Self-belief—The first and most important step is to work on your self-belief. The most effective way of doing this is to be realistic about your strengths and weaknesses. Concentrate on both but don't think of them in the same way. Your strengths give you confidence and your weaknesses act as an anchor. So, turn the negative into a positive by having your own self-development plan to increase your skills in the weaker areas. This will help to build confidence overall and maintain that important positive attitude. We all have different ways we like to take on new information, so make sure you work in the way that is most likely to get you the results. For me it is reading, writing and web-based interaction with other businesspeople.

- Don't just think inside the box—We need to think about the full range of possibilities that can be used in our daily routine. Some call this thinking dimensionally rather than being myopic. Take marketing or sales as an example, instead of having just one message innovate and come up with 100 ideas, even if you only use one or two, this really will help you to start thinking beyond current boundaries and increase your positive attitude. We are all hard wired to succeed and it's our attitude and those doubting voices in our head that restrict our growth. Don't focus on the problem focus on the opportunity to improve. In my own life I have found that problems have a way of sorting themselves out if you maintain a positive outlook and constantly work toward your primary goals.

- Think like an entrepreneur—One of the greatest things about being an entrepreneur is the freedom it gives you. If you're not taking advantage of this, then change right now and start leading the way in ideas and act on them as rapidly as you can. Constantly be thinking about the product or service. The way you market, sell it and re-invent these methods, keep innovating and keep moving.

- Change the rules to give you the advantage—Competitive advantage is a necessity to have in business. If you want to win then don't be dragged by the crowd to play to their rules at their level on their playing field. Think it through, plan, innovate and give yourself the advantage. What I am saying is there are no rules, think outside the box. A word of warning, thinking outside the box does not mean you can forget about being ethical. Always act with the highest levels of ethics but think innovation. Think about pushing the envelope be bold, be daring, be successful!

Understand the law of attraction

When you embark on a journey of self-development and development for your business, it's important to understand the law of attraction. The greater the effort you out into your journey, the better the results. As these results continue to build, you'll begin to understand the law of attraction. You'll start to see the more you work at it, the more good fortune and opportunities you'll attract. Once you gain enough momentum there's simply no turning back, your route to success is assured! The more you do, the more you attract. The more you attract the more attractive you become and so the circle for success is gaining momentum.

Beware the circle can be broken, and its worst enemy is the out of control ego. Power can and does corrupt. Someone has to be the leader but that does not give you the only voice, business should be a team effort!

Understand too the importance and power of multiple minds working on the same aim or problem together in harmony. That is much better than just one mind or a collection of minds at odds with each other! Harmony is something that you should seek but not to the detriment of the team's ability to innovate. This is a difficult but doable balancing act. You want to avoid the country club effect, where people just agree like nodding donkeys. You do want group consensus but not to the detriment of innovative thinking, conflicting views discussed respectfully is a common theme in most exceptional teams and businesses.

"Choose your team with care, it's not about friendship it's about performance. Don't pick yes men pick free thinkers who have the same goal as you!"

Step 12: Plan your end game first.

This is a very important step, you need to do this before you do anything else, because this one action will have a direct influence on all the other actions you take!

So, take a time out, go somewhere quiet and take a long look at yourself, your business and where you want to be, what you want to do, when you get there. Get this all clear in your mind and plan your attack before you do anything else.

When I look at most of the businesses I meet, many, far too many, of them seem to just drift almost by accident into what it is they are doing. Conversely some of the most successful businesses all seem to have the same thing in common, they start their journey already knowing what the end game is going to look like and from that point each planned step they take is toward that end game.

When I first started in business, developing the various plans that were needed was often a challenge and in the early days I rarely followed the plan once it had been designed. Instead the noise and distractions of the daily battle that is business got in the way. I see the same symptom in many other businesses that I meet along the way.

As the years have passed and my experience grown, I now fully understand the importance of all planning activities and now will invest time into making sure plans are developed, tested and most importantly of all executed.

Having no plan is like setting sail with a cargo but not knowing for which port you are bound and with no navigation charts! If you know your destination and have a map to get you there your chances of success are significantly increased. So, I say get planning, long before you start the journey!

"To help with this try using an upside-down to-do list. Write where you want to end up and then list backwards all the steps that came immediately before. Keep doing this until you get to the actions you need to take today. Turn the list around and follow each step-in turn. Stick to it and you'll get there!"

Step 13: Now create a great strategy.

Armed with a vision of your end game now you can put together an inspirational, innovative strategy to help you get there. I think the best way to do this is to start to reverse engineer, in much the same way we did for the backwards to do list. So, start at the ultimate aim back to the start of the journey.

So for example, if part of the plan is to have a certain amount of cash in the bank or a certain profit margin or value to the business, reverse engineer that amount backwards to your position right now, so you can see what it is you're going to have to do to get there year-on-year, month-on-month and day-by-day.

So, let's say you were turning over 100,000 and at the end of three years you wanted to be turning over 1,000,000, the way to do this is to work it backwards, using figures you know you can handle. Your plan is to show what the growth looks like for the difference between the two figures, in this case 900,000. Oh yes, be ambitious, but make sure you can support that ambition logistically, so plan a strategy for that too!

The key is you want your growth to be predictable and controllable. The only thing that is going to stop you is your belief. You need to be motivated and maintain the drive to achieve this. Having the idea, having the plan is the easy part; being driven and inspired for the entire journey is the tough bit, which is why not everyone makes it.

Do yourself a favour and be one of those that heeds the message and put the effort in, not just now, not just this week or month but for the duration, breathe life into your plan and strategy and live it every day.

Strategy is a big subject and one that I will be covering in a later book but for now you have enough information to make a difference and that is a good start.

"Strategy consists of the competitive moves and approaches that you employ to grow your business, attract and satisfy customers and successfully conduct your operations to achieve target levels of performance!"

Step 14: Make your marketing work.

I could rant a little about marketing and the number of smaller businesses that just don't get this right! Instead I am just going to tell you that marketing is and always will be at the centre of your business and everyone else's business too. The greatest sales success will come from those that invest in building a community through great marketing, content and expertise. If you do nothing else get this bit right and suddenly sales will be easier.

I often say to people, in my talks, that nothing in business happens without sales, and that is true. However, if you look beyond the sale in any really successful business, you'll find marketing at its very centre. Many experts have written many things about marketing and what it really means to business.

I believe that marketing has but one purpose in business and that is to make selling, I mean overt selling, pressure selling, obsolete. This is simply done; you just need to really understand who your customers are and what makes them tick. Find out what it is they want and then demonstrate that you know them, know what they want and make it readily available to them, this is done by using marketing techniques that demonstrate to your target market just that.

Here's a marketing mission that should fit all businesses where generating more sales is concerned, this is the same mission I have used in my e-book about social media marketing and all my past businesses and you're welcome to use it too:

"Make selling superfluous. Do this by knowing and understanding your customer so well your product sells itself. Marketing results in a customer who is ready to buy. All that is needed then is to make the product available to them."

Now that you have a sensible marketing mission, which is based on the wise words of the irreplaceable Peter Drucker, you now need to get the most you can from the marketing activity you undertake. The secret is to try a combination of activities and assess those that work the best for you and increase the activity in these areas, drop the ones that aren't working so well.

Step 15: Be seen as the expert.

Make it another objective in your overall mission to be seen by your target market as the expert. Demonstrate this expertise and leadership to your market through your marketing activity.

Most of us are operating in busy sectors with plenty of competition to monitor and in some cases be concerned about. Your aim is to be seen as the trusted expert in your market by all those that are and could be your customers. Here is a fact that many smaller businesses miss, it's simply this:

The moment you position yourself and your business as a credible, trusted expert, leader and adviser, you'll gain the markets attention, keep up the right activity and continue to demonstrate your expertise and you'll soon gain their trust and custom. Instead of selling to your market, engineer it so that they come to you to buy. Change your tactics from those overused sell, sell, sell, to the much under estimated tell, tell, tell!

Remember people hate to be sold to but they love to buy and so what you should be doing is creating an environment in which people want to buy. People have changed the way they buy. At the centre of their journey is a hunger for information, mostly gained online.

Step 16: Front to back marketing.

When I look back at my various projects both as CEO and Mentor, I clearly had the greatest success when using a 'Front End' and 'Back End' marketing strategy. Let me explain this in more detail because it can work for you too.

It is simply based on the understanding that when a customer first hears your sales message. The reality is in most cases they will feel at risk before they know more about you, through the selling and marketing process. As the marketing content increases their knowledge of you and the sales process underpins that marketing, they will begin to see, that what you are promising actually is what will be delivered, when and if they make the purchase.

"The worst thing you can do is over promise and under deliver – far better to under promise and then over deliver. That will give you a differential that few businesses have achieved."

So how can a customer know, before experiencing the result you promise? Every business I know of, promises great results; the reality is very few deliver on their promise to a level that is exceptional in the eyes of the client. Think long and hard about this and make sure you're not one that underdelivers on the promises made. If by chance you are, then let's work together in the Rainmakers Club to change this as soon as possible.

Look at what happens when the customer does receive the promised result from the sale you've made to them. That person then becomes a trusting, willing and active ongoing customer and provides you with a flow of additional sales and profits over a good number of months or even years.

The fact is that the majority of small businesses will experience the largest proportion of their marketing budget spent on the attempt to acquire new customers. The reality is most of that budget will go to waste. It has little or no effect. It is falling on deaf ears or perhaps misunderstanding ears.

No matter how much belief you may have in your product, no matter how delighted your existing customers are with what you sell to them, you'll find it hard to attract new customers that you need so much to develop your business. You'll probably also find it difficult to differentiate yourself from your competition. The solution to all this is simple, just create two clearly defined and different strategies to grow your business and gain competitive advantage. The strategy I suggest is split in the following way:

Front end—customer acquisition.
Back end—customer lifetime value proposition.

This is based on the understanding that most of the money your business will make will take place in the back end of the business rather than the front.

The key to this is to make the front end so attractive to the target market to buy from you for the very first time, that they find it almost impossible not to do just that. In this way you get a much better ROI (Return On Investment) on the cash that needs to be spent on the front end. Over time this will mean that an increasing number of people will be persuaded to buy from you rather than from the competition.

Having bought from you they will learn about the experience of using the product or services supplied by you and see that the promises of the front end were fully fulfilled. As a result, the majority of customers will appreciate and value you and continue to buy from you as well as spread the word to others they are connected to.

This continued buying from you is the back end and where most of the money is in most businesses. I believe the best way to gain the greatest advantage at the front end is to create a price differential, making the initial purchase very affordable rather than a high price compared to others in your immediate market. The rule is don't try to make too much money at the front end.

I have used this system myself in many of my businesses. I do this by giving the experience at the front end using low cost options with great information. Those that have agreed to buy go on to buy other affordable materials on a low-cost high-volume strategy.

Once the experience is complete some of the businesses will go on to request more paid for services at the back end.

Once you have this system up and running you have to make sure you spend enough time working intelligently and relentlessly on the development of the back end for without it the entire model will surely fail.

"The longer the customer spends with you the more value they will create for you. Therefore, find a way to get them into your buying process as early as you are able and then keep them there by creating repeatable value for them."

Step 17: Create a culture of coaching.

As you build your team around you it is essential that you create a culture of coaching throughout your entire business. Unlike training coaching should be a constant activity that all your team can take advantage of when they need it most. The coaching I am talking about doesn't have to be done by a coaching professional although there is certainly nothing wrong with using the services of a professional coach from time to time. I am talking about the creation of a culture of internal coaching, where members of the team assist each other in the development of skills and weaknesses on the job.

I remember the first time I took on this task. I had no idea how to go about it or if successful would it make the difference I was hoping for. Over a few years of wanting the same culture in all the teams I was involved with, I managed to refine the process to the point where I am now confident that given the right people, I can introduce this culture in a few short weeks. I do this by simply introducing a reward system that creates mutual reliance and performance to gain the full reward. This is one of the defining characteristics of the Rainmakers Club, along with everything else I talk about in this book.

The simplest version of this method is to have a financial bonus based on individual, team and group performance encouraging cooperation and coaching within teams.

Step 18: Your payday.

Don't just read these things commit to putting them into practise, my biggest wish for you is that you put plans into action as a result of this book, that you work toward your exit plan with passion and diligence that brings certain success. Your exit plan can see you with true financial independence and that is worth working toward, don't you think? That level of independence can and should be your ticket to do all those things you really want to.

The exit, in most cases will be based on you making significant gains as a result of employing the traits, hints and tips throughout this book. You can make it happen if you're minded to. You can make it happen if you take the decision to step out of the mainstream and become exceptional and that all starts with taking time to invest in the right activity, not just for a day or a week but all the time in everything you do. Key throughout this is your ability to communicate well, sell, and build enduring relationships and it is these skills we also want to look at now as they are an essential part of being a Rainmaker, of making rain in your business. Let's take a look.

PART TWO

Communicating, Selling & Creating Enduring Relationships.

The Ten Rules of Relationship Selling

During my career I have always sought to improve my understanding of the skills and activities that create and attract success in business. One of the things I have learnt is that the basic skills required for relationship-based selling are key to success and that every person in business should take the time to learn and refine their selling skills. In this part of the book we are going to take all the hints and tips from part one and merge them with the basic skills required for successful selling. My experience in sales has built up over the years, predominantly by learning from the best. I have learnt ten key rules that for me tell you all you need in a snapshot; all need to know to be an exceptional salesperson based on the promotion of enduring relationships.

Rule 1—People not Products.

"The most successful businesspeople understand that it's all about people not products. Concentrate on the people not the products, because people still buy from people. In most cases people they like, even online selling now requires personality!"

Rule 2—People don't like being sold to but love to buy.

"Think about it I bet you're the same. Don't sell; instead create an environment that promotes the natural desire in people to want to buy. Then make sure it's you they want to buy from, by demonstrating your expertise in your content!"

Rule 3—A sale is always made.

"Selling is just communication and there will always be an outcome or if you prefer a sale! You don't need to get the deal every time, you just need to take the next step forward toward the ultimate goal a new and loyal connection and or client.

Rule 4—Always be prepared.

"Never go to a meeting or make a call without being prepared and well-practised. Do your homework. A little preparation and planning goes a long way toward success!"

Rule 5—More sales are made through friendship than salesmanship.

"Take time to really get to know the people, friendship will lead to more sales, repeat business and referrals, your life blood in business!"

Rule 6—Have a great elevator pitch.

"You only get one chance to make a first impression, make sure the first thing you say sets the right tone and creates some curiosity. Inspire people to want to know more and ask you the right questions to inspire action!"

Rule 7—Get your prospect thinking as if they already have the product.

"Tell a relevant story about what it's like to own one. Concentrate on the Features Advantages and Benefits that they are most interested in. You'll know this from the great questions you've asked when getting to know them!"

Rule 8—Practice everything.

"Selling is the greatest communication skill and like all top performers to be the best you need to practise and then practise some more; practice makes it look natural and seamless!"

Rule 9—Always have an end in mind.

"When you get the job right, you'll probably not have to close because you've already been asked for the outcome you desire. If that is not the case then you close to get a positive outcome, that is what they are expecting you to do!"

Rule 10—Control the journey.

"Let the prospect talk, in fact let them do most of the talking and you do the listening. Control the journey with well-placed open and closed questions. Open to get the data you need and closed to confirm facts and control the direction and pace!"

Selling a dirty word or must have skill?

"Anyone with the skills to sell well will have a job for life as long as they concentrate on the people."

There are many people, in fact an alarming number of people who see selling as a bit of a dirty word. I guess that's because they either remember the bad old days of pressure sales, or they have heard the horror stories of bad sales habits or sharp practice.

The reality is that selling is a vital skill, I would argue that we all have to sell every day and some of us are good at it and others not so good. A CEO has to sell their ideas to the board and the staff. A staff member has to sell their request for a pay rise or more investment for the department. Selling in reality is nothing more than smart communication and looking after the interests of the people through the provision of suitable solutions.

Selling isn't a dirty word at all, done correctly it is an essential skill that will keep bread on your table for life! It will also make you many friends but only if done the right way. I truly believe that there is only one way to gain true success in business and that is to learn the art selling. Learn to sell with great respect for the person or people you are selling to and remember your greatest priority is the people and not the product, the solution that fits them perfectly and not the commission. Do it for the buzz and not for the money and the money will follow in any event and you'll feel better for it! Selling is a must have skill for any business owner.

Making Rain the beginning and end of business!

The reality is that sales (done really well) are the beginning middle and end of all business and it is true to say that nothing in business happens without sales. It should therefore be one of, if not the most, important element in the operational side of business. That is why sales skills are so very important. Perhaps the most important, save perhaps for marketing, so closely related to sales. Therefore, a good rainmaker is going to be one of the most highly prized assets for any business, with great skill in sales and marketing.

"Without sales nothing and I mean nothing in business happens, as my old friend said if you need more cash in the business, then sell more!"

It's no good coming up with a great product or a great idea for a business if you then don't have the skill to sell the idea or product. The success you achieve can be attributed to a number of related activities. Depending on whom you talk to, you will get to hear many different views as to which of the elements making a great business are the most important.

In reality all the elements are important, but it is right to say that nothing in business happens without sales and the best sales come from marketing, great marketing will make selling so much easier. This is a subject that I feel just as passionately about as sales they go together like a dovetail joint.

No matter how great the idea, how good the product, if they are not being sold in the right quantity the business will go nowhere. I am going to give you a quick tour of those skills that all the superstars demonstrate, they will help you to accelerate your sales performance by understanding the skills and process better when added to the personal traits also covered in this book you will increase your value to any business. Perhaps I will introduce you to some new ideas, most likely it will remind you or endorse things you already know but may have forgotten in the heat of battle and we all do that! If you need a quick fix and want to know the secret to selling right now, then here it is: There is no secret, just hard work, the right mental attitude and loads of preparation, practise and planning!

Think of selling as great communication!

The first thig you have to do is get rid of any barriers you may have built, that prevent you from seeing yourself as a person who sells. If you run a business, you must be in sales! I can remember, on more than a few occasions, delivering sales training or coaching to different companies and always having one or two people in the audience who would state that they were not a salesperson, or worse still that they had no interest in selling. That's because their perception of sales centred on an image of the guy with case full of samples trying to get past your front door to sell you something you didn't need, didn't want and quite frankly didn't understand! That's not what we are talking about; we are professional businesspeople with pride in what we do. We care about the people first, the right solution second and well, if we do a good job a guilt free reward. If that's not you, you might be reading the wrong book or perhaps living in the wrong century! So, for those of you that agree with me lets read on, for the others who don't, well to be frank you better read on too!

"Cut through all the jargon! Selling is nothing more than really good communication with a logical structure, that is why we should all learn to sell."

Change is constant and the way people buy also changes, the more sophisticated technology becomes, the greater the level of information available to those buying and at the same time the less they want to be pushed and the more they want to be led by an expert. The real skill to selling is not 'foot in the door' tactics but smart communication. That's right as far as I'm concerned, selling is nothing more than communication that is very well done and that's what we are focus on, great communication, great sales based on a process that makes perfect sense to the internet savvy buyers of today.

In today's business world we all have to sell! Even those who would say with great conviction that they are not salespeople are going to be called upon to sell, perhaps not in the traditional way but sell they must. Every time you talk to another person, friend, family, colleague, stranger or boss about something which you would like them to agree to or with; or react to in a certain way, you'll only succeed if you sell them the idea in such a way that they can see the benefits. Then they will want to respond in the way you're looking for! That my friend is selling!

I know this can be a contentious point and there are many counter views to this but talking generically and ignoring, for the moment, the subjects of leadership, Influence and other complimentary skills that help in great communication, the truth is that if you want to get any idea across or motivate someone to take a particular action, you are going to have to sell them on the idea.

The world of sales has changed. The true leaders in sales today are the true experts on their subject. No longer the provider of a predictable sales message but a true expert. They have personality people like them, and they can communicate at an above average standard. Increasingly entrepreneurs, engineers, chemists, technicians are becoming the latest generation of exceptional salespeople; at the same time large numbers of traditional salespeople are falling off the edge of the world!

I remember on one occasion I needed my engineering team to amend one of the services we were supplying to our customers, but I needed the engineers to undertake some development to make it happen. They needed to be onside and therefore I needed to sell them the idea to gain their complete buy-in. In reality doing this used the same process as the one I use to sell a product to a prospect or existing customer. You see there really is no difference it all comes down to the same characteristics and traits. It comes down to communication, passion and knowledge!

I can remember that one particular engineer, with complete passion and an unrivalled knowledge of the product also had a natural tendency to like people; he became our top consultative salesperson.

"It really is about communication, about people, about using well-chosen words to motivate the right actions from those you talk to."

Most people would think nothing of standing at the bar trying to sell to their best friend the advantages of their new iPhone or selling them on the idea of a weekend break to go see a concert or soccer match. It is all just selling; it is all just smart communication. You're more likely to get what you want if you understand the person you're talking to. If you can generate motivation, if you ensure that they understand you and they can see there is a win for them too, that is what I call selling, what I call good communication!

Spot The Difference!

Sales V's Communication.

Having said that selling is based on well-executed communication, I want to clarify, there is a difference between normal daily communication and sales. The difference between selling and normal communication all comes down to process, planning and preparation.

To sell really well you need great communication skills, the big difference between selling and conversation is that with informal communication we communicate without always having the need to gain something whereas when you communicate in sales there is always a point that requires a positive action of some description. Let's dig a little deeper into this and gain more insight into this way of thinking about sales and communication. It's these views that I have based my entire career in business on and built more than a few successful sales teams on for both my own business and the businesses of others on both sides of the Atlantic.

Presentation skills, presenting to groups of people is another form of selling that I have great passion for. Presenting and Selling are very closely linked to each other and have little in common with simple communication between people in everyday life. I have found in business the skill of public speaking to be a significant asset and a great producer of sales leads. I therefore urge you all to practise and refine your public speaking skills as part of your sales development.

If I had to identify, outside of the really obvious things, the difference between communicating on a day-to-day basis and selling it always comes down to research, planning, preparation and closing! It is these four things that truly differentiate selling (and presenting) from standard day to day communications.

I feel I should point out to all the old school sales people (no offense intended) that when I talk about closing I am not talking about getting the sale but more reaching your objective, either the major overall objective or one of the multiple steps you may have to take to get there; all of which are objectives in their own right, or as I am calling them here closes.

"The really big difference between conversation and selling is the amount of preparation, planning and research you should be doing before you start."

If you already have some degree of interaction with the person you ultimately want to sell to, maybe you were introduced to each other through a mutual friend and you want to pick the phone up to talk to them about something in particular, just normal day-to-day social stuff, you would do just that! There would be no need to do any preparation or planning, just say Hi and then tell them what it is that you wanted to tell or ask them. Plain and simple communication. Oh, and please remember it only qualifies as true communication if information is flowing in both directions! Too many salespeople fall into the trap of giving mini lectures rather than joining or starting conversations.

If you use social media, and most of us do, you'll know to get followers and build your connections you need to join in not just broadcast but receive and react too. Those that I meet who have few followers tend to have either just started or are not engaging. The same these days is true of sales. We need to get used to having conversations on Facebook, LinkedIn, Blogs and many other similar platforms, so we can engage inform and connect with those that we want to make clients.

We need to be a little bit sensible about jumping in too soon with the familiar conversational style and understand the difference between a conversation between people who already know each other or people who are connected in some way on one of the many Social Media sites and building the first tentative steps in rapport.

If you've tried to be too familiar too soon with someone new, you would quickly notice that you were burning all but a few of your leads because you were treating a complete stranger as if they were someone who you'd known for some time. Some would say that approaching a stranger and being able to talk to them as if they were a long-lost friend was a demonstration of great self-confidence and that may be true. However, this skill is not effective on its own and you'd do well to remember that before you treat that person with that degree of familiarity you should first break the ice and get to know them on a very basic level. It is the things you learn about them, from them and share with them that will give you the ability and credibility to break the ice and become more conversational.

The only people who can get away with the familiar approach from cold or nearly cold are those that have some kind of celebrity status. They can get away with it because the more famous they are the more you already know about them, it's as if you've already gone through the getting to know you phase of relationship building.

In the real world we have to work at this to start with and steadily build a relationship based on trust. Now I am no celebrity, but I can give you an example of how this works. I was writing a daily blog as the CEO for a web company a while back. The more often I wrote about a day in the life of the CEO, the more people followed and some even started to comment on the posts.

A few months into this blog and I found myself in Birmingham, England, for a series of meetings at a Holiday Inn. I walked up to the main desk of this particular hotel, one I had not been to before, and to my amazement the receptionist, again I had never come across her before, said; 'Hello Chris, how's the neck now? Are you back at the gym yet?' She did this because she had been reading the blog and from this, she had learnt about a neck injury I had sustained and how that was keeping me from the gym. She felt like she knew me despite the fact we had never met!

I saw a similar thing at a sporting dinner, this time I was introduced to the spouse of a colleague and we politely shook hands and exchanged very polite unfamiliar pleasantries. Within seconds she was introduced, for the first time, to Frank Bruno a well-known ex world heavyweight boxing champion. Because he was so well known she greeted him like she had known him for years kissing his cheek and saying; "Hi Frank, you look great!" When I later asked her about it she explained that she had seen him so many times on different media vehicles she felt she knew him.

For us mortals we have to put the work in! We have to do our research, preparation and planning and then, with a fair wind and some focused work, we will get to the same point of familiarity that will make the sale possible.

Sales communication requires more work, before during and after. I want to share with you those skills that will set you apart from the rest, by developing the true sales skills, those that will make you better than the average and with practise as good as the very best. Understanding these skills is vital, the more you know, the more you understand, the better you'll be at communicating, selling and relationship building!

"Selling does involve a certain amount of luck. However, it is also true to say the harder and smarter you work the luckier you'll become."

So, to recap the difference between communication and selling starts with understanding that you can't be a great salesperson with just the gift of the gab, it helps but that is all. What you really need is knowledge of the product, the market, the people involved and the confidence to use it conversationally at the right time with the right people and to understand the importance of trust; the ability to build relationships based on a sincere desire to help others. If you're in sales now and don't have that natural and sincere desire, you might need to think about a career change, you won't last without it!

Average Sales V's exceptional Sales.

I don't want to give the impression that what I am writing about is the only way to sell, nor do I want to try to say that my way is the best way. It all comes down to how you want to operate. I do believe that what I am calling my way is not really that at all. I have adopted it from the best sales experts and businesspeople I know who use this way of selling very successfully. I just think you should listen to the rules, tips and hints, really listen, take them onboard, make them your own and watch your business rocket skyward! This book in its entirety will give you a significant edge in business and in sales, it may even help with personal relationships.

When I first started in sales I worked with major national salesforces, they taught me a sales process that was all about the product. In most cases this was delivered by insincere people who pretended to care about the person, this was not an efficient method and not many salespeople lasted the course as a result. Most of the people I met were what I would later call sales nomads, who went from company to company selling for a few months and then moving on, with no loyalty and no passion!

It was common in many major B2C industries using the same methods, which were all about targets, it was all about moving as much product as you could. The people on both sides of the sale were not important it was the figures that counted!

It was not a great time for sales and not a time I would want to see again. It did get me started and I can see why figures have their place but not to the detriment of the way people are treated. Numbers should be the indicators for hiring, firing, mentoring and training. I can still remnants of this type of 'selling' in many call centre's working on cold data but even then they need to concentrate on the people and the right motivation. Many people who work for call centre's do have the right motivation, but I have seen many cases where it is knocked out of them and replaced with metrics, quotas and the wrong management devoid of leadership!

"Numbers and activity are important but not more important than being a good person with sincere desires to help people, don't let the numbers take over. Use them as a coaching tool not a sledgehammer to crack a nut!"

For the most part this book is about you becoming an exceptional businessperson who understands the human side of business or if you prefer an exceptional communicator! Average and exceptional selling do have many things in common with each other, what makes them different and why I say you have no option but to follow the path of exceptional is simply that average has no real shelf life and although you may sell a bit you'll never have longevity and you certainly won't make many enduring friends along the way. No friends will mean no referrals. No referrals will mean no prospects and of course no prospects mean you have no prospects!

The old model had the characteristics of being relentless obvious pressure, you can see the sale and the close coming from a mile away, I suppose there is some honesty in that at least! The exceptional or new way however is more in tune with people than product and therefore I characterise that as being relationship oriented and reliant on the interaction of the people involved. My personal experience is using the old way I got average results and I had to work very hard to get those! While the new way resulted in more business, more connections and better relationships. Many of the sales I make using these methods are closed by the customer before I get a chance to ask for the business. What a great situation to be in, don't you think?

You could argue that both methods do share the same navigation process but that at certain points in that navigation the detail behind the individual elements is quite different as the level of detail and relationship required for the exceptional way is much higher than that of the average way.

"The average way has its place, but it will certainly not work with high value or more intangible product sales. The more intangible the product the greater the skill required to gain the sale."

The 'Old' way was almost completely product based and questions were filtered toward the product. The 'New' way is all about problem solving, needs and solutions, all about the people and all about the relationship. In summary, the main differences between the old and new. The old or average way is very much oriented toward the product and the new or exceptional method is all about the people and the best possible solution.

For example, the old way of prospecting was to just qualify the person, ensuring they were the right one to talk to for the purposes of selling the product. Whereas the exceptional way is to find out as much as you can about the person, their motivations and or the business so that you can engage them in quality conversation about who they are, what they do and what they want. Making it all about them and not about you.

Once in front of the prospect the old way is to ask questions that direct the client to a certain kind of answer that will result in your product being the subject for discussion, finding out about just those items you need to know to demonstrate the suitability of your product.

The new way, on the other hand, is not filtered and comes from a genuine interest in the other person and a genuine desire to help, that desire requires a deeper understanding of what makes the prospect tick.

When it comes to the identification of the prospect and what they might need, the old way is product based, whereas the new is based on a true interest in what the prospect thinks, feels and needs. With the need identified the solution is presented, if it is the old way then it is very product specific and the new should talk about a range of alternate solutions rather than just the product in your bag!

When it comes to the close, the old way assumes the ultimate close is everything. The new way often results in no close being needed because the prospect asks to do business with you because you've ticked all their boxes and demonstrated your interest in them, your knowledge and your expertise!

In reality most salespeople are caught in the middle, almost as a hybrid between old and new. The important thing is no matter where you are, make sure that you take account of the person first, the product will look after itself, or it should do. If you feel the need to sell the product hard maybe just maybe it's not the right fit, or you've got some ticks missing in some important boxes.

Understand people are different.

The best way of selling is understanding that people are different and working with the difference. The old way was to go through the process and get to the close as quickly as you were able. I'm not suggesting that the old way does not work or take account of people. I am however suggesting that it doesn't take enough account of people and their differences to help you gain really exceptional results.

"I am not a number I am a free man! I don't fit a box. If I buy from you it's because you understand me, and I feel you have my best interests at heart."

I can remember my training with the TSB and another well-known Insurance company, both of whom ran well-respected sales training schools. So good were these schools that it was not unusual for people to join the business just so they could get the training. I say that because I was one of them! Interestingly none of this training, despite how good it was, ever mentioned the difference an individual's personality could and should make to the way in which a sale is made.

I am sure that in the past I have lost many a sale, not because I can't sell but because nobody ever told me about the impact of personality. I was too busy trying to close, to make target, to take time and think about it! You just don't know what you don't know. As one of my mentors used to say to me "Remember Pigs don't know Pigs stink!"

Once you understand that people are different, life suddenly becomes so much easier and not just for sales, let me recap from earlier in this book about some of these major differences. Let's keep it simple, more for me that for you. People can be split into generic personality types and these different types all react to conversations and sales presentations in different ways. If you can identify what personality type the person, you're talking to is, then you can avoid some of the issues they may have with you if you're a different personality type to them. So, it is more complex than we are dealing with in this book as some of the recognised instruments used in profiling, including the Rainmakers Club profiling tools use 16 segmentations. For this book we are only looking for the fundamental differences to watch out for, these are:

- **Action or Reflector**
- **Big Picture or Detail**

- **Toward goals or away from problems**

People are either going to be Action people or Reflectors, when it comes to making a decision and those that are action oriented will become frustrated by those who are reflectors and vice-versa. The action person will make a quick decision based on what might be described as a reflex reaction or instinct made up of their experience. The reflector will want to take their time and consider all the options, consider all the possibilities and make a decision in their own time.

There are those who are Big Picture people and those who are Detail oriented. The big picture person will look beyond the field they are currently in and beyond the hedgerow toward the far distant horizon. The detail person will want to see every possible detail, every blade of grass and examine them at great length. These two different personality types will react against each other if you lack the understanding of what makes them tick. The detail person having no interest in the bigger picture before they understand the finite detail and the big picture person not wanting to be held back by all the detail, they just want to get on with it, although later the detail may become important to them.

There are those that have Goals and move toward their goals and all that they do is based on achieving that goal. Then there are those that move away from Problems leaving the current situation not to chase the goal but to move away from the problem.

Now imagine being one and not the other and imagine how you would respond if the person selling to you was the opposite, you would soon get frustrated and the sale would be lost. If the person took time to understand you through good question technique and research, then used that information to present to you in a way that appealed to you, imagine how much better that would be. It won't surprise you to learn that I'm an action, big picture and goal-oriented person and that probably comes across in all that I do including my writing! Now you know that you can pick up the phone and sell to me in the right way, once you know what I need!

The Basic Sales Process

Let it guide you not restrict you.

Knowing the basic sales process will not make you a great salesperson but it will certainly help to make sense of the routines, which are the foundation to a good sale. The sales process is a very valuable guideline and, in most cases, should be followed as a guide. It is logical and will create a journey for the customer that makes sense to them. Done well it puts them at ease and protects them from buying things they don't need, want or understand.

The sales process will protect you from those who just want to waste your time and have no intention of buying, but again only when done well! However, just because it's a valuable guideline it doesn't mean each time you go into a sales meeting you need to follow the process to the letter. Now and again you might not need to go through the entire process. Now and again you might have someone in front of you who just wants to buy. That being the case, just make sure they understand what it is they're getting.

Do this by satisfying yourself it is good advice for them and complete the deal on that basis. If you think you have a better solution or if you think it is just wrong to use this solution, let your values guide you. Do not be afraid to enter into a conversation that respectfully points out the true situation. By doing this you might lose a sale, but you'll be true to your values and make a friend at the same time. A friend, who will at some point do business with you. A friend who will refer others to you! The best way to handle this situation is to use the process to establish the need and then present your version of the right solution.

"The best sales are the ones that are done because the customer has a need for the product, and you can both clearly see it is the most appropriate advice."

We all know the person just asking to do business is not going to happen that often, unless this is an existing client doing repeat business. Most of the time you should stick to the process. Practice makes perfect and so practise using the process, make it conversational, professional, relaxed, confident and learn it inside and out. Most of all make it fun; make it enjoyable for you and the customer. Selling should be fun! Buying should be fun and this process is designed to be used in conjunction with the creation of an atmosphere in which people want to buy. Creating the right atmosphere leads to enjoyable sales and that is where true sales success comes from!

Research

I believe the first step we should take in any sales process is research in most cases this should be the initial activity, to help you prepare and equip you with the right information. Because with the high levels of information available on the Internet, research has become the most valuable tool for the sales professional. In no time you can have all you need to make an informed initial approach. The research is where you find the right people to talk to, through a number of channels. These contacts will then be converted into a series of leads and the smarter you are with your research and marketing activity the more qualified leads you will generate.

The greater the qualification, before the approach, the bigger the number of conversions into sales. The more quality sales you have the greater the revenue, reputation and brand value you create! Great business all comes down to the conversion of leads into quality sales and repeat business.

A large part of sales success comes down to marketing and as the business world relies more on technologies and our buying habits change, leaning heavily on the Internet and information, marketing becomes increasingly important. We will leave marketing for another time, but it is worth pointing out that if nothing happens in business without sales, not much happens in sales without marketing. Prospecting is simply to identify a number of targets likely to benefit from your product and engineer a personal contact strategy. Prospecting is a vital part of your preparation and good solid research will help to ensure greater success.

I feel, as a potential customer there is nothing worse that meeting a sales person who has taken the time to make an appointment to see me, who then arrives at the meeting, right time, right place, looking good and then enters into a whole range of dumb questions that he or she should have found out before arriving at my office. To me it indicates a lack of interest in the task. I'm not talking about the personal stuff that I would expect to be questioned on but things like, 'what is it you do?' 'Do you have a website?' seriously you'd be amazed how many times I have been asked questions like that!

I think the one that stands out the most in my recent memory is the sales guy who called me and said I am in the area is there any chance I can pop in and have a chat next week? I agreed, there was no harm in listening to what he had to say. He opened the meeting by handing me his card and saying so Chris what is it you need from me? I looked at him and said, 'knowing who you are, and your agenda might help!' In reality it was too late the damage that bad first question caused was not recoverable.

I can remember once being approached by a salesperson from a bank who asked me for a few moments, I agreed and the first question they asked me was; "When was the last time you had your financial planning reviewed?" If they had 'Googled' my name before they picked up the phone, or even just looked at the company website, they would have discovered I was the CEO of an Independent Financial Adviser Company! With that small but vital snippet of information they would have either had a totally different opening, or perhaps not bothered at all!

"There is nothing worse, or more insulting than having a meeting with a salesperson who has clearly done nothing to prepare for the meeting and illustrates the point by asking dumb questions!"

Basic information should be researched before you go to the meeting as part of your standard procedure, make it a habit of yours. I went to a sales meeting for a new client a while back, I was not familiar with the sector and so I made sure that during my prospecting phase I did my homework. By the time I got to the prospects office I was able to hold a conversation that proved I was interested and proved I had taken the time to learn about their business and learn about their sector.

I could talk about their last year of trading results, I could tell them what the entire sector was worth and the most recent financial trends from 2009 right up to 2012. I was able to comment on their web offering, its ranking and congratulate them on their SEO. Now how do you think that made the prospect feel compared to being asked a whole bunch of dumb questions? The simple model I use for prospecting is broken down into two stages.

Stage 1 is simply to go through your list of potential customers and do some very basic research on the web to assist you in the qualification of the lead. Make sure the person you are aiming to talk to is the right person to contact. Ask this simple question, will they be able to take you onto the next stage?

If it looks simple and obvious, that's because it is. The trouble is, in my experience, not many salespeople invest enough, if any, time in this simple but vital activity. Instead they prefer to play it by ear and maybe fall into the trap of asking dumb questions, or worse still, make inaccurate assumptions and lose what could be significant opportunities.

Just a quick point here, the right person at this stage of the process might not be the decision maker for the eventual sale but might be the person who can introduce you to the decision maker. Treat the gatekeeper or introducer with the same respect and importance as you would the ultimate decision maker. They deserve your respect and, in any event, can be most valuable to you. Have the approach that everybody knows somebody you'd like to know and then you can't go wrong.

"Be respectful to everybody you meet and never say anything you would not want to be repeated!"

Armed with some basic information to qualify the lead and some valuable and interesting subjects to talk about with your first contact or gatekeeper, you have a good starting point for the conversation that will start the relationship off on the right foot. With practise and good research, you'll find that the first approach will generate many meetings with the right people and will be the start point of your sales acceleration to exceptional and sustainable performance. With a meeting arranged we can start onto the next stage.

Stage 2 the second stage and do a much more detailed search; this is your opportunity to get down to the really important material that will make a difference at point of sale. Whenever I do this research, pre-sale, I follow the same format, that enables me to make sure I get a good picture.

When the meeting takes place, it is clear to the person I am meeting that I have taken an interest in the person, the team, the business, the industry and the competition. Having this level of intelligence is so much simpler than it sounds and takes no more than a few minutes if you know where to look on the Internet.

My first stop is to Google the name of the person that I am going to be talking to and the name of the company. I do this not because I couldn't be bothered to find out the company URL but because I am looking for other content that might relate to the business or person. An example might be articles; social media pages or blog posts anything that is going to give me useful intelligence about the subject.

I will of course also go to the web site and have a good look around and see what I can learn about strategies, tactics, team members, product information, personality and marketing proposition. I will also look at their Vision Mission and Values; this will give me a valuable insight into the objectives and culture of the business. Using Google™ again I will look for industry statistics that are going to give me a heads-up on the state of play the recent history and performance figures as well as anything else that might help me, for example; demographics, new technologies, ideas, new entrants and mergers.

I will also spend some time looking at the most obvious search words on all the popular search engines including YouTube™ to find out who else is working with them and who else is in their arena. This then gives me a window into the competition, more really useful information before I venture into a sales meeting with the prospect.

My final actions are to check out Companies House and some of the well-known business networking sites including LinkedIn™ so that I can see who knows who, which can be invaluable information, particularly if I can discover some common ground to use as part of the icebreaker! I also like to look at industry statistics for an even better feel for the landscape.

"This is also a good time to set up some Google™ Alerts to keep you up to date post the meeting, you can never have too much information."

With all the information lined up I now have a great picture of the prospect and the space in which they operate. The great thing about this kind of intelligence is it is reusable when I see other businesses in the same space, not to gossip but to demonstrate understanding. It also works well if a referral is given by this prospect into someone else that they know in the same sector. Job done, it's time to move on to the next phase of the sales process.

Know your client—The Fact Find.

I have always called this phase of the process the 'Fact Find.' In my first sales job, the company made the mistake of turning this phase into a form filling exercise. This was partially due to the need for compliance with what was back then new legal requirements and the need to make sure the entire sales force kept to the record keeping and evidential regulations.

The problem with that system was the business would provide the salesperson with a form to complete. These were never that well-constructed and invariably did not leave enough space for all the information, worse still they almost encouraged an interrogation with a series of closed questions that did little in the way of building the relationship. I guess this could have worked if the sales team had been trained and coached to only use the form as a guide and still invested time in making the process conversational. The adviser was more interested in keeping the management happy by completing the form than building rapport with the potential client.

The purpose of this stage of the process is for the salesperson to get to know the prospect through a series of open and closed questions delivered in a conversational way. The rule I want you to remember is; to get you have to give first and therefore you should make a point of not just taking but giving information too.

This should be done as part of a two-way conversation. At this stage it is important to avoid the temptation to give product related information, which will sound more like a pitch than a conversation, running the risk of losing the prospect along the way; because as a rule people hate to be sold to, although they do love to buy.

Your primary aim should be to gather as much information as you can about all aspects of the individual insofar as it is relevant to the job in hand. That job is the building of a relationship and that is designed to lead to the eventual sale. This is achieved through a combination of open and closed questions and a bucket full of active listening. A word of warning, do it because you want to learn about them so you can do the best job possible, do it because you want to help, be sincere in your actions and your motivation. Never just go through the motions, you'll get found out and let potentially great opportunities walk out of the door into the arms of your competition.

Let's briefly talk about some of the core things you will want to know about your prospect. There are two fundamentals to this, first there is the personal facts that will give you all you need to build rapport and get to know the person, which after all is the backbone to the sale. You need to know what makes them tick at every level.

Then there are those facts that let you understand how and why this person buys. This is the same kind of information any marketer would want to know so they could design a focused campaign. Here are pointers to the information it would be useful to understand:

- When do they buy?
- What do they buy?
- Why do they buy?
- Where do they buy?
- How do they pay?
- What do they pay?

Open Questions.

During this phase open questions should be used wherever possible, they promote conversation and get the potential client talking about the things that motivate them, things you need to know. An open question is one that requires your prospect to give a detailed open answer. In other words, not just a yes or a no. A typical open question might be: "Tell me about your family?" You can see how a question phrased this way will encourage the respondent to give a wide-ranging conversational answer, making conversation rather than conducting an interrogation. This is a really important part of the relationship building process, which is what business is all about.

"Tell me about your family?" Will start a conversation, whereas "Are you married?" "Do you have children?" Feels like an interrogation.

Closed Questions.

The closed question does the exact opposite of the open question. The closed question is posed in such a way that it generally only requires a yes or no answer. Like the example already given. Asking; "Tell me about your family?" Is so much better than; "Are you married?" "Do you have children?"

You can also see from this that you would have to ask far more questions that were closed to get the result you would from one well-placed open question. However, the closed question does have its use when you need to collate key facts. My personal preference is to always mix them up, open and closed and that way you can keep the meeting conversational and control its pace by using the occasional closed question.

I do also use closed questions at the end of a meeting just to tie up any areas where I may need additional information. Closed questions are good for taking control of important moments and changing the pace of the conversation.

Control should be used with care, remember this is not about power it's about building relationships, remembering they are the most important person in the room.

"Don't take it for granted, practise open and closed questions with your friends to hone your skills."

Active Listening.

I know we have talked about this briefly earlier in the book, but I have included listening again because you would be surprised at the number of people out there that are so used to listening to themselves that they have forgotten how to listen to others and I don't want you to be one of those.

Some people will multitask and scribble away while the other person is talking, which is just as bad as not listening in some ways and does not promote conversation. It takes your mind off what is being said and also acts as a distraction. If you need to take notes at the time of the conversation, learn to take notes while maintaining the maximum eye contact and using affirmations.

"The cardinal sin when listening is to simply use the time to decide on what you want to say next. Leave that thought; it will take care of itself when it's time. Instead concentrate on what is being said."

In sales it is not enough to listen, you have to show that you're listening too, not just because it is a good technique, which it is, because you are sincere in your desire to learn and you respect the person talking to you. Active listening requires you to keep a degree of eye contact; to use body language to show that you are not just listening but interested.

If you are on the phone you will have to use your voice to confirm to the person on the other end that you are listening. If you're using Social Media or chat technologies, you can use symbols and comments to do the same. This is not done by interrupting or talking across them, it is done by acknowledgment signals, like, 'Oh I see' or 'I understand' or 'that is interesting.'

We all know you can learn things by listening and you should not ignore the power of a good listener. I saw the results of a University study recently where it was made clear that listening was key to success in communication. A group of people were asked to vote on whom amongst them was the best communicator. The results were a surprise to them all. The person deemed to be the best communicator was the person who by some margin did the least talking but the most listening!

Identify The Need.

During the last step of getting to know your potential client you will have started to understand what it is they may be looking for. This next phase is all about identifying exactly what it is your client needs from you and indeed if you are able to help. During this stage you will need to ask more detailed questions to get a real feel for what it is the client is looking for. Once this is established, I would recommend you confirm this back to the client to ensure that you have got all the information and detail correctly interpreted before you continue.

Depending on your product, you may be able to continue with the sale at this point, or you may need to close the meeting to prepare a suitable recommendation, either way the process is still fundamentally the same. You now have to design the potential solution for presentation to the client either now or during a future meeting. If your process is one that requires you to come back for additional meetings, you'll still need to leave with the commitment from the client. So, after confirming the exact nature of the need, close the sale down by gaining the commitment from your client that they will see you again. Explain that you will be able to present to them the solution that you've designed for them at the next meeting.

I would always make sure I left with a confirmed appointment for the presentation, making sure that I had left enough time to prepare for the presentation. Once back at the office I would always make sure the client received a confirmatory letter, email, text or some other suitable communication technology to remind them of the next actions and appointment.

Present The Solution.

Whcn presenting the solution, you still need to make it conversational and not just a string of business or product related jargon. As a rule of thumb, it is good to only use the jargon that the client is aware of or would use in their own business. If in doubt use no jargon at all, far better to be understood than lose the prospects attention due to jargon, so keep it simple!

Where possible use visual aids to help with the presentation, the more senses you engage the better. The art of presenting has many rules some of which are covered in this book. The key is that you need to keep the presentation fluid, and understandable to the audience, it needs to show the client how the solution solves the issues that were previously identified as needing to be dealt with. It is during this stage you should ensure the client has a full understanding of the solution, the best way to do this is to split the different elements of the product into three related sections; these are called features, advantages and benefits.

Feature—Advantage—Benefit

This is how it should work, or at least this is the way that seems to work the for most of the business personalities I know and look up to. Once you have worked through the first feature (this should be related directly to the established need of the prospect) you explain the advantage that it gives and then how that will benefit the potential client. Once completed you start again with the next feature and so on.

"The more information you give during the Features, Advantages and Benefits, the less likely it is that you'll experience objections later in the process."

When you have gone through the main features you can talk about the financial aspects of the sale. Many salespeople prefer to call the price something else, like the investment, I guess this is just personal preference, whatever your preference, cover the cost and any payment plans that might be available. Unless you want to hold back on any plans and use them to handle a price related objection from the potential client. A price related objection towards the end of the sale indicates you didn't cover all the points in enough detail earlier in the process. I personally bring price into the mix early so I can directly relate them to the features, advantages and benefits and concentrate on the value proposition. I also make sure that in the early stages of the process I establish affordability. This is a subject that is avoided by many. Not me! If you think about it the earlier, you deal with this the better. It saves wasting yours and their precious time.

Now it's time to invite questions, questions the client may have relating to the product or price, some of these might be what we call objections, objections are covered in the next part of the process. Objections can be raised at any time during the process and so be ready, be prepared and be practised in the art of handling them. The sooner in the process you can deal with them the better. In the ideal world you would cover enough detail throughout the process to negate objections completely, something to aspire to.

Things don't always go to plan though so you need to be prepared. The difference between an objection and a question is simply that the question is a quest for more information while the objection has the potential to be a reason not to buy.

The Close.

Closing the sale is the area that creates the greatest issue for most people in business, regardless of age, gender and levels of experience. There is nothing to fear, all you are doing is bringing the meeting to a point of focus that was the entire purpose of all the work that came before this moment. In some cases, you may not even have to close, that is the ultimate compliment to your handling of the process!

The more experience I gained in sales the more often I found that I didn't need to close, because during all the previous stages I had covered the points that were needed. I invited all the right questions and handled possible touch points before they became objections, so all that was left was for the client to ask for the business.

Having said that, there were just as many times when this was not the case and it was down to me to close the sale and in so doing invite any last-minute doubts or objections the client might have. Providing these were all handled, the close would happen, if all the bases had been covered correctly.

I think it's important to understand, for those who are just starting out in sales or still learning to refine their skills, the close will be in your favour if you cover your bases, in other words the client will say yes to you.

The more you cover during the presentation, the more questions you encourage. Once the questions are dealt with and the better your initial research and fact finding was, the less likely you are to have to close the sale for yourself, the client will do it for you.

When I first started out in sales, I can remember vividly my sales training, I remember I had problems with the close. I was fine in role-play and in the class, but in front of real people I found it difficult to get to the close, and the people in front of me were not helping. At the time I didn't really understand why. By the end of my first year at the sharp end I was getting the sales but was still not happy about my performance, despite finishing near the top of the performance charts with 140% of target.

I was soon to discover why I wasn't closing well; it was all to do with me not being happy with the way in which the product was sold. It went deeper than that; I had a bee in my bonnet about suitability of many cases I was asked to close and deep down I didn't believe in the product, I was not on the right bus. You see I couldn't say I was in the best place for me; therefore, my closes didn't happen the way the book said they would.

The book wasn't wrong my attitude was. Sales is not just about the product or your knowledge of the product it is very much about your mental attitude, your passion for what you are doing and the product or service you're selling. We'll come onto that in more detail in the next section. There is a key lesson here and that is simply never sell something you don't believe in and feel passionate about and make sure you are in the right frame of mind.

"No matter how good a salesperson you are, you'll never hit exceptional results if your head is in the wrong place, you need to get the attitude right first! You need to love the people and the product."

Despite the very best of training, my mental attitude, had an impact on the way I presented, moreover, it made the close very difficult for me to execute. Sometimes I also felt like the emphasis at point of close was not a natural conclusion to what should have been a very pleasant and rewarding exchange for both parties, with complete satisfaction all round. There was too much emphasis on target and not enough on relationships. Of course, there has to be balance between the objectives you are working to.

If you close a deal with pressure, sometimes called the hard close, the sale will not stick at worst or at best you will only ever sell the one product and the client will not remain a client for long. A good example of this is the troubled Financial Services sector of the mid-eighties where nearly 40% of sales that were closed did not complete their term and more that 20% of transactions didn't last one year. It was these figures that originally created the need for a cooling off period of 14 days on all insurance sales during the eighties! A significant number of people took the option not to go ahead within the 14 days after the salesperson had left the building. Simply put, they hadn't sold the product based on a true need.

"No gimmicks, no tricks, give them all the answers, give them confidence, show them you care more about them, than the sale, then just ask for the business; assuming they don't ask you first!"

I am not going to share with you all the things I was taught to get the client to say yes at the close, because I don't believe that you should have to do anything other than ask if they have any questions, give them all the answers and then ask for the business, if they haven't already asked you! No tricks just a simple, logical and expected end to a good quality professional presentation.

Objection Handling.

A significant part of the journey is the ability to handle those objections that will be raised by the client during the presentation and particularly at the point of close. This is their last chance to reassure themselves that they are making the correct choice and your chance to shine. This is where the true salespeople will stand and be counted!

It has been said many times an objection is a buying signal and should be treated as such. I am not sure that I fully agree with this, I think sometimes objections are just things that the customer is not happy with or does not fully understand. I also believe that if not handled well, the sale can go very wrong at this point. An objection is your prospect asking for more information because during your presentation you've not covered all the bases, they needed covered, or they lack full understanding of what is on offer.

Let's look at objections and handling them in a little more detail. First let's talk about why an objection is raised, what is the motivation behind the objection? In the worst case the motivation could be that the prospect is looking for a chance to say no through objections because they are just not interested in what it is, you're selling. Some people will use this tactic because they find it difficult to say no thank you directly and have to look for more indirect methods such as raising spurious objections. In my experience if you have done your homework and gone through the sales process this would not happen. It is more likely to happen if your process was flawed, for example if you hadn't done your research well and were not talking to the right person.

Another reason might be that the prospect is concerned about something they have not disclosed, despite your best efforts, the more the prospect trusts you, the more they will open up to you. This is why relationship building is so important. In many cases this might be avoided by ensuring that during the process you concentrate on the quality of the relationship all of the time the presentation you cover all the features advantages and benefits based on the information you have gathered about the prospect in the 'Know your client' phase. Price is often an objection and is best dealt with by ensuring you check ability to pay early in the process (Know your client phase) and deal with the price early in the presentation and concentrate on the value.

"The more you cover in the process leading up to the close, the more you listen and the better your questions, the less likely you are to get objections!"

Done well you'll have already asked the right questions to establish how the prospect is feeling about the subjects you are covering and any concerns they may have. There will be times when an objection based on price does get through the net. Handling it is simple, use the techniques I am about to introduce to you and tell them the truth. Concentrate on the solution and why it works, use examples and confirm how they feel with more questions. Always focus on the value to them, based on your knowledge of their need and situation. You can see from this, if you don't know them well at this stage, you're heading up a dead end! Hence the emphasis on great questions and loads of listening leading up to this point.

In the ideal world the objection is raised because they have a real interest in what it is, you're selling but just need to clear up some last-minute doubts. When dealing with objections regardless of the motivation behind them you should remain professional, calm, considerate and likable. How you handle them is important, not just to the outcome of the sale but to how you are seen and the reputation that you build.

The way you conduct yourself during the sales process will say an awful lot about you, your character and your business. Remember the people that say no will also talk about the experience and contribute to your reputation and brand value. That is why it's so important to focus all the time on all the people regardless of outcome. The first thing to know about handling the objection is that you need to:

Listen—Seek Clarity—Search for more objections— Answer or defer

The listening part is obvious I know, but you need to remember that you have to demonstrate that you've heard what the prospect has said to you, no matter if you are in a face-to-face meeting or on the phone, the same rules apply. When the objection has been delivered to you, make sure you clarify it by repeating your understanding to the prospect. Sometimes it's what lies beneath that you have to get to, in other words the objection they verbalise may not be the true objection.

"Sometimes the objection raised is not the true issue and so you need to use your instincts and experience to ensure you have all the information; ask; other than this is there anything else preventing you from progressing?"

It is my personal preference to find out if there are any other objections the prospect might have along with what they have already told me. I like to get them all out in the open and then deal with them. If you don't have all the information to hand to deal with the objections, don't bluff, defer the answer and gain the commitment from the prospect to continue the conversation once you have completed your research. In this event the commitment to the next meeting becomes the close. Here are my top six rules for effectively handling sales objections:

Rule 1—Get all the objections out in one hit—If you handle the first objection and then you are presented with another, which you handle, then another and another, you will multiply your chances of losing the prospect and the quick answers may come across in the wrong way (too smart, too rehearsed). For me the best way to do this is, after the first objection has been explained and clarified, you would say something like:

"Other than the price is there anything else that might stop you from going ahead with this?"

Your aim is to repeat this process until the prospect is saying that there are no other issues that would prevent them from doing business with you. Now handle all the objections one at a time to the satisfaction of the prospect. Once you do this all that is left is to do the business.

Rule 2—Test the prospects commitment—Do this by simply asking them:

"If I can deal with this issue (these issues) to our mutual satisfaction will you be able to go ahead?"

This is simple and effective; it will certainly confirm those that are really serious about doing business with you.

Rule 3—Challenge the objection—If the objection is based on something that is just not true, perhaps based on a common opinion that is not fully accurate. Maybe something a competitor has said or done, maybe a previous bad experience of a similar offering. Now is the time to challenge the objection in a softly-softly manner, try using, Feel, Felt, Found, this is a very well-established technique, some might even say old school:

*"I understand how you **feel**, many others have **felt** the same way as you do but once they had experienced our solution they **found** that . . ."*

I can almost hear some of you saying, this method is as old as the hills, which is about the same age as me! Guess what? It works and if you practise and make it your own, using your own words and personality, it will work even better!

Rule 4—Reverse the objection—I personally use this method the least but it is still up there with the best. The phrase you would use If the prospect said:

"I don't have the time to use this"

You would simply come back with a phrase that started with this answer (only if it fits like a glove):

"That's exactly why you should be using this."

Then go on to repeat the appropriate features, advantages and benefits to show why the solution is right for them.

Assuming your product, when implemented was something that would save time, you could use this phrase to handle the objection and then go on to explain your point in greater detail, focusing on this issue. As with all these techniques, practise makes perfect.

Rule 5—Outweigh the objection—This is a very traditional method used when handling objections that are related to the price. The idea here is to compare the price with other similar priced solutions that do not have the same value. So, for example if you are selling advertising space in a book that has a 12-month shelf life for a similar price for an entry in publication with a shelf life of one month, your proposal potentially outweighs the other.

Rule 6—Minimize the objection—Again this is mainly used for price objections and requires you to think about breaking the price down into component parts to emphasis the value and reach of the solution. I have used both 5 and 6 for the same objection very successfully.

I use other methods too, it's worth experimenting and finding methods that work for you and give you the success you are looking for. Here's another example that I have used with success:

When presented with an objection I might say something before I answer the objection that gains commitment from the prospect taking them closer to the close before the objection is handled. I might say:

"If I can provide you will all the evidence you need to prove this is not the case, would you be prepared to make up your own mind?"

You can see that this approach makes it quite difficult to give the answer no. This is not a trick it is simply gaining commitment, which places the prospect in the right frame of mind. The key to objection handling, like so many other things in business, simply comes down to practise, research, preparation, sincerity and honesty, above all honesty.

"Sell because you love it and focus on the people not the product. Don't take short cuts, never do anything other than tell the truth. Gain a reputation to be proud of!"

Consolidate The Sale.

The final part of the ideal sales process is the consolidation, while the simplest part of the process; it is still vital to the overall success of your sales career. The purpose of this part of the process is quite simply to make sure that once the deal is done, the client understands what happens next. Has any paperwork they may get post sale been explained to them in advance? Do they have all the information needed to take full advantage of customer support available to them? When the client has just agreed to buy is the time when they are at their most responsive. They have the deal done they are fully satisfied with the product and they are full of expectation, that is why it is so important to make sure that there are no surprises for them around the corner. Anything they need to know about post sale must be fully explained and all questions dealt with before you ride off into the sunset.

This is also a great time to get the client to think about people they know who might also benefit from a meeting with you. Now is the time to ask for the referral. I would do this by asking a few questions to get the client into the right frame of mind before asking for the referral. My mentor in my early days of selling always said to me that I should get two to three referrals for each close I completed, and, in that way, I would never be short of sales leads. I still agree in the principle but in the real world the key is to ask but not expect and remember to gain you first need to give. Here are the questions you might want to ask, use these as a baseline, as always adapt them to suit your own personality, make them your own:

Q: "Have you found going through this process of value?"
A: "Yes" (if you've done a great job there is no other answer to this question, or for that matter any of the questions).

Q: "Are you happy with the result?"
A: "Yes."

Q: "Do you think that other people in a similar situation to you would also benefit from this?"
A: Yes.

Now you can ask for the referral. I would usually ask them to tell the referral that they have given me their details but I would always ask the client not to mention too much about what I do, just the highlights but do take time to explain what I don't do, no strong-arm tactics, no foot in the door! Every happy client has the capability to be a brand ambassador, remember that, it is so powerful and will certainly keep your attention on providing exceptional customer service.

"You should really be thinking referrals from the very beginning. The better the relationship the more referrals you'll get, all you have to do is ask!"

The Principles Of Exceptional Sales

Get your attitude right first.

You should never and I mean never go into a sales situation, be it face-to-face or on the phone, video or other technology, without first getting your mindset right. How you are thinking has a major influence on how you feel and the sales results you achieve, more so than you probably realise. If you start a sales call or for that matter any kind of meeting, feeling like it's going to go nowhere, that is exactly where the meeting will end up, nowhere! For me I would say the perfect mindset is one where you are feeling happy, friendly toward people, positive, full of enthusiasm, full of confidence in yourself and the product.

"Your mental attitude is important, make sure yours is always positive. Never go to a meeting thinking you will fail, that's a sure way to attract the wrong result. Get yourself a mentor, better still join Rainmakers Club!"

I think attitude of mind is a subject that is not given enough emphasis during sales training and for that matter any form of business coaching. Many people have written about the importance of a positive mental attitude and others have written about how powerful the human brain is and that it's possible to achieve anything using the power of your mind and attitude. This works for good and bad; you do become what you think about. It was Earl Nightingale who wrote, 'The Strangest Secret,' where he maintained you are what you think about. Napoleon Hill and others have all maintained and proved the same is true.

I think the first time I really understood what Napoleon Hill and Earl Nightingale and others were talking about was when I was at the height of my fitness and the height of my game in Rugby. The night before a game I would always get an early night not because I needed the sleep particularly but because I wanted some quite time alone with my thoughts. I would lie there and visualise the match running through my part in the game. I would imagine playing the entire game in my mind.

I am convinced that my performance was better because of this visualisation and the moves that I imagined the night before crept into the game, many times and what is more important, the moves worked! Mental attitude is a vital element to your success, without a shadow of a doubt.

Today I still use the same techniques before I do any of my public speaking engagements; I also use it before any sales presentations or a game of golf. To be fair I probably need it most for the golf! I didn't realise it, but I was using this technique long before I was taught about it as a business skill by my mentors.

I remember using this technique in the Army as a patrol commander. I used to find some quite time and visualise the patrol before the event and rehearse my reactions to a range of possibilities. In that way I always felt prepared and always felt confident in my leadership.

In the Rainmakers Club we have an entire library on the development of emotional intelligence and mindfulness to help our entrepreneurs and enterprising people to get the best possible performance from themselves and their teams.

Now you need some belief.

With your attitude right it is now time to work on that belief system of yours. To be that exceptional business owner, entrepreneur and sales professional, you need to believe in you and what you are doing. I have heard some say it doesn't matter what the product is, I can sell it. I have to pin my flag to the mast and say that I am totally against this view those that say this may be able to sell anything to anybody but in my experience, these are risk takers that don't last too long in any job. They tend to take many risks with their own reputation and may even have no worthy values. Often these types of salespeople end up being very nomadic going from job to job, or project to project and quickly lose their drive.

I do know that some sales experts can demonstrate their skill in sales by selling anything, but this is not the same. I can sell anything as a means of demonstrating the skills I coach on. This is not the same as selling a product day on day that you do not believe in or for that matter selling for a company you don't believe in. When I demonstrate selling anything, I am not selling the product I am selling the method and it works because I believe in the method.

"If you're serious about your business, serious about selling then you need to make sure you have four things all in perfect balance; your attitude, your belief in the product, your belief and love for the company and your love of the people."

The client that buys your company's product will first buy you, the way you look, talk, act and treat them will influence this first and most important sale. This doesn't change, even if you sell online, the same rules apply. They just change to design, navigation, content, and interactions. Once they have bought you, they will move on to the products and the company. That is why the first thing you need to do is have belief in yourself, belief that you can do this, that you are good enough, that you'll be the best. Add this to a belief that your product is the best in the market, the best value, the best for the client and that it is supplied by the best company, with the best record and the best ethics.

With all your positive beliefs in place, you can spend all your time concentrating on doing a great job for the client, for you and for the company, happy days! To achieve this level of belief you need to be doing what you are most passionate about and what you are or can be best at doing. If your heart is not in it then don't do it, find something else to do with your time. This is not a rehearsal and you only have the one life, use it well! If need be going back to the section of the book that introduced you to the three circles test and remind yourself of the questions and the answers that you gave.

I personally think it is very difficult to maintain a positive outlook and be constantly inspired and motivated to give the very best all the time if you're not in the dead centre of the circles. There have been times in my career where I have found myself in the wrong place, letting financial inducement or need push me away from the centre. Those occasions have never been the happiest of times, but they did focus my attention to getting back to where I belong. You should do the same if ever you stray from the centre of your journey!

Assuming you have your head in the right place and you are happy with your lot, the next thing you need to concentrate on for exceptional results is that of building rapport, become a master at this essential skill, it will work for you in more than just your business life, of that I am certain!

Build rapport early.

You need to engage the client; you need to build some rapport with them and the sooner you get this done the better the sale will go. As you walk through their door, or when you speak to them on the phone they will be forming an opinion about you and this opinion will set thc tone for the rest of the meeting and perhaps the relationship, so you need to get it right.

You can start this process of rapport building by finding some common ground, find something (other than the product) to talk about, make sure it is something that interests them; this is where the value of good research comes into play. Remember that in most cases people like to talk about themselves and so if you can get the client doing this during the early part of the meeting, you'll be giving yourself a significant advantage.

I think the worst thing you can do is to start the meeting by talking about you and your company, no, start by talking about them and their company. That's the way to get the meeting off on the right footing. Now, I appreciate that you have to tell them who you are, where you are from and what you want to talk about, if they don't already know this but then stop and ask open questions about them. Use your research and find subjects to get them talking and build that relationship. Be honest, be sincere, be natural, show them you are someone worth having as a positive connection, a friend.

"Many businesspeople spend far too much time talking about themselves and their product. That's because we all like to talk about us! Change the tactic, talk about them and listen to what they say."

When you arrive at your meeting, armed with all your research, assume that you have been the subject of research too. You can test to see if this is the case with a few well-placed questions. I would assume they have done some research and use that activity to help in building rapport, for example contact points on subjects like values, mission or history.

Because you will be researched too, it is important not to just think in one direction. Most of us tend to concentrate our attention on the research we want to do. Here's a very valuable tip for you; research yourself and your business on a regular basis to see what is being said about you. The last thing you want is to be in a meeting when some research you are not aware of is used and you get caught out! When you use social media, make sure you keep in mind business and reputation and don't put anything, including pictures and video, online that you wouldn't want to be seen by others. Your prospect is bound to, look for you on social media! The rule is never say or post anything you wouldn't be happy for your customer to see or discuss with others.

Selling is all about the motivation to buy.

When I talk to people about marketing or business planning, I always tell them the importance of understanding their target market, it is no less important in sales to understand why your target clients buy. In business planning I tell my clients they need to be able to answer these vital questions: Who are your buyers? Why do they buy? When do they buy? How do they buy? Where do they buy? How much do they pay? How do they pay?

I think as an exceptional salesperson you'd want to know this too. The most important of these in my view is the 'Why?' If you can discover this your sale will be ten times easier than if you don't know.

This 'Why' is so important that it remains the theme from the beginning to the end of the process. It is the 'Why' that dictates my strategy of always talking about the client their needs and later the solutions rather than my company, my product and me. I want to take a little time to consider some of the possible reasons why the customer may buy, where does their motivation come from. Once you know this you can concentrate on these motivations to increase your sales successes. The other elements, for example where and how they buy are also important but the why is the key!

The best way to uncover these motivations is through good quality research and by asking a series of smart open questions with a few closed ones thrown in to control the pace and content. In my own career in sales I always start by undertaking research on my target and in that way, I avoid asking them questions they might consider to be dumb, or a reflection of the lack of preparation or care I have taken. Before each meeting with my prospects I do all, I can to gain the maximum amount of information needed to start the process of building rapport.

It is also worth considering that most of the salespeople out there are average and many of them are doing the same thing as the majority, concentrating on the selling rather than on building relationships. That gives you a great opportunity to build your differential by concentrating on the relationships before the sales. Stay the course and you'll soon discover this will give you more sales, more longevity and a far better reputation.

"Don't follow the pack, their short-term wins will not last as long as quality sales skills and quality relationships."

Here is my list of things you should find out and understand about your prospects. If you can take the time to gather this important information at the same time as building the relationship, believe me you'll move still closer to be that exceptional salesperson leaving the mediocre behind you:

- What are your prospects main motive for buying?

- Understand their experience and particularly their experience of the sector you represent.

- Find out how much they really know and understand, you should never underestimate their level of knowledge.

- Find their true needs, how will they use and benefit from the product you have on offer?

- Just as important to what they need is the more emotional side of sales what do they want? We don't always buy what we need!

- Other possible motivations to consider include; greed for something, their passion, wanting something as a result of a fear of some description, vanity, the desire to impress, peace of mind and maybe the pursuit of a particular outcome.

- What is their 'reason why?' You need to understand and uncover the true reason why, if the sale is to progress. The more you can get to the truth the more you are able to mitigate the risk that the prospect perceives, which holds them back from the ultimate buying decision.

You'll find over time that the motivations between people for a particular product are very similar, it has to be that way as the product will have been designed with specific features, advantages and benefits which act as boundaries within which there are a finite number of motivations. Collate and learn these and prepare good quality probing questions that will get to the heart of the matter in each presentation you do.

Learn how to ask the right questions.

If you ask the wrong questions, surprise, surprise, you'll get the wrong answers. I think you'll start to see by now that quality questions are at the very heart of selling. As you ask the questions this is what happens; the sales process slowly and surely gets converted into a buying process. With the right questions you'll uncover facts and motives for buying that will assist you to get the right results.

In essence the best way to ask questions is to ask them in such a way that the prospect starts thinking about themselves but answering with your preferred result in mind. Here's what I mean; you ask questions that make them think about new information relating to the product, how they would use it or what they think about it. This gets them thinking of themselves and gives you all the information you'll need at the same time.

Asked right, your questions will give you a picture of what they consider to be of value and benefit to them, which will motivate them to want to take ownership. The biggest sin you could commit at this point is to ask stupid questions. Make sure your questions are well thought out, intelligent and make the effort to avoid the obvious.

Your competition will be using the obvious you need to try to be different, being different matters as much as being professional. Oh, and by the way, being professional doesn't mean being boring or predictable, you can still have fun and be professional.

"The secret to really good sales is to always concentrate on the people and put your effort into the creation of an environment in which those people want to buy."

Take time to ask the prospect for their opinion, do this as often as you are able, it makes all the difference and at this point in the process it is the only opinion that should matter to you. Not forgetting of course that finding out their opinion is a great way of testing the water before a trial close.

When seeking the opinion do try to avoid the obvious, in other words don't ask, 'What's important to you?', that is just being lazy. Use your imagination and ask other questions, make them open, to get the prospect really talking to you.

Preparing for the questions and answers before the call is really important, there are many ways you can prepare, I prefer to ask myself some simple questions about the prospect and if I am not able to answer them, I will do all I can to find the answers before I go on the call or pick the phone up to them. The kind of thing you need to know is; what is it that has the greatest effect on their business? How did they do last year and how are they doing this year so far? What is their main mission for this coming year? There are some other really important questions you'll need to have the answer to as well, questions like:

- Are you talking to the right person, can they make the decision, or will they be able to push you further up the chain to the person who can make the decision?

- How would they benefit more, through production or profit as a result of buying from you?

- What is the range of possible motives for buying?

- What is their current level of experience of the solution or alternate solutions?

- What, if any, degree of urgency is there to buy?

Make sure that you are prepared for any questions that the prospect might have for you too, this means really be prepared. If it were me, I would make sure that I had as much information with me as possible so that I could handle the questions. The more prepared you are the better. The more prepared you are the more impressed and engaged the prospect will be with your performance and that will give you better odds of getting the result you are looking for.

"Being fully prepared for your sales calls is essential, if you are to be really successful. Deliver your answers with humility, nobody likes a show-off!"

It is true to say that the way in which you ask, and answer questions will determine the way you're seen as a salesperson and the reputation you build with your customers. If you get this part right along with the other key skills you will see your sales performance increase, that I can promise you.

Keep those eyes wide open all the time.

I think we all know how important it is in sales to listen to what the prospect has to say. However, it is often the observational skills that can let the salesperson down. I would say that your abilities to observe are as important as any other skill we talk about. I learnt quite early on in my Army career that we think we are observing and miss much. Just like we think we are listening and miss entire sections of the conversation and buying signals.

Some of the more obvious things you should be doing include making sure that if you're including in your research clues that you can turn into icebreaking conversation. For example, I am always on the lookout for things that I might have in common with the person I am about to meet, sporting objects, pictures, diplomas and many other personal items that give me a window into the person's personality and interests, many of which can be found on social media.

When you enter their territory you should be thinking what might we have in common to help build a relationship, where might there be connection points? Remember people may buy products but for the most part they still buy using their instincts about the people involved in the process. Even if they don't buy directly from people, they buy on common ground and values, that's why it is so important to work on your online persona too, give your business a likable personality.

The more observant you are the more you can learn and the more you will understand about your prospect. The more you understand them the better you'll be at communicating with them. Observation is more than just looking, ask yourself are you just looking or are you observing and then thinking about what you have just seen? Are you thinking about the prospect as you are observing the things around you? When you have seen something are you getting inspiration, from the observation, on things to say and do? To be a great salesperson you need to be answering yes to all of these questions.

If you take steps to be really observant, you'll have a significant advantage over most of the competition and even colleagues too! That is quite simply because in most cases people are somewhere in the middle of seeing nothing and only seeing half of what is out there. Good observation gives you a significant advantage over most people.

"Actively look for touch points and common ground and then use them to help lower the barriers and engage in true conversation. Don't do it as a process, do it because you really are interested and really do care about people!"

Being observant does take some practise, like most skills if you stop practicing, you'll surly lose your edge. I remember how much training I was given, in the infantry in the early days, to practise my observation skills, I also remember the significant difference between the results I got when I first started and the significant improvements after a few weeks training. Being part of an elite fighting force, they did not leave it there, I was subjected to constant training to keep me at the top of my game, just like they do in sport! To become an exceptional salesperson, you need to be constantly practicing your skills, there is always room for improvement, for all of us.

You only have to fear yourself.

There are many challenges encountered in running and growing a business, but I truly believe that sales should not really be one of them, providing you have got the product and or service right. You wouldn't think sales would be something to be scared of, I mean six active service tours, that might be something to be scared of, jumping out of a perfectly serviceable aircraft at 12,000 feet and relying on some silk and string to keep you safe, that might be something to be scared of too. Scared of sales, you wouldn't think so would you?

However, many people are scared of selling, oh they don't mind the conversational parts of the process, they don't even mind talking about the product but when it comes down to closing the sale the fear takes over. You already know my personal opinion is that selling is just great communication and therefore nothing to fear, we should all want to be the best at the selling part of running a business that we can be!

The key is to make sure you know all there is to know about your product, your target market, your customers, your competition and of course sales. I can certainly help you with the last part; the rest is kind of down to you. The more you know, the more you practise, the more you prepare, the less fear you'll have and that's the same for so many things in life, not just sales. Get rid of the fear, it takes up far too much room, replace the fear with confidence. Get your confidence levels up through knowledge and practise. Incidentally the same is true for presenting to large groups. You'll always get nerves, that is natural, but you shouldn't be scared!

During the learning curve! You'll get things wrong, we all do and that is how we learn and develop, so embrace that part of your exciting journey. Just remember if you make a mistake do not blame, simply take responsibility for the error, identify what you did wrong, learn from that and then do it differently next time, practise makes perfect and the blame game never works to your advantage, it just burns precious time and tarnishes reputations!

Taking ownership.

This thing that we seem to have in abundance in many companies both in the UK and the US is a culture of blame. I have already mentioned this, but it is so rife in business I want to emphasise the message to you.

Blame is just going to drive you into ever decreasing circles and will create even greater failure in the long run. It can also destroy business relationships. Blame and autopsy is a waste of energy and achieves nothing positive. Take responsibility and learn, explain where you went wrong and demonstrate what you will do to prevent the same thing happening again. Keep the entire journey positive.

If you make, this really simple to say but hard to do, change in your culture you will be much closer to sustainable exceptional performance than ever before. The reason is simple, if you take responsibility, forget blame and concentrate on learning and development, success will become more frequent and sustainable. The alternate journey can be seen going on around you each day, where blame is the norm due mainly to out of control ego's not willing to take responsibility.

In my leadership talks I demonstrate the difference between good and bad leaders using the analogy of windows and mirrors, briefly covered earlier in this book. The Windows and Mirrors concept was first introduced to me by one of my American mentors when I was CEO of a business in Pittsburgh PA. I have to say I had never considered this aspect of leadership until she introduced it to me. I can tell you for me applying this in my daily life was a game changer for me! I would love for you to give it a go and see if you can gain the benefits of making this more than a way of behaving, make it a business wide behaviour, it can become a significant advantage to sales and general performance. It's worth looking at again:

"The difference between the average businessperson and the exceptional includes this; the mediocre person makes a mistake and looks out of the window for someone to blame and when things go well looks into the mirror to congratulate themselves. The exceptional person when things go wrong looks in the mirror and takes responsibility and when things go well will look out of the window for someone to share the congratulations with."

Exceptional sales and businesspeople all share this common trait of taking responsibility for their own actions and then learning from the experience rather than expending energy in finding 101 excuses and others to blame for the failure they have just experienced.

"Learn the difference between windows and mirrors. Mirror for responsibility and window for encouragement, not the other way around!"

Build relationships and earn their trust.

The key is understanding the difference between making the sale and earning the sale. For what it's worth, I think sales should be earned not made and I say this for this simple reason; sales come as a result of building a relationship. If you just sell something it will get you a commission, if you build a relationship with the person first, built on trust, you'll not just get a commission you'll earn income. In fact, you'll earn multiple sales from the same person both through direct sales and through referral. It's all about earning their trust building the relationship and as a result earning year on year income not just a one-off commission.

Relationships do take time to build; they don't just happen as a result of the first meeting or at the first sale but are built up over time. Most people will say and do the right things leading up to the first sale but then once the deal is in the bag, they simply move on leaving all that great work of building the foundations of a good relationship to wither and die. Exceptional people understand that this is just the beginning and despite getting the sale continue to build the relationship to secure future sales and referrals.

It is really important that you take care not to damage the relationship-building element of your sales skills when under pressure to make quota. Care should always be taken to protect and develop the relationship not damage it for a quick win in times of pressure.

On the subject of quota; the best way to is to have targets based on realistic levels of activity to hit the number of sales required and then make sure you always make time for the pre-sale activities! Don't get lulled into a false sense of wellbeing as a result of a good sale. Get straight back to the job in hand!

Don't talk about being the best, be the best.

As the old saying goes the proof of the pudding is in the eating. So, don't waste your time telling people how good you are, instead show them. Make a point of collecting as many testimonials as you can, not just about the company or product, which most people in sales will or should do. Be different and get testimonials about you, your performance and the product, remember people still buy from people.

The good thing about testimonials is they are a real asset in the handling of objections raised during the sales process. Get a variety of testimonials using different media, that would be even better, video testimonials can be really powerful. Testimonials are the proof that you are who you say you are and that your product does what you say it can for them.

"Becoming an exceptional salesperson is the same as becoming exceptional at anything else, it takes talent and much hard work. You won't become exceptional in a day, but you will if you put the effort in day after day."

To be a great businessperson you need to be a salesperson, you need to have great values.

I often mention the importance of a business having the right values and then living by them as they are at the centre of the development of reputation and brand. Values are also very important for the individual too. It's quite interesting that few caching professionals take much time talking about and developing the right values in the people they work with. There are a few of us out there that see this as a vital part of the development of an exceptional business and salesperson. Here then are the standard values that make a great professional, in my opinion, and I urge you to try to adopt these as your own, if you're not already doing so:

Be different—Actively seek to create a difference between yourself and the competition, a difference that can be seen by your customers.

Create loyalty—Through your actions and the way in which you treat your customers and prospects. Loyalty is more valuable to the sales professional than mere satisfaction.

Be engaging—Your communication style is all important and has a direct effect on results, become a student of presentation techniques and always make sure your sales message inspires action, use great questions and ideas, to drive them into the buying process.

Never stop learning—Never stop seeking out new information and ideas to enhance your skills and experience. Leverage the experience of others; this is the driving force behind the Rainmakers Club and in particular the 'Inner Circle.'

Be approachable be a friend—People like to do business with people, make it easy to do business with you.

Don't take yourself too seriously—Business and selling should be fun, buying should be fun too, so don't take yourself too seriously, have some fun and understand the power of humour in the right balance in your sales presentations.

Be creative, think creative—The more creatively you think and the more creative you are in your presentation the greater the differential that will make you stand out from the crowd.

Always ask for the business—With a great presentation asking for the business is a natural, welcome and expected conclusion.

Be confident and believe—To be an exceptional salesperson you need to have exceptional self-belief that will come with confidence, that comes from good old-fashioned hard work, preparation and practise. Don't confuse confidence with arrogance. Confident yes and a little bit humble to keep that ego in place.

Planning is key—Most salespeople don't spend enough time planning their work. Planning is key, doing the preparation work before the sale will significantly increase your sales performance.

Avoid blaming others—Don't waste time looking for people to blame, either take responsibility or just keep quiet and put it right, you'll keep and make more friends that way and friends create selling opportunities for those they like and trust most.

Create more time for you—Make the personal choice to spend a little time each day on increasing your knowledge and skills.

Always concentrate on yes—Most of my colleagues who specialise in sales coaching agree that the maintenance of a positive yes attitude is key to success and is also very infectious to those around you.

The Rules Of Selling

The golden rules that most people miss.

When I first set out in my business career, sales were my first port of call. On day one of my new career I knew very little about real business and even less about how to be an exceptional salesperson. My first sales manager was wiser than I gave him credit for. At the time I felt a bit cheated, I asked him for help with my sales. I told him that I was uncertain of what it took to be a great salesperson and needed him to share with me the secret to his success. He simply said to me there is no secret, just dammed hard work and treat each opportunity the same way you would if you were selected to play rugby for your country.

Above all make sure you concentrate on the simple stuff; you can never afford to get the simple things wrong. So here I am more years than I care to remember from that first encounter and now rather than feeling cheated I find myself giving exactly the same advice to all those people that I have and continue to mentor in sales and in business. So, the golden rule is this:

"Concentrate on the simple stuff and do it right every time. When you're not selling practise and develop your skills, treat selling as a skill that

needs to be practised all the time. Learn from the world of sport! The greatest players are great because they practice, they don't just turn up on the day, they practice before the big games, each sale is a big game."

I remember a dear friend of mine, Paul; he is sadly not with us anymore. He used to ask questions to find out how everyone else worked and when he was given a good idea would assess if that would fit his style and then practice it and then practice it again.

He was also a great example of making every sale the most important sale. The entire sales team were at a bar celebrating a record year and also waiting to find out who was the winner of the most sales for the year. We got a call from Paul, he apologised for being late he had just one more meeting he had to attend and would get to us as soon as he could! At 23:20 he turned up and when most of us were ready to go home. While we were all having a party, he went on one last meeting, one last sale that was worth only a few pounds. From there he went to the office to catch the last internal mail and then finally came to celebrate. That year he was the top salesperson in the entire company by a significant margin! The client he saw wrote one of the nicest testimonials I have ever seen. Paul was rewarded with a very good bonus and a trip to Hawaii, all for just a little extra effort.

We have already talked about the importance of having the right values now we are going to talk about the basic rules of exceptional selling. As you read these, you'll start to think I know this, or this is all very simple and obvious. You'd be right to think that, and you'd also be right if you thought about how few people you know in business who follow these oh so simple rules to exceptional sales. It's because so few people follow these rules that there are so few exceptional salespeople out there and why the majority just that aren't good! You now have a personal choice to make, exceptional or mediocre? If I were you, I would pause now and give that some real thought, it might make the rest of this book as valuable as pure gold!

Find yourself a positive attitude then keep it going (all the time).

I know, we have mentioned this before, but it is mentioned again for good reason! To be fair this first rule would have its place in any coaching book about any subject in business, that doesn't dilute the importance of this rule. It is by design that it is the first of my rules of exceptional sales and business in general. The more committed you are to have a positive outlook and attitude toward your life and the people around you, the greater success you'll experience.

Without this you will never make it big, oh you might get by but to be fair if all you want is to get by then stop reading this book and go watch the big game and all those successful players and their positive attitudes. If you still don't want some positive attitude, then get back to the couch and watch some a soap or reality TV! Having the right attitude is so much more powerful than people understand. Positive people really do attract positive outcomes. Remember nobody likes to be around negative people, interestingly even negative people dislike negative people, the ultimate paradox!

We all need to believe in something—At the very least make your something you.

Self-belief is very important; the way we think about ourselves has direct influence on the way be feel, work and indeed the levels of success we experience. Most of us would agree that the way we feel has a direct influence on how we act day to day. We will have all experienced times when our confidence has been a little low and as a result, we seem to perform under par and even make more mistakes than usual, we seem to hesitate when normally we would not.

This is nothing new and many others have written in detail about this, such as Napoleon Hill and others, well known for their inspirational books on the subject of success and the importance of that positive mental attitude. I would add their books to your 'must read' list. It's not just in sales and business that maintaining self-belief is important, high levels of confidence are needed for all walks of life, if you are going to experience the success you seek. Your levels of self-belief will directly affect your confidence levels. This book is about small business sales and personal success and not psychology, but it is worth looking at a few quick wins for getting your confidence up. Your levels of confidence will help you no end in the battle to maintain a positive mental attitude during your journey to exceptional business, exceptional sales, exceptional value and exceptional performance.

I would say that step one is to like who you are, if you don't, make those changes first. Learn to like you, to do this make sure you are a likeable person, do the right thing. Take a look at you from the outside in and be the person you most want to be! Embrace the hints in this book and change the habits you don't like.

Now that you've made those changes and you like what you see, it's time to make sure you really know your subject from every possible direction. The more you know and the more you apply that knowledge, in the right place, at the right time, using the right language; the greater your confidence and self-belief will become. Learn things from a variety of angles, for example when you look at your products you should understand them not just from the perspective of selling them but also from the perspective of a user of the product and how they will benefit from the solution and the challenges they face. Feel how the solution will benefit them and live that experience. People that can do this will come across as so much more passionate about the outcome than a simple traditional sales pitch.

So surround yourself with the right people, fill your mind with thoughts that are positive and visualise your success from doing the right things all of the time, the more you think, the more you visualise the future you desire, the more you increase your odds in your favour!

"There is no getting away from the fact that you will attract what you think about, it's a rule of the universe. Take a look around; the world is full of evidence that you really do become what you think about. If you're walking along a plank six feet off the ground and you think I am going to lose my balance you probably will. Life is that plank!"

The key message here is that at the very least you need to believe in yourself, if you can't take that all important first step then you'll have a difficult, if not impossible journey ahead of you.

Back to those important P's.

Earlier in this book we talked about the important of preparation and planning, this is in my blood, thanks to my early Army career. I learnt the importance of planning in every aspect of my training and active service. I learnt the power of planning preparation and practice from a variety of instructor courses I was able to complete and from my own passion for presentations and public speaking. These were great days where I learnt the art and science of presenting and the importance of self-confidence and leadership.

Today I am just as vocal as my first instructor was about the vital role planning has in all walks of life and in particular business life. The way this lesson was communicated to me and the other fine soldiers I served with was to drum into us that in all that we did we needed to remember importance of planning, preparation and practice.

Prior **P**reparation and **P**lanning, **P**revents **P***** **P**oor **P**erformance!

I have used the stars to save the blushes! The real key here is to point out to you, if you don't have a plan then how can you ever get to where you want to be. You should have a minimum two plans of action, long-term and short-term. The long-term plan is all about where you want to be and the short-term plan is all about how you're going to get there, or how you're going to start the journey.

To start the process, you could do worse than to adopt a technique known as the 'Broad Concept,' this simply requires you to think in these terms:

Where am I now? **W**here do I want to be tomorrow? **W**hat is the best way to get there right now?

It's worth remembering that your objectives remain the same but the route you take can change to fit the circumstances. Plans have to be active, both proactive and reactive and therefore will from time to time have to change to achieve the mission in the most effective and risk-free way. Therefore, we say the best way to get there right now because we build into this the expectation that things will have to be amended along the way, to suit new and unforeseen circumstances. Just a quick reminder on my view of risk in business; taking risks is fine as long as they are calculated and planned, so they have the least possible impact on the overall goals.

We would never set out on a long road trip without a route in mind and without a map or navigation system to refer to. A ship's captain would never take a ship packed with a valuable cargo out of port without knowing where he was headed and you should be the same don't set out without a route map and an objective in mind, but be prepared to adjust your course from time to time to meet the ever changing environment. We call this a business plan!

Never stop learning.

During my time in the Army I was constantly learning, in fact I would venture that I learnt more of use in life during that period than I did all the time I was at school, a time when learning should be at its height! When I left the Army, from the moment I left I embarked on a journey of learning. Here I am today many years later, still learning and helping many others to learn too from within the Rainmakers Club. The journey of being an exceptional person in business does not end, there is always more to learn and more to share with others.

When it comes to the lifeblood of business, sales, it is really important that you understand the sales process and know the fundamentals of the required selling skills and techniques, these baseline skills will give you the best of starts and for those that have been selling for a while and may have a few bad habits, the fundamentals are a great way to get back on track. The baseline skills are important no matter how long you've been selling. You should never have the attitude that you know all there is to know. Instead have the attitude of wanting to know more and never stop looking for new knowledge, never stop learning. You should put some effort into allowing yourself time each week, after hours or at the weekend to enhance your knowledge and skills. Read books, read articles, blogs and listen to podcasts and other media to help you develop your skills and knowledge.

"Once you are doing the job for real this is not an excuse to stop training. You should actively seek to learn new skills. Never stop learning, each day commit to learning more."

Think people, think needs not products.

To be a truly exceptional performer you need to get the basics right every time, this means making sure that you know what questions you need to ask and really listen to what the prospect is saying to you. It doesn't finish there, you need to be reacting in the right way too. Always focus on the true needs of the prospect rather than your needs and your product. Putting them first is a key component in exceptional sales performance.

There is a temptation, as you gain experience, to cut corners in the belief that you know what the client needs before they have even opened their mouth. This is a big mistake; you need to let them tell you. Never prejudge the prospect, if you think you know, keep it to yourself until they have told you. This will create a much better relationship and take them deeper into the buying process than if you do all the talking and telling. Remember that people don't generally like to be sold to, but they do enjoy the process of buying something they want. Let them make the discovery that they want to buy, don't tell them!

Be motivated for the right reason.

Nobody wants to be sold to by someone who shows no spirit, no passion, no motivation but it does have to be the right kind of passion and motivation. Have a passion for helping people and providing truly suitable solutions matched to real needs, not on a desire to earn commission!

There is nothing wrong with wanting to earn good money and pushing to earn more but make sure the real buzz comes from helping, which leads to earning. Most of the really successful salespeople that I connect with share the attitude that the money is a very attractive side effect to them doing a great job for people they really want to help.

The alternative, being commission driven has no real longevity and you'll end up a sales nomad moving from company to company year on year with no real loyalty, not the best of reputations and no long-term relationships developed and earned.

Think longer term.

Building enduring relationships is like the pot of gold at the end of the rainbow. Exceptional businesspeople always think about the longer-term relationships rather than the immediate win. There is nothing wrong quick wins, however if you concentrate on that outcome alone it maybe all you get, whereas if you concentrate on relationship and true needs you'll still gain the win and much more you'll build an enduring relationship with loyalty, repeat business, reputation and referrals. Anyone can make a sale but only the few get the full range of rewards gained from taking the time and making the effort to invest in people. The benefits are clear for all to see, all you need do is look at the most successful salespeople and you'll see they have a career for life based on quality, skills and a great reputation! It is no coincidence that many great salespeople go on to have sparkling leadership careers as executive officers and directors.

"Making time for people, making time to build relationships is the key to the pot of gold."

Make sure you're on the right bus.

My first sales job only lasted for one year, at the end of that year I was on about 140% of target and could have stayed on and done even better in the second year, which would have been very good for my pocket. I made the bold decision to leave for two great reasons; first and perhaps most importantly I left because I did not have complete belief in the product I was selling. I knew that when I was closing the client down to one of the products in our range of solutions, there were better options out there that would probably be far more suitable than the ones I had but company regulations prevented me from talking honestly about that. The second reason was my belief that the pressure we were put under to make target was encouraging a poorer standard of advice.

"Making the transition to exceptional will require you to be totally committed to the solutions you sell with great passion for the people and the company you represent."

The more I learnt about the products and the more I learnt about the competition, the more convinced I became that I could do better. I needed to be independent. That is where my business career really took off and where my love affair with helping others first started.

It is vital that you believe in your product that you believe that you are working for the best; without this belief you can never truly excel in your sales career. Like all things this will be part of your journey and so you might be able to tick all the boxes right now but the more you learn the more you will want to progress. As you develop you may find your thirst for knowledge grow and your hunger for more success increase ten-fold. This book and the Rainmakers Club should certainly feature in that growth.

Care needs to be taken plan your path to incorporate an increase in performance and responsibility challenge yourself and you will see some spectacular results. The key is resilience, get up one more time than you are knocked down and soldier-on.

As a business owner never ignore your dissatisfaction with the status quo work on inspiring development and change from within. It is the change and development, as you gain experience, that will help your own business become the success you desire. This is a vital part of your business development that needs to be embraced.

Look at it this way if you don't have that essential belief in you and you are sincere and motivated and thinking of the client, then your sales will suffer because this lack of confidence will be communicated to the client and they will not have as much motivation to buy.

Get your attitude right.

We've already touched on the importance of motivation and preparation. Attitude goes hand in glove with these elements, make sure you are ready for the sale, make sure your attitude is right. Your mood will have a direct effect on the way the prospect is going to feel about you and the sale. How you are feeling will have an effect on those around you and the higher profile your role at point of contact the greater the impact.

As the boss if you go to the office in a bad mood, you know this will have a direct effect on your staff and how they act with you and each other. If you go in the next day, happy and full of the joys of spring imagine the difference. Always, always have a bright, positive, sunny outlook; you'll go far in sales, leadership and business for that matter with this approach. Getting your attitude right is so very important to success. It is no coincidence that the most successful people are also the ones with the best attitude and have charismatic personalities.

"Your attitude will dictate the way you look, talk and act. Make yourself as attractive to others through your attitude."

Make sure you're talking to the right people.

In some sales books I have reviewed the author tells us not to waste time with people that cannot make the ultimate buying decision. I do understand this, but I think it sends out the wrong message, so I want to look at this in a little more enlightened manner.

Sometimes it is not possible to talk directly to the decision maker, sometime more than one person is involved in the chain and they cannot or maybe should not be spoken to on the same sales call. So, I would like to amend that view and say that you should make sure you are talking to the right person for the stage you are at in the process. The right person is someone who has the power to take you to the next stage of getting the deal. So, the rule is to qualify whom you are talking to and then take the meeting to the next logical level.

If the person you are talking to is a rung on the ladder, the close for that meeting is to gain their commitment to take you to the next level. Don't waste time if the person in not able to do that, always qualify with the right questions. I would go further and say that regardless of the position of the person you are talking to, always treat them with respect. You never know whom they might know and when you might meet them again and need their help!

Buy a good watch.

This may be a bit of a throwback to my military days where it was drummed into me that you always turned up five minutes before the parade, since then I have always tried to be on time for all my meetings. This usually involves me calculating travel time and then adding to that for any unforeseen events. If all goes well, I arrive early, which is never a problem as there are always things to do and I never go anywhere without my iPhone or

Tablet. If I get caught in traffic then I still have a chance of making it on time because I prepare for unforeseen delays, if I arrive early, I just get on with some work.

"If you turn up late for your meetings you will be sending the wrong message. Worst case your prospect will think you don't care."

If you do turn up late it can say much about you without you uttering a single word! It can say you don't have respect for the person you're meeting with or you're not well organised. In my view lateness is to be avoided at all costs and on most occasions the simple act of planning ahead can reduce the probability of being late significantly.

If you are late making sure there is a very good reason is essential. Call them before the appointment time and let them know you're going to be late, apologise and then do it again when you arrive. Now get on with the meeting and make a great job of it. Buy a good watch and make sure it is right, plan all your meetings and factor in for traffic or any other travel delays. Work hard to get there on time and safely!

Looking good, feeling good.

An old friend of mine used to say to me, 'When I dress important, I feel important.' He had a point to be fair. I believe that first impressions are very important, I also believe that you should dress suitably for each meeting you attend. It's not that difficult to find out what the suitable dress code for the occasion is going to be. The most important thing is to be clean and always look the part, dress and act like a professional, remember if you look sharp and in place, it's a positive reflection on you and your business.

Even if you are making contact on the telephone, or the web make sure you have the right attitude positive and sunny, as this too will set the tone for the meeting. When I am making sales calls on the phone I prefer to be standing and I always make sure I have a smile on my face so that my attitude comes across on the phone. You don't have to stand, some of us just prefer to do that. I know others who like to walk around but I would suggest the smile is a good idea, no matter what.

I have already told you that the Army drummed into me the importance of planning and preparation and I just wanted to share some results of my own preparation for this book. When I was thinking about all the points, I wanted to cover to give you the best value and the best possible chance for success, one of the things I did was some research to really test and check my own beliefs.

On the subject of your attitude having a major effect on the people you talk to, I wanted to prove this under extreme circumstances. What better way than to make a series of calls to people that I knew to be quite negative in general, for them things were always grey!

I made ten calls to them over a period of as many weeks. For the first five I mirrored their dour attitude. No surprise for guessing they showed no change, although I did come away feeling a bit low sometimes but only for a moment. For the final five I changed tactics and was positive and upbeat. By the time we got to the tenth call when they answered they still answered as if the weight of the world was on their shoulders but as soon as they knew it was me you could hear the change in their voice. They instantly adopted my tone and we all came away feeling good!

I have called them since the research and the habit has stuck, we always have a very animated and upbeat conversation, once they have established who they are talking to. I think that is proof enough. Later I did share with them what I had done and why. Of course, they also got a thank you letter and a signed copy of the book.

Always take time to build rapport.

Resist the temptation to talk about you or your product, before you think about starting any kind of pitch you need to first get the trust of the person you're talking to, make them feel like the most important person in the room and get to know about them and their company. Build their confidence in you as early as you can in the process by concentrating on them.

"Lower their barriers to make the sale easier. Do this by demonstrating your expertise, your human side, your passion and sincerity."

Life is not a rehearsal, so enjoy it.

The reality is most of us will spend more time working than anything else we do, so remember when at work you should be able to enjoy yourself. Use a little humour where and when it is appropriate to do so. This will greatly assist the progress you make with your prospect and the tone of your presentation. It will also make you feel more relaxed and enhance your confidence, it gives them confidence in you.

Make the entire experience as memorable as you can, this helps to build your reputation. Humour is a great tool for relationship sales but don't overdo it. Don't tell jokes that are not appropriate to the situation and the level of your relationship with the client or potential client. Use wit and learn from the best. Most good humour is based on observation, don't be political, racial or sexist but be topical. You can learn from the best by watching some of the great stand up artists and you will soon learn it's all about engagement and timing. If you can't do it don't try it and instead rely on your expertise, happy outlook and sincerity. You can still make it enjoyable for you and the prospect.

Using humour effectively does take time and practise, so be patient and invest time in developing the skill. Don't use it in sales meetings until you are sure you have it pegged. Start by practicing with family and friends. Do be aware that your friends and family will want to make you feel good, so make sure you watch for honest feedback and not just ego stroking. Don't use it with clients until you are sure you have got it right!

Know all there is to know about the product.

I believe it is vital that you know all there is to know about your product, industry and market from every possible angle, the more you know the better. Understand the product from top to bottom, inside and out, above all understand how it is used by customers and how they benefit from it. With a comprehensive understanding of the product the market and the industry you will have all you need to handle any question that is asked of you during the sales process. You'll also have all you need to handle even the toughest of objections should they arise, the more you know and the greater your understanding the more confidence you'll have and show. That confidence is infectious and will help in the creation of more sales.

You should avoid though, the temptation to show off your extensive knowledge and make the presentation all about you and your expertise. Instead use this information sparingly and only where it serves a positive purpose in the journey to the eventual sale. You need to know 100% but may only need to use a proportion of that knowledge during the sale. The important thing is it gives you the freedom to concentrate on the sale and the confidence to answer any questions the prospect may have.

Always think FAB (Feature, Advantage & Benefit).

When you get to the point in the sale where you need to talk about the product rather than the prospect and their needs, make sure you always think FAB, that is features, advantages and benefits. Explain a feature by pointing out what it does and then explain what the advantage is for the client and how that acts as a benefit to them and then repeat for all the main features that you feel need to be presented to help gain the sale.

In most cases the prospect is going to be more interested in how the product benefits them rather than how it works from a technical perspective. Think of it this way if you wanted to make holes in a wall to put some shelves up and you didn't have drill, you might go and buy one not because you wanted the drill but because you wanted the holes and that is the benefit of the purchase!

Honesty is always the best policy in sales.

Some of the people I met in my time in financial services, not so much in the independent sector but certainly in the larger insurance companies, were what you might describe as less than ethical in some of their practises. I am not saying they were bad people, in most cases they were very young, just starting out, knew no different and in many cases just following the training they were given. I remember some of the tricks they would use to get the sale and how they would manipulate and spin the truth, in some cases invent the truth to fit the sale. This in my view is the biggest sin you can commit as a professional who cares about people.

For me the only way to sell is the ethical way, the right way! The right way is to always tell the truth and always act in the best interest of the potential client. If you tell the truth you will never be put in a position where you are unable to accurately remember what it is, you said. Tell the truth and build a great reputation and get referrals or tell lies and lose it overnight. Once lost you may never get it back. The professional salesperson always tells the truth to their prospects and clients, because they are never lacking in confidence in their solution and its suitability. Those that lack this confidence are more likely to disguise the fact with stories that stretch the truth or are simply fiction.

Engage brain before opening mouth.

Make sure you think about what you are going to say before you say it and just as important make sure that if you say you're going to do something, that you do it and do it to the timescale you promised. On that subject it is better to overestimate delivery times and then beat them than to underestimate and create disappointment. So, in essence never over promise and under deliver, better to under promise and then over deliver. That does not mean exaggerate timescales otherwise you will just lose out to the competition. Great reputations are made from realistic goals that are met. You will never be remembered for what you said you were going to do; you will be remembered for what you did!

"If what you are about to say does not add value to the conversation and can't be delivered you should probably not bother to say it."

Get into the habit of pausing before you say anything. So, if you are asked something, even if you think you know the answer, I want you to get into the habit of pausing. That will be a good start! Next, once you have this sorted, use the pause to think about what you are about to say to make sure it is appropriate and fits the situation. In other words, engage your brain before you open your mouth!

Many people in business, including me, can fall into the trap of doing far too much talking and in many cases doing it just for the sake of talking, rather than adding real value to the conversation. It is a hard habit to break because we are naturally talkative and, in some cases, we have been trained to do all the talking. Trust me this is not the way to get sales! It is far better to listen and only talk when you are adding value to the conversation.

Speak wisely about the competition.

Part of being a professional in business is having a good working knowledge of your competition. You will frequently come across the competition during your sales presentations. The temptation might be to say something less than complimentary about them, but this is to be avoided. Remember about engaging brain before opening your mouth. The rule I use is simply this: if you have nothing good to say then don't say anything!

When I am in a situation where I need to talk about the competition, I always concentrate on saying something positive about them and never get caught saying anything that could offend. You never know who knows who and your comments might backfire! You'll be seen as significantly more professional if you refrain from insulting the competition or calling them into question in some way. You can still talk around any issues and emphasise the differential without the need to bad-mouth them.

It is best to always assume there is an existing relationship or indirect connection with the competition! In my early days in sales I saw a colleague make an error of this nature and the situation was never recovered.

My colleague was talking to the decision maker of an engineering business about gaining the contract for the supply of cutting equipment for them. At the time they split their orders between three of the competition. One of these businesses got more of the order than the rest and they happened to be the most expensive of the three and had a bit of a reputation of not treating their employees so well. They had a higher than average turnover of staff too. During the presentation my colleague was gathering information and the subject of the competition and pricing came up. This is where it all started to go wrong. My colleague mentioned this other company and the fact they were more expensive and then went too far by stating he could never work for a company like that and continued to comment on the quality of the leadership, based on gossip he had listened to relating to staff treatment. What he didn't know, because it had not come out in the previous conversations, was the link between the supplier and this company. It happened that they were related through family!

"You may be in competition with others but rise above the temptation of using gossip or speaking ill of them. Let the others do that and you stand out from the crowd with your integrity intact!"

You can imagine what happened next! No business was done, and he was not welcome back at the prospects business. In reality this could have been avoided in a number of ways; more questions may have identified the family link in the early part of the process, certainly not listening or using gossip would have avoided the situation and finally not saying anything other than positive things about the competition would have worked. It may not have resulted in business, but it would have protected his reputation and kept the door open for the future.

Later my colleague asked me what he could have done differently, and I told him exactly the same. He took it well and then asked if I could give an example of how I would have handled the situation? I told him that to avoid any comment was best but if you need to make a comment then make sure it is positive rather than negative, without being dishonest. For example, rather than mentioning not being able to work with a company like that because of the reputation I might have said.

"I have heard many things about them, and they could even take credit for where I am today, as they were my motivation to get into this business and be the best we can be."

With regard the price issue I might have said,

"We all have our own pricing policies, but I always feel it's not so much the price but rather the value that should be assessed. They have many clients, as do we, so I guess we have that quality in common."

As you can see there was no gossip, no defamatory statements and nothing for anyone to get upset about either and so the sales presentation continues, and the chances of an order have not been diminished. You might even have just won a fan and increased your chances; you'll never know unless you try!

Collect great testimonials.

As I have said before you shouldn't tell people how great you are, instead you should show them through your actions. Another way to show how good you, your business and your products are is through testimonials. These can be worth many sales for you as they are direct evidence, from satisfied customers, of your quality. Make a real effort to collect as many of these as you can as often as you can. Don't sing your own praises, this will come across as arrogant and will alienate people. Instead let others do it for you, while you remain modest and humble.

"Take your smartphone out on customer calls and use it to record video clips of your customers sharing their thoughts about you and your company!"

Get a mixture of written and video testimonials. Video testimonials are quite easy to do these days all you have to do is take your smartphone with you and ask the client if you can film a clip of them sharing their thoughts about your service. Make sure you get the very best from your testimonials use them as a marketing tool to gain new sales leads.

If you are short of testimonials consider contacting a client and offer to save them some time by writing the testimonial for them, all they need do is agree the wording and agree to put their name to it. You'll be surprised how many clients will be happy to do this.

Recognise buying signals.

During the sales process your prospect may say things that are direct indications that they want to buy, we call these buying signals. Make sure you recognise these; you are being told that the prospect is ready to buy. This is why I always say, listening is usually more important than talking, where sales are concerned. Listen to the prospect, really listen.

Sometimes the prospect might raise what we call objections; these are either reasons why they may not go ahead with the purchase, or a simple need for more information. In many cases, when all the other elements of the sales process have been followed and executed professionally, these too can be buying signals. The prospect is showing their interest by raising the questions that need to be addressed before they get to telling you yes. So, make sure you take time to understand all the possible objections and practise delivering the right answers. At the very least prepare for the obvious ones like, price, timing or budget. Also be aware that many, if not all, can be avoided during the presentation by covering all the bases!

Know your client—Confirm affordability—Understand their decision-making process—Understand their needs

Anticipate and overcome.

By asking the right questions gathering all the information you'll be able to effectively anticipate objections and deal with them in the presentation before they become an issue. That said, you will still get occasional objections that need to be dealt with. There will be times when the objections may be a smoke screen and you'll need to be able to recognise if it is the real thing, or just covering the real reason for raising the objection that has yet to be voiced.

"People don't always tell the whole truth; part of the skill is finding the true reasons for the objections. You'll need to drill down to get to the heart of the matter. When you can do this your sales will increase."

Those that aspire to be exceptional will need to have the confidence to really drill down to get to the true objection, the root cause of the issues. The next step is to overcome them, using all their skill and knowledge of the product, market and competition. They can also use their experience, gained from others who have felt the same way but discovered the true value of the solution on offer. Like so many other aspects of business and the sales process this takes preparation and practise. Make sure you become expert and well-practised in the area of objection handling, a key skill.

Ask for the business then keep quiet!

It never ceases to amaze me the number of people I come across who are trying to earn their living and develop their future through sales and yet they find it difficult to do the most important part of the sale, ask for the business! This could be for a number of reasons which we will look into. However, for now I just want to say if asking for the sale seems to be too simple, that's because it really is that simple.

If you did the job well this is the one question your prospect will be waiting for, because by now they really want the product. So be confident and ask for the business. Once you have done that shut up and wait. My first sales trainer told me the same thing and it is as true today as it was back then. He used to say to the class; "The first one to talk loses the game!" The only change I would make to that is to point out this not supposed to be taken literally and it's not a game it's the life blood of business, your business.

I do use silence after a big question but not to the point that it starts to get uncomfortable. So, when I have asked for the business, assuming my prospect hasn't already asked me, I wait but before it gets uncomfortable will say something like, so what do you think?

Get used to silence by practicing, when you first start a 5 second wait will feel like 30 seconds. The more you get used to it the better you'll become at using pauses and silence, the more you use this technique, the more success you'll have. This is also a very useful presenting skill too.

Sales rarely happen on the first meeting.

You may not get the sale on the first meeting or contact, you may need to have multiple contacts first and that is quite simply because people like to buy from people they like and trust, and before they do that they want to know a little about you, they want you to know them and they want to know they can really trust you. So, with that in mind do not be down hearted if you can't close on the first, second or third contact, concentrate on building the relationship; first gain their confidence and then ask for the business. So be prepared and plan for multiple contacts and always follow up. Your personal rule should be to have no loose ends where your prospects and customers are concerned.

The number of contacts you need to make before you get the sale will also be influenced by the type of product you are selling; how complex it is, the company you are selling to and their procedure. Some of the more complex sales can take months to come to fruition; these are usually the very high value sales with many complicated stages. The good news is this will give you plenty of time and opportunities to really get to know the client and build a great relationship with them.

It's not you it's just timing.

Most people hate the feeling of rejection and the same can be said for anyone who has the responsibility for sales. I would go as far as to say most of the salespeople that I know are far more sensitive to rejection than everyone else. It is the fear of rejection that takes the biggest toll on sales, with more salespeople avoiding the close for fear of rejection than any other reason for not getting the sale. So, in this regard the key is to recognise the role your ego takes in this process. It is your ego that gets bruised when rejection comes to call and therefore it is your ego that stands in the way of completing the sale. To solve this issue all we need to do is realign the way you interpret the rejection.

"When people say no to the sale. Providing you have followed all the rules there is little chance the person is saying no to you forever, they're just saying not right now."

The first thing I want you to consider is: Providing you are following all the rules and putting people first, building rapport and trust, it is not you that is being rejected, just the offer you are making at that particular time. They are not saying 'no' forever but 'no' for now. The other thing worth pointing out is that we all have key performance indicators (KPI). These arc metrics that will tell us our close ratio amongst other important information related to our performance. I will use my own KPI as an example I know that I will close one in three presentations that I make and therefore I know that for each sale I need to be rejected twice, I have to get rid of the people that are going to tell me no, before I can get to the sought after yes. I also know that if the average value of each sale is £5,000 that every time I am told 'no' I am earning in effect one-third of £5,000, i.e. £1,666.66, with that at the forefront of my mind I quite welcome no, because that is another £1,666.66 in the bank! That also means, the next sale is just around the corner, as long as I keep up the activity. I appreciate this is just a psychological trick, but the KPI is fact as is the average sale value, and it helps to position it this way.

That is a key point; in most failing sales careers I will find a lack of the right activity and a complete lack of attention to personal performance metrics and investment in their improvement. If you want to improve yours then register with **Rainmakers Club** and Join our community of small business owners all on a journey to exceptional and sustainable results, to learn more and improve!

Keep your eye on the ball, all the time.

I often tell fellow businesspeople entrepreneurs and others at my speaking events that they have to embrace change and that change is inevitable, those who can accept it, adapt and roll with it will have greater success than those who don't. As is often the case we find the rules that apply so well to business management also apply to sales. You will find your market changes, techniques change, technologies change, and products change. My message is don't take your eye off the ball, embrace the change and roll with it, if you fight it or ignore it, you will start the long and painful journey of failure, like so many before you.

Never venture beyond your Values

Some businesspeople feel the need to sail close to the wind and bend the rules to breaking point many will go beyond breaking point. They might get away with that once or twice but eventually their actions will catch up with them.

The risks are too great and like your own personal values you should never venture beyond the left and right boundaries of the rules that protect you. Guard your reputation as if were the most valuable thing in your life, it's not far from that and deserves the attention. These boundaries I speak of are your personal values. Business is important but should be done well and with integrity. Work inside your core values and watch your reputation and fortune grow, step outside and you are on the slippery slopes to nowhere!

Always be the good guy and really mean it.

In most cases sales are never a one-man job often others are involved and so it is really important that you make the effort to get on with the people around you. Particularly those that have an effect on the sale and the customer. Like so many other elements in business, being sincere truthful and dependable are vital to your reputation and development.

Work hard & work smart.

This next point is still as true today as it has always been. There is no such thing as pure luck but there is such a thing as hard work and the relationship is clear and simple, the harder we work the more luck we seem to get. So, your success will be defined by the amount of effort you put into your skills development and the amount of work you put into the vital task of selling.

"People say you should work smarter not harder. The reality is if you look at the truly successful, they all work harder than the average person and they all work smarter too!"

If you haven't already done so, get hold of a copy of Napoleon Hills book 'Think and Grow Rich.' I am suggesting this so that you really put some time into understanding how important the way you think is. Luck is a fine thing but only the foolhardy will sit back and wait for luck to come calling. The lucky ones are those that put the effort in and keep on putting it in all the time. Take a look around you at the people you know who are successful and you'll see that they all put the hours in and work hard but they also work smart too! Hard without smart and smart without hard is just not going to work in the long term!

Remember windows and mirrors.

Practice accountability and take responsibility for your actions. Above all share the wins with those around you and enhance your reputation and success still further. The blame game is not just negative it is distracting and damaging. Remember when things go wrong don't go to the window and blame go to the mirror and take responsibility, then fix it. The opposite is also true when things go well, forget the mirror for self-congratulations, instead go to the window and share the congratulations around, because you are never alone in business.

If at first you don't succeed try, try again.

This above all things is my own personal mantra. I truly believe as long as I get up more than I get knocked down I will succeed. Being persistent is a fine art, get it wrong and you become a hinderer, a problem, get it right and you'll start to win more than you lose. The true art is finding the right balance and be persistent with character, charisma, humour and sincerity. Think of being told no as a challenge rather than a rejection and watch your sales grow. My belief in this is very strong, I want you to believe it just as strongly!

Understand KPI, use the power of numbers.

If you don't already know your KPI, then make an effort to find out, understand the power of numbers. The more you understand about your numbers the better you can plan your success and the success of your business. Make sure you understand the formula to your own sales success. How many calls do you need to make to get the number of appointments or opportunities to deliver a proper and full pitch? How many pitches does it take to get a close, what is the average value and how many do you need to meet your own income goals? Once you understand your own formula work to it and work on improving it too. Figures are an important item in your toolbox, just as they are for

"I have been asked what one thing I do that makes the most difference to my sales performance? There are many things like getting the right attitude but without doubt the biggest was understanding the numbers and making them work for me!"

With the technology that is available today there is no excuse for not knowing your numbers, record them daily and keep them on your Smartphone. Most good CRM systems will have mobile applications for use on your phone, so you need never be without your latest performance metrics.

Have passion and show it.

Have you ever been to a presentation where the speaker is really passionate about the subject they are discussing? Now compare that to a presentation that you've witnessed that lacked passion. Did you leave one feeling cheated, bored, or demotivated and the other uplifted with a feeling that you gained from the experience?

People will experience the same if they are the recipient of a sales presentation that is just going through the motions, or one based on belief and passion for the product and above all the prospects well-being. You need to have a passion for the solution, if not there is no point in even turning up. Deliver the presentation with passion, be creative and professional, show sincerity and you'll be remembered. Being memorable is very important and very easy for the exceptional sales professional.

"Passion for something is infectious. If you show your passion for the solution and the prospect, your chances of success are increased significantly."

Selling and buying should be fun.

With a passion for what you do you'll enjoy the entire process; these feelings are contagious and if you come across as passionate and happy in your work this will be reflected back. Your prospect will start to enjoy the process too, which is important if you're to get the sale. Happy salesperson equals happy client. Business is tough, it's hard work and can be challenging, don't make it harder by having the wrong outlook.

In any one day as a business owner you could experience every human emotion, from the pits of despair to the heights of elation. Despite all that, business and in particular selling should be fun. There is nothing wrong with having fun while you're working. The clue is in the words, having fun, yes but still working, still doing a great job and still being successful! Learn to enjoy what you do, learn to encourage others to feel the same way. Make meeting you a pleasure!

Consequences.

I just wanted to say a few words on the consequences of not following these basic guidelines for a professional outlook on sales. If you fail to follow these basic guides you will, over a time, begin to fail, slowly at first and like most failures quite suddenly it will all be over, and all be too late. Ignore these points at your peril. So, your action plan for now is to:

- Have a plan and stick to it—Fail to plan, plan to fail.

- Always do your best.
- Always take time to learn something new.
- Make sure targets make sense and then commit to them.
- Keep to targets, if it means extra work, then do it.
- Always maintain a positive attitude.

The thing about failing is there really is nobody else to blame, even though many a mediocre businessperson would have you believe that their failure is in some way the responsibility of others.

Any failure can be damaging to your attitude and confidence and we all have to go through that, without the failure we would find it difficult to learn. The failure is just a moment in time, learn from it, dust yourself down, stand up, put a big smile on your face and start again, twice as positive, with your new learning and greater strength!

On the other side of the coin we have success, which comes from self-confidence, experience, positive actions and a constant positive outlook and above all hard work, much hard work. We have all experienced failure and it can be hard to get back on the horse once it has thrown you. Just do it, that is the mark of a successful person. They won't let the failure get them down; they turn it into a positive, learn and move onward and upward!

Join the AA (Attitude & Action).

In this case the AA I am referring to is two essential elements in the formula for successful sales, I am referring to your attitude and taking action. Maintaining a positive mental attitude is important and is without doubt the force behind your success. Positive attitude is not something that you can treat as a part of the process of selling it is so much more than that, it's a discipline that needs to be maintained everyday no matter what is thrown at you, make your glass half full never half empty.

"You've heard it all before, but have you acted on it too? Actions do speak louder than words. Don't just talk about it, do it and do it well!"

I was talking to a guy at a networking event I was a guest speaker at; during the conversation he complimented me on the presentation. He then puzzled over what made a successful person successful when compared to others who on the face of it appeared to be exactly the same but without the success, was it simply a question of luck? The answer was quite simple, and this is where the second 'A' comes in. The difference is quite simply action. Taking positive action not just talking the talk but walking the walk too.

You'll find this often; the difference is some talk about it and others do it. You need to be one of those that does it not just talk about doing it. Actions speak louder than words. My words in this and my other books and presentations would mean nothing if they weren't preceded with successful action. Talking about what you have done, to help others to share the success, is infinitely better than talking about what you might do or might have done. We are very much what we have done and not what we say we are going to do and that is how we will be judged too, on what we have done not what we said we were going to do!

When our peers judge us or form an opinion about us it will be based on our actions not our intentions, it will be based on what we have done not what we say we are going to do. We leave that to Del-Boy and the Trotters (Cult UK Comedy about a family of market traders always talking about being wealthy and always getting it wrong).

Why some fail?

You become what you think you about most.

The human mind is very powerful and has a direct influence over what happens in your life. Most people in business, when asked if they have a positive attitude, will say yes, however many who say yes are just saying it rather than living it. You can't just say you have a positive attitude you have to work at it, and it starts from the inside. You are what you think about and if you spend all your time thinking negative thoughts, thinking, I can't do this, it is highly likely that you won't. On the other hand, if you approach it with a positive spin, telling yourself you can do it and then visualise the actions needed to achieve the goal, you stand a really good chance of success.

I can personally vouch for this, I use the same technique for all my public speaking engagements for a few days before the event I visualise the presentation and what I'm going to say, where I'm going to stand and how I will handle a range of possible questions. Preparation and rehearsal for sales is necessary for all aspiring exceptional salespeople.

If I had to pick out the main things you could do to make a difference and avoid the possibility of sales failure, I would say make sure you expel all the negative stuff and concentrate only on the positive. If you feel that you have any weakness in your attitude, and you want to improve your sales fortunes then you could do yourself a real service by simply committing to follow these important pointers:

- When things go bad, you take **responsibility** and don't get pulled into the blame game, it never helps.

- Understand that your life and career is a series of choices, you need to make a choice. Sitting on the fence gets you nowhere. Mistakes are fine as long as you **learn** from them.

- Trust your **instincts**, more often than not you'll be right to do so and when you're not, learn.

- Avoid those who just want to rain on your parade. Avoid negative news and don't join in with gossip. Instead spend your time doing something more **worthwhile**.

- Sometimes bad things happen, each time this happens to you look for the **opportunity** in the circumstances and make it a learning experience too.

- Take time to **invest** in yourself, always look for new learning opportunities.

- Always make the **effort** to help others and always give value first. **Concentrate** on saying what and why you like things and avoid talking about all the things you dislike.

- Don't keep score when helping others, do it because you want to, because you **care**.

Bad moods are a waste of time effort energy and will not help you with any kind of victory, **smile** and get on with it.

Sales hero, born or taught?

This is a question many have asked. Are great salespeople born with a talent for sales or is it nothing more than a set of skills that can be taught? To be frank It is a combination of both. Salespeople aren't born but nor is it all down to training. There are key skills that you need to learn and then develop to become a great salesperson. However, the very best salespeople do all share some vary similar personality traits which influence greatly how good they will become, these include:

- They enjoy working toward their own **goals**.

- They have good **self-discipline**.

- They have high levels of **self-motivation**.

- Learning and **developing skills** is a constant desire.
- They enjoy the process of building new **relationships**.
- They **like** who they are.
- They enjoy **meeting** and the company of people.
- **Challenges** are sought after.
- **Winning** is important to them.
- They are able to maintain a **positive attitude**, even in rejection.
- Although not usually **detail** oriented, they can handle it.
- They have high levels of **loyalty**.
- They are **enthusiastic**.
- They are often very **observant**.
- They are great **listeners** and good at communication.
- They work hard are **persistent** and seek financial security.

All the other things that you expect in a salesperson like the ability to handle objections or close the sale can be taught. The very best salespeople will have most if not all of these characteristics before they even know the formal skills of selling. How do you fare against these traits? I wouldn't worry if you don't have them all, the key is that you recognise a fair share of these in yourself, more importantly that others notice them in you. We do tend to have a slightly warped image of ourselves!

"It is probably not good enough to believe your own PR, you may think you're great, what really matters is what others are saying about you."

Now that we know the base traits needed to be a salesperson let's look more into why salespeople sometimes fail to get the sale when on paper they are talking to the perfect prospect.

I was thinking about this and I can't remember one occasion in all the sales training sessions workshops or seminars I have been involved in, where a salesperson spoke to me, admitting that they had lost a sale and it was all their fault! I have however, spoken to many who have told be about the external issues that they had faced, which caused, or contributed to the failure of the sale. During my journey in sales I have witnessed or fallen foul of a whole bunch or sales mistakes that are usually the real cause of a sales failure, when the odds should really be in favour of the salesperson, the most common of these are listed below.

Being too soft on the prospect.

I am not suggesting you need to go in hard all the time and just become a throwback to the high pressure techniques of yesteryear but I am suggesting that you need to focus on getting some kind of commitment from the prospect before you start to give them all the value without a commitment to reciprocate.

We have all been there, where you make a call or go to see a prospect and during the conversation, they say something like; "That sounds great can you send me an email with all the information, or can you send me a brochure?" There is nothing wrong with doing this as long as it is not all you do. At that point you should say something like; "Sure so why don't we put a date in the dairy to discuss this in more detail once you've had a chance to review the information. How about next Tuesday at the same time or would Thursday be better for you?"

Get the commitment before you give away all the sweeties in the jar. Make them happy, yes, give them what they want, within reason, yes but don't give and then walk away without some kind of commitment in return. If you send the mail and then wait for them to come back to you, it's best that you're not holding your breath!

Don't talk about it, just do it.

This refers to the salespeople who when they enter a situation where a sales presentation needs to be given, they start by talking about themselves, this is to be avoided. Instead think about asking the right questions about the prospect, so that you can establish their feelings, their needs, their opinions and their background. You'll get your chance later, for now it's all about them. If you follow this, I promise you you'll be doing much more and much better than most of your competition, because they will all be working with bad habits. They will be cutting corners and concentrating far too much on themselves and their products. I find it really interesting that most salespeople know all this but when it's time to go to work they don't do it. Instead they revert to the lazy bad habits. Habits that have a negative effect on their sales performance.

Don't say it unless you can do it.

I have said earlier in this book, never over promise and under deliver but always place yourself in a position where you can exceed the prospect or customers' expectations. If you do, during a meeting or telephone conversation say that you're going to do something or structure the deal in a particular way, you need to make sure, before you complete the meeting, that you and the people on the other side of the table all have the same understanding.

Make sure you commit this to notes and then send a copy to the prospect so that you reduce the chance of being misunderstood, in this regard written confirmation is key. Your mission is to avoid the need for the prospect or customer to ever have to say to you, "I thought you said that . . ." If this happens it can only lead to trouble or a backwards step in the relationship.

Never get caught being unfair!

Remember the key rule, People do buy from people and then only people that they like, so that means your prospect has to like you. A sure way to get a knock back is to be insincere and another sure way is to get caught saying bad things about the competition. No matter what you might think of them or what you might think the prospect thinks of them, never get caught being negative about them. So, the rule is don't put them down be positive and only say things that are true and not idle gossip or negative.

"By now you've won their hearts and minds and started to build their confidence in you, don't blow it by showing your dark side and bad mouthing the competition."

Make sure you really understand your differential and use that to create the right kind of distance between you and the competition, not forgetting to show the benefits to the prospect, without the need to revert to cheap shots. Now is not the time to start a war of words with or about the competition. All you'll achieve between you is to drive the prospect into the arms of another.

Never send marketing material followed by a call to see if they got it.

This will just make you look silly, it's not helpful and you could quite easily be seen as a bit of a nuisance, which will do nothing to help you get the sale you want. If you want to contact them do it because you have prearranged a chat or call to offer some ideas, or to ask some really good questions. The sort of questions that will get them thinking about the next step. Be smart and be professional all the time. When they ask you to send something agree to send it but agree a time and date to follow it up first.

You don't need to sell your soul to get the business!

If price becomes an issue don't give something away immediately. Never and I mean never ask a prospect, "What do I have to do to get your business?" Rather than ask this question and get back some really predictable retorts why not just be completely honest and say something like:

"Let me tell you what has made others buy from us over our competition, because in truth we're not the cheapest and there's good reason for that . . ."

Now concentrate on the features, advantages and benefits and get them to think as if they already have the product, make sure you bring their attention to the value proposition so cost ceases to be an issue, or at least is greatly reduced as an issue.

"Too many salespeople come in early with a price deal or discount, use this sparingly, have confidence in the value of the product and validity of the pricing policy."

If you do ask your prospect what you need to do to get the business, you're likely to get all the usual answers relating to bringing the price down, offering extended warranty for free, or significant discounts on orders that just aren't big enough to warrant such treatment. You work for a great business selling a great product and it is priced the way it is for a good reason. Have the confidence and tools to demonstrate this and motivate the sale on your terms but make them fair.

Don't forget, they've heard it all before!

I have no doubt that when you talk to your prospect, they will have heard it all before and that is a potential point of failure, try to be different, give them the truth about your business before you get there. In most cases if you are selling B2B they will have done some research on you already. Rather than going through the usual pitch; influence them to ask questions that result in you demonstrating how the product will work for them in particular.

Get them to tell you about their experience with similar products so far. This will work so much better than going into the same old pitch material about why they should be considering your product over all the other possibilities.

"You will gain much better results in B2B sales if you create a differential by telling the prospect the truth, don't sugar coat your sale."

Never assume the prospect hasn't already made their decision.

I know on the face of it this may sound a little strange to you, however this happens more often than you'll realise. It is quite possible that the prospect has already made up their mind about the product; maybe they just need that final confirmation that the decision they made was the right one. If you approach them as if this is just a pitch it is quite possible to lose the sale against all the odds.

The way around this is to assume nothing and make friends with the prospect as quickly as you can. By doing this you'll find out so much more than the pure sales method. Once you've established the rapport you can ask them smart questions to find out exactly where they are in the decision-making process, giving you the ability to adapt your presentation to suit the circumstances. I have used this method for some years in B2B sales and I have to say, for me it works perfectly. If you're new to this technique give it a chance to work for you. Practice, after all, does make perfect.

Keep giving value all the time.

No matter how many times you make follow up calls to the client, you need to make sure you always give value, yes even after the sale has been made. Give and keep giving, this is the way to get more sales and really great referrals. If you do the opposite, which in most cases is what the mediocre do, you'll find yourself getting fewer and fewer sales over time.

Don't ask predictable questions that are all about you and the money, just concentrate on giving value. Selling is all about people, relationships and needs. Everything else is just white noise.

Build the positive, then dump the negative.

If I had the power to change one thing in everybody it would be to get everyone to think of their glass as half full rather than half empty. I have found in business that far too many people concentrate on the 'can't' instead of the 'can.' This attitude acts as a kind of inhibitor or anchor to success. The same is true for sales, when we concentrate on the negative, we inhibit the success we should be having. If you continue to have negative thoughts it will have an effect on the way you act and soon people will start to feel it too. Most of us like to surround ourselves with positive people, so make sure you're one of those positive people. Don't think why can't I get that person on the phone, why won't they return my call. Think positive, act positive and be positive.

"Negative repels and positives attract. Success is far more common in those that attract than repel. Contrary to belief they do not attract because they are successful as much as they are successful because they attract!"

We all have things that go wrong from time to time, the important thing is how we deal with them and how that affects the people around us. Let me share something with you that is probably my pet hate. I really dislike the blame culture particularly in business. In my view this is one of the most negative traits you can come across in business today! So, my message to you is to stop blaming the situation you are in on others, stop blaming the circumstances and stop blaming the people around you. Instead start to take some responsibility for the situation and then do something about it, in a positive manner. You have so much more influence over what happens to you than you realise.

The other thing I want to say is, the better you know your clients the less you will have to handle the problems. Others who don't take time to do this will have to spend increasing amounts of time handling the problems. Whereas if you take the time to really know your client and really understand them, understand their personality, you'll be able to deal with issues before they become issues.

Sometimes the simplest of things can make a difference to you and assist you in becoming that attractive positive person. For example, rather than feeling negative because you can't get hold of the customer, take time to find out the best time to contact them and call then. Simple? **Yes**. Effective? **Yes**. Positive action? **Yes**. My rule for this is you can never know too much about your customers or prospects.

Another thing I want to say to you is, there is nothing wrong with being persistent, I believe that the tenacious salespeople are far more successful than those that give up on the first unanswered call or the first 'no.' There is however, a balance to find, tenacious yes a nuisance never!

Being tenacious is good but know when to stop.

I come across many salespeople who give up too soon, who don't understand how much a customer or prospect has respect for the salesperson who demonstrates a bit of staying power. As long as it is not over the top and they always demonstrate the greatest respect for the prospect or customer. A friendly warning, as important as it is to demonstrate this tenacity, it's equally important knowing when you've gone far enough, never go too far.

Research has shown that in B2B sales and in some of the more intangible B2C sales it takes between five and ten exposures before the sale is made and so tenacity is very important and the salesperson who can hang on in there, even when the prospect is saying 'no' to start with, will gain the sale. It is only a negative right now and all things being right this will become a yes at some point in the future, assuming you're talking to the right person and there is a clear need for the product.

Think CPD (continuous professional development).

If you take time, like I have, to really look long and hard at those salespeople who are starting to fail, a key characteristic most of them have is their reticence to seek out new learning all the time, rather than just the occasional CPD they are almost forced to do. Having the attitude where they actively seek to undertake training and learning is what the more successful people do but that is far too few in reality. Many do nothing or only get involved if they are told to do so by their boss!

When I was full time in sales, I used to spend quite a bit of time reading and honing my selling skills in the evenings and weekends. I got into this habit long before I began my sales career, it was a habit instilled in me during my time in the Army. Once the habit was set, I never looked back, seeking out new knowledge has become second nature to me, it is a passion that has become one of my biggest assets in business. You can never have too much information. Try to get into the habit of reading, researching, listening to seminars on subjects that will help to improve your skills and knowledge. You'll never know it all, so keep looking, keep learning, keep improving your game.

Think solutions not problems.

Some of us are positive and some of us are not, without doubt those who are positive, the ones who always see things as an opportunity to be addressed rather than a problem, have a far better chance of sales success than the negative people. If you're not already doing so, concentrate on being solution oriented rather than seeing things as problems. When things happen, the way I see it, you have these choices; build the circumstances into a barrier to prevent your progress or create a ladder to the next level.

Engage brain and think about the impact.

Once we have you thinking about solutions rather than problems, we need to make sure that you avoid the other things that many of the unsuccessful salespeople do. Put as simply as I can, I have already said you need to engage your brain before you open your mouth to speak. It goes beyond that you also need to always think about the impact and knock-on effect of what you're about to say.

"Always consider the impact of what you are saying on the people around you!"

You'd do well to remember that everything you say will have an impact on someone, your aim should be to ensure you have the right effect on the right people at the right time. Please don't just say stuff for the hell of saying it. Never set out to hurt the people you are communicating to or about, it's not nice and will never bring you success. It might make you feel empowered for a moment, but the moment will pass quickly, leaving only regret and a damaged relationship.

You as a customer.

How should you be treated?

Most of us would say exactly the same to the question of how we want to be treated when we are the customer, interestingly in practise few sales professionals act in a way they would want to be treated if they were buying. The reasons behind this could be many things; I think the main one is the pressure to sell. It makes people forget to have the right levels of respect and at the same time being professional. It turns them into a relentless closing machine with no true regard for the people. Conversely if you take a look at exceptional salespeople, these are the ones that are earning five to ten times more than the mediocre salespeople that make up over 90% of the sales population. In the exceptional you'll find a completely different approach that is always people oriented, with the product bringing up the rear.

Here then is what I would like to experience if I were the customer and therefore the way I try to treat my prospects and customers all the time. I find it interesting that during the many sales recruitment projects I have been involved in for my various customers over the years, when asked for the most important element in the sales persons tool box, most would say listening and yet not really listening turns out to be the most prevalent sin committed by the majority of salespeople at all levels.

The reason listening is so important is that people buy from people, moreover they will normally buy from people they like. A sale will always take place you will either sell the prospect on saying yes to you, or they will take control and sell you on no. I maintain that more declines are the outcome of the sales process, where there has been a lack of initial research and a lack of listening to the prospect than any other reason for sales failure.

"Always remember how you would want to be treated if you were the customer in your meeting and then make sure you are treating your customer in that way."

Therefore, my number one tip for the salesperson is understand the importance of listening! Not just because this is how you learn about your prospect or client but because you know how you would feel, if you were in conversation with someone about something that was important to you and you discovered they were not really listening to you. As a professional salesperson you'd not want to make your client or prospect feel that way, would you?

As a customer I don't want any bull, I just want the facts, not some story that is designed to fit my needs but the cold hard facts about the solution, the good, the bad and the ugly. For me honesty should be a given, there is no value at all in telling me things that are made up. I don't need you to tell me something that you label as honest, if you say, 'to be honest'. It makes me feel like anything you've said before without that descriptor has not been honest. If you always tell the truth you don't need to say to be honest, do you?

As a customer I want you to demonstrate to me in all you do you have integrity, I want evidence that you act in an ethical manner, if you have values, make a point of being seen to live and act by those values. I have often found that those people who need to talk constantly about being ethical are often the ones that are not! You'll find the same in the Army those that do most the talking have probably done the least, watch out for the quiet and humble ones!

When you're selling it to me, make sure you are thinking about me and not the product, in other word concentrate on the benefits to me not the generic benefits. If I am buying a computer for my writing, I want to know all the benefits that match my proposed use not all the benefits for gaming. In other words, tell me how the product is going to benefit me with my writing.

If you're going to make claims about the product or service, you're selling to me, give me some evidence to show that it's true. Maybe a testimonial from an existing user supported by an article or some other form of media in support of the claims that are being made. The last time I was looking at buying a car the salesperson gave me a copy of a 'What Car' magazine article in support of his claims about its performance. If you're going to use a testimonial use one that is based on similar needs to those of my own and demonstrate how it worked out for them and build my confidence still further.

I also like to have some form of evidence that the support I am being shown during the sales process will continue after the sale and during the life span of the product I am buying into. This can be demonstrated as above by a good testimonial and through reputation. Build up a database of satisfied customers who will talk about the good and how they have been helped, no smoke just true hard facts.

Although price may not always be the issue particularly in sales that are part motivated by status, I will still want the salesperson to demonstrate to me that the price is fair and that I am getting a good deal. Then talk to me about payment options to make sure I am getting the best possible package designed to suit my needs. Don't let me find out later there was a better option for me!

"Give me the best possible deal, the best possible options and in return I will promote you and do more business with you, I will show you the same consideration and loyalty you have shown me."

Show me sincere passion for the solution show me that if you were in the market for this product you would buy this above all the other options and why you'd make that choice.

Help me to make the right decision by re-enforcing the choice I am about to make. You can do this through talking about the specific features that relate to my needs, the needs you've discovered by careful questions and active listening. Relate the features to the specific advantages of the feature and make sure you relate that to the benefits for me specifically. This will increase my confidence in making the purchase.

I am happy if you have a different opinion to me on certain aspects but if you need to communicate them to me as part of the process make sure you do it with respect and not as an argument. You might well win the argument but if you are winning with a confrontational style you will probably lose the sale.

Try to keep things as simple as you can, not because I won't understand the complexities but because the more complex you make it the less likely I am to buy from you or the more questions and possible objections I will raise.

Although I want the truth the whole truth and nothing but the truth when I am being sold to, I don't want to hear negative things about other people or the competition and particularly about my business. This is a sure way to lose the sale. Also please don't talk down to me you may know more than I do about certain subjects, but I am not stupid, and I don't want to be treated that way. If you do, I will simply go and buy from one of your competitors who treats me right, or maybe even your business but through someone else, anything not to see you again!

From time to time I will make a mistake, I've always said show me a person who doesn't make the occasional mistake and I will show you a person who is doing nothing. If I do make a mistake in a purchase before seeing you, I don't need you to make me feel worse than I already do, I know I made the mistake I don't need to be told it again by you. Instead you could always make me feel a little better by concentrating on showing me I'm not alone and others have done the same.

It is important that as a customer you listen to me. When I am being sold to and I decide I want to buy, then that's what I want to do, buy. However, if you're too busy going through the pitch to listen to me asking to buy then you'll probably lose the sale. So, listen and if I want to buy stop the pitch and close the deal.

When I am spending money on something I want to buy, it should be fun it should be an experience that I enjoy. So, as the salesperson you need to ensure that the process is an enjoyable one and use some humour too. Use it at the right time and for the right reasons. If you put me in a good mood, I am far more likely to buy than if you put me in a bad mood or bore me. You can also do this by taking a real interest in me. I believe that selling is all about people not products, people buy from people they like, they like people who are interested in them.

I already said I am not stupid and don't want to be treated that way and so don't say things just to try to get me onside, I will be able to tell if you're just saying it for effect. It is vital that you only say things with real integrity and sincerity. Oh, and when you start to sound like a salesperson with relentless time worn sales terms that I can see coming a mile off you'll lose me. So, concentrate on having a conversation with me, it takes at least two to have a conversation. I'm not sitting in front of you because I want a lecture.

Always, and I mean always, deliver what you promise me, therefore never over promise and never under deliver, far better to under promise and over deliver. If you can do that, you'll have a client for life, and I won't be shy in talking you up to my contact base. Above all I want you to help me to buy the right solution and not to just sell to me, remember the golden rule, I don't want to be sold to, but I do love to buy stuff.

I personally think that if you are not already using the positives and expelling the negatives mentioned above in your sales technique then you should read them all again and commit them to memory and habit. Start using them today to improve your sales performance, make this part of your sales philosophy. The better you become at this, the less your prospects will be tempted to use their ultimate deal breaker, saying no to you and buying from someone else!

"Treat the customer right all the time, better to under promise and over deliver than the other way around!"

What about me!

How do you want to be treated?

The other side of the coin is how do you want to be treated by the customer? Why is this important? I think if you understand what it is that you want too, you can start to act in a way that is going to promote these reactions in your customers. I think it would be correct to say that we do have the power to change the way we are treated by behaving in a way that promotes the right responses.

If I sit down and really think about how, as a salesperson, I would want to be treated, my list of things would look like this, how does it match with your own expectations? Perhaps the question should be, are you treating salespeople who contact you in this way, and if not why not?

I guess the main thing is, I want to be shown respect, sales are not a dirty word it's what makes the world go around, nothing and I mean nothing in business can happen without sales so treat me with the respect I deserve. If you do that, I will concentrate on being the best I can, a professional hard working tenacious and honest salesperson with heart. How can you demonstrate this respect to me?

Well, I think a good starting point might be to return my calls when I contact you. I know for sure if you made a call to me, you'd expect me to return it, so you should do the same. This is a key point don't moan if you don't get your calls returned if you're not doing the same, if you think it's because you're more important, we may need to check your ego!

Don't block me out and lose your opportunity with short-sighted instructions to your gatekeeper not to let me talk to you. I understand that sometimes it might not be the right time to talk, that being the case just tell me the truth and give me a chance to call and talk another time. Don't say no before you know what opportunities I might have for you. Give the gatekeeper the responsibility to keep opportunities open so you don't miss a thing.

Please, please, always tell me the truth, don't string me along, don't fear my reaction to the truth, don't sugar coat it. You can inspire this by doing the same and build a reputation of being honest and trustworthy and say it as it is but always with respect. Don't get caught operating outside of your core values.

If you can't make the decision or if you need others to share the decision tell me early to give me a fair chance to present to the right people. Just like I would with you. To be fair as a salesperson you might want this but in reality, you should always get this simply by asking the right questions and getting honest answers.

If for some reason during my presentation to you I go off target or even if I am right on target and hitting the mark don't wait give me instant feedback so that I can learn as I go and make sure you get the best possible value from me. Also, when I am presenting, I want to know that I have your full and undivided attention. Don't take calls or read emails and text messages while I am talking to you. How would you feel if I was doing that while you were talking to me?

"If you concentrate on me, I will do the same to you and we will all get on fine!"

If you have reservations about the solution I am presenting to you, if you have a feeling or a reason for not going ahead with my recommendation, please take the time to tell me the real objections so I can deal with them and provide you with complete satisfaction. Never play games with me, tell me as it really is and tell me how you feel about the product, even if you're not going to buy, I want to learn.

Find the motivations

How to get from conversation to sale.

To go from conversation to sale you need to identify and understand the motivation for the purchase in the person or people you are presenting to. That is why it is so important for you to listen. You need to be able to identify the clues to the key that will open the door to a sale. There are a number of ways you can do this. They all involve asking a series of questions that open the prospect up giving you the important data you need. Gather the information by asking a series of open and closed questions, open to get the prospect talking and closed to control the pace of the conversation and to clarify key details and confirm your understanding.

- Ask questions about their situation as well as status, the history of the business where it came from where it is going, what is their vision for the future of their choice?

- What is their biggest success in their business? What goals are they looking to achieve in the current year?

- Ask direct questions about their motivations, business and spare time?

- If they could do whatever they wanted to, what would that be?

- How do they plan to meet their key objectives and goals, how do they plan to achieve their vision for the future?

If you are having the meeting at their home or office, be very observant; take a good look at the surroundings for clues to other motivations, things like pictures, awards, certificates etc. If you're online then visit their social media to get the same kind of information. This all sounds very simple, very obvious but still the majority of sales people pay lip service to their fact gathering or in some really poor cases they don't even bother to find a motivation they just talk and talk about the product as if that is the most important thing, when the reality is it is the people who are the key not the product.

The really hard part is not the observations, or the asking of the right questions, in the right way, it's the listening for those keys, the keys to the door of the sale.

The answers you get are the clues to the sale, that is why it is so important to listen and then be able to interpret and either use or park the information to get closer to the sales objectives, which need to be a mirror of the prospects objectives, otherwise there will be no sale!

It is unlikely that just one of the points I am about to make are going to give you the full picture to enable you to move toward providing the ultimate solution. However, I do believe by taking all of these points into account it will be difficult to fail. So, your aim should be to use all of these in your journey to the sale.

- Often the first response you get is a reflection of the subject that is at the forefront of the prospects mind. It may not be the full story, but you can be sure that it has an important role to play in the sale. Of course, the question asked will influence the response and so skilled questions are vital in gaining a true picture of the prospect's motivation.

- How things are said is also important in the interpretation of the data, listen to the tone as well as the words, listen to the volume and for the passion. Add to this, if you are face to face or using Skype™ or FaceTime™, the body language, which can also give you a good indication on how the prospect is feeling about the words they are saying.

- When the prospect starts to give you long responses and is even using a story to illustrate the response, you can be quite certain that this is a subject they care about and feel motivated by, another great clue for you on your route to the sale.

- Does the prospect repeat themselves? If they are repeating the statements often, you can be sure that this is a subject that is at the forefront of their mind and is important to them. It might also show you that not only is it important to them, but they might think you are not getting the message or giving it enough importance in the conversation. Let them know you understand the emphasis.

If you want more then simply ask. Not only will you get the answer, you'll also show your prospect you care, giving more touch points for the two of you.

- Always look for the emotion attached to the words these are always clues to how you should progress with your presentation.

Some people will lie so while you are listening and watching their body language, watch out for the person who suddenly starts to give you loads of superfluous detail and is finding it difficult to maintain eye contact with you. The chances are they are not telling you the whole story!

Once you start to do this on a regular basis it will become second nature and you'll see an improvement in your sales, you will need to work at it and establish this as an habitual activity for it to work for you all the time. Don't give it up, keep doing it until it is part of you, part of your technique. Once you have started to identify those subjects that matter, it's time to push on further, to really get to the bottom on the clues and keys you've just been handed. Here are just a few ideas to push you on still further toward exceptional performance:

- Once you have asked questions that require the prospect to drill down further into the things, they feel are important; questions that will draw out the reason for the importance and the impact it has or might have on the prospect. Ask as many questions around the subject as you can, questions you think are important, to give you all the information to present a 'best or most suitable advice' solution to the prospect.

- Take time to practise this technique by testing different formats to questions in normal conversations to extract more information. Get used to using them so that they become a very natural part of your selling technique.

- Established the motivation don't be afraid to use them on more than one occasion during the presentation. Reaffirm them, listen and watch with care to the way in which the prospect reacts.

- Be prepared to include a trial close during this process when you feel the prospect is motivated you could use phrases like: "If I offered you a solution would you be ready to commit to it." Find variations that will work for you, the important thing is to trial close to test the motivation.

Things you should also be aware of are sensitivities the prospect might have surrounding the very item you've identified as their motivator, so recognise the signs and if need be back off, don't push too hard.

"The trial close is a very valuable tool to judge the prospects commitment levels to the sale."

Go on make friends

Why networking works.

There is an old saying in business that all things being equal people prefer to do business with friends and all things being not so equal people still like to do business with their friends. Okay we may not be talking about lifelong friends you want to spend your weekends with, although there is nothing wrong with that either. Your inner circle of friends can usually be counted on the fingers of your hands. Here we are talking about doing business with people who like you and that you like, which helps to motivate them to buy from you rather than from someone they don't know.

That is why it is so important to base your sales on friendship rather than a number of different sales techniques that you can read about on the web and in many of the books that have been written about sales. There are many activities that you should embark on to generate the interest and leads for your product but I believe the two most important activities are building a database of contacts by demonstrating your expertise or the expertise of your business and networking, building relationships and reputation for being knowledgeable and helpful, a source that can be trusted.

Networking works but only if you take time to concentrate on the right activities and concentrate on giving value to the others in the group. I deal with Networking in more detail later in this book. For now, though I want to point out that networking events and online networking is a really great way of building a web of contacts, who over time can get to know you and you them. This gives you, and them, important data, building initial trust and rapport, all vitally important elements in selling. Networking is also the perfect solution for initial prospecting. My only reservation is that too few people know how to network effectively, and many go too far which works against us all, as it will put the entire group on their guard. It's not about pitching and collecting business cards. It's about relationships.

"Networking is so much more than just collecting contacts, it's about building relationships."

While it is really important that you have complete faith and a passion for your business and product, along with belief that you have the best there is to offer for your market. This is not why most people are going to buy from you. Having said that, if you don't feel that way your negative feelings will be telegraphed to the prospect and they won't buy, even if they are a business friend. The reality is that well over 50% of sales are made on a friendly basis. That means if you are not taking the time to make friends first, you could be missing out on over 50% of your performance potential. So, start today using social media including physical events in your local area!

Advantages of making business friends.

If you think about your best clients, they probably became your best clients because of the relationship you've built up with them. If you were business friends with them too you would probably eliminate some of the barriers you'd normally encounter with selling, such as price checks and maybe even negotiating. With a great relationship there is also room for the occasional mistake, providing you're honest about it straight away, you fix it and keep them informed and onside.

If you could get all your clients on to the same level of relationship, you'd start to see other benefits, for example you might even be able to eliminate the threat from competition poaching your client with a better pitch or special offer. With a really strong relationship nothing should be able to take the client away from you, unless your business is not keeping up with the market or has chosen the wrong strategy, or you forget how to be a dependable friend!

You already know that my number one rule of sales is that people, on balance, don't like to be sold to but do enjoy buying, which is why it is so important to build the relationship. Don't be one of those salespeople who believe the only reason to call on the client is to make the sale; nothing could be further from the truth. Calling on the client to build the relationship is a very valuable activity.

The only way you are going to achieve more business connections, more friends, is to put in the effort and put in the time. Take it slow and have patience. If you think this is a waste of time and you need to concentrate on selling not building your network, you should seriously consider your future, you might not be cut out to be a business or sales professional and may not last too long. As an entrepreneur it is so very important that you understand this!

Here are just a few suggestions for the kind of activities and places you can get involved in to make more business friends and build the relationships:

- Networking events
- Running seminars
- Guest speaking
- Breakfast, lunch and dinner
- Membership of online and offline networking clubs and associations, including social media.

Remember if your efforts in networking are not working, the most likely cause is that you've failed to give first and may not be offering enough value to be accepted into the network of people. Take your time, don't push too hard and always give value first.

Your best prospects.

Your best new prospects are quite possibly your current clients. The reason many people in sales will tell you this is because it is quite simply true! Consider these points that you already have in your favour:

- They already know and like you.
- You've already built the relationship and have good rapport.

- They already have confidence, trust and respect for you.
- They have already bought and have direct experience of you and your product.
- They will take your calls and return your calls when messages are left.
- You know they will pay and they don't need to be sold to.
- They will be willing to listen to new presentations on other products.

Your next best prospects are the people that you have started to build a relationship with through your on and offline activities and networking. You won't have built the same level of trust and confidence as your best customers and they'll not have the direct experience of your product but with any luck you'll have demonstrated your expertise and begun to win them over.

It's really obvious when you think about it, why bother cold calling for business if you have built up a web of contacts by networking. Think of all the people they know who prospects could be too. Think about the power of referral, the power of introductions, the power of testimonials and the power of word of mouth. The power of you giving value first to build the reputation that promotes referral.

Getting more value from existing customers.

This is possible if you have more than one product to sell, or if you have opportunities for up-selling, or upgrades to existing products they are using. There is also the possibility that you could sell the same product again if there is room for expansion into other areas of the business, other locations or even partner businesses.

Don't forget your client has the ability (all you need to do is ask) to introduce you to other individuals and businesses who could also benefit in the same way as they have from your products. You just need to get them to agree they have had great value from you and then to agree that other companies, or people in similar situations would also benefit. From there it is a short trip to asking for the introduction. Get them to tell the new prospect that you'll be getting in touch, to prime them, make sure you tell them to tell the new prospect, not what you do but rather what you don't do. In other words, you don't sell, sell, sell, no high-pressure sales techniques, no foot in the door, just good quality advice and solutions.

Possibly the best way to get to this point tactically is to get your customer to meet you for lunch, get them out of their office and away from the daily noise of battle, onto neutral ground. Give them some more value! Make this a tangible activity that you excel at, rather than something that you bolt onto the end of the process. It is that important and that much of a game-changer that it deserves your investment.

"Breakfast and lunch meetings are fine. Just make sure you order your food with your objective in mind. If you want to be talking don't eat messy or complicated food!"

It will be easier in this environment to uncover any new business opportunities. Also think about introducing them to a referral from you, remember it always pays to give value first. Then you can start the process of asking them for referrals. If for some reason they are not prepared to do this, take the time to drill down to find the true reason why. This might turn out to be an opportunity for some candid comments for improvement. Think about it, either way you win.

You also need to understand how important it is to continue to build the relationship with your clients, regardless of making another sale or not. Being in front of them builds on the relationship and creates more goodwill. Please avoid the attitude I see far too often, where the salesperson feels as if the only reason to call a client is if they have something to sell otherwise it is a wasted call, oh how wrong they are!

I look at it this way I would much rather have 100 loyal clients that I could count on and who could count on me than have 1,000 cold prospects to pitch to, wouldn't you?

Just a quick word on taking your client out of their office for a meeting. Wherever possible try to limit the number of distractions they may be subjected to while you are out, you want them to be concentrating on you not the view from the window behind you! I would suggest you need to think about you too regarding distractions. You need to make them feel like the most important person in the room. So, to do this when you are in conversation with them maintain eye contact and switch your phone off or at least put it on silent. Nothing says you don't care quicker than letting your phone have priority over the person you're with!

Build consistency

Have a great week.

Is there a secret to sales success? Is there a secret to getting consistent sales performance? You're going to hate this bit because the answer to these questions is simply no there is no secret to sales success or consistent performance! There are only four elements you need more than the ability and desire to sell, having a great product and detailed market knowledge and they are:

***Being organised—Binge disciplined—Working hard—
Concentrating on the right activities***

Let's deal with organisation and discipline first. It is important you understand that selling is as much about being organised in your work as it is seeing the prospects and closing them down. Here are my top tips for getting into the habit of becoming more organised:

One touch is best—Time is a precious commodity in business and therefore should be treated as such, distractions and procrastination is your enemy when it comes to sales consistency. One of the ways you can make more time for sales is to make sure you reduce the number of times you touch something that needs your attention, the fewer times you touch it the more time you save and the more efficient you become at doing those, hopefully, important administration tasks. I say hopefully because if the task is not important, then why are you investing your time in doing it?

One touch is all about having the discipline to complete the work once you've picked it up. If you're not going to complete it, then don't pick it up. I should point out that some tasks cannot be completed in one go, in which case you'll need to touch the task more than once. If it requires stages, don't start if you're not going to complete the current stage.

However, the principle still applies, in this case you decide the number of phases you need to complete the task and you work to achieve just one touch per phase. In so doing your in-tray will not overflow and you'll have a constant flow of completed tasks without wasting too much time.

Before my mentor told me this, I used to spend time going through the same papers repeatedly over a few days, giving them a priority and placing them in neat piles. At the end of the exercise I felt good, as if I had done something worthwhile. The reality is, I had made no progress at all, just shuffled papers from one part of my desk to another.

Work to priority—We've established that one touch is best; the next thing to recognise is that you should always ensure you attribute the right priority to the tasks that you undertake. The temptation is to concentrate too much on the easy tasks, leaving the more difficult ones till last. Don't do that; eat your greens before the ice cream as my Mum would say.

If need be go back to the section of the book that introduces the system I prefer to use and remind yourself of the A, B, C, D of work priorities. I use a system of alphanumeric to designate the urgency and importance.

Make a list—I like to start or finish each working day by making a list of all the tasks I need to complete during the next working day. My list is always based on the above priorities and I have to say I find it quite satisfying each time to cross another completed task of the list. Having a list also helps me to keep to the priority system because I, like many other people, am very capable of falling off the well-planned wagon into the seat of your pants camp. We all do that from time to time, it's called being human. Don't beat yourself up too much, just get back on it and move on.

"The key to consistency is found in your activity and using all the time you have doing the right things. Avoid the temptation to always concentrate on the easy or pleasant tasks. Sometimes you have to kiss a frog or two!"

Understand the 80/20 rule—My final top tip for being organised is to understand the 80/20 rule knowing the difference is key. It is a universal rule that just seems to be true time and again. 20% of my effort will be responsible for 80% of my production and the remaining 80% will only generate 20% of the results. So, concentrate on the important 20% and if you can increase those activities and decrease the others.

We now move on to good old-fashioned hard work. It is however more about understanding your own success characteristic than it is blindly working at full pelt the entire time. Know what works, know your own KPI (Key Performance Indicators) and work to them, always striving to improve. Let me give you an example of some simple KPI:

When I worked for the bank in their sales team, just after I left the Army, it was drummed into me that KPI was the window to my sales performance and I would find the answers to all my issues within the KPI. This is something I totally agree with and I urge you all to embrace your own KPI and use them as a platform for improving your performance.

I knew that to finish the year on a minimum of 100% of company target exactly what level of activities I would need to do. My KPI from the previous period gave me all I needed to work that out. Back in those days my KPI looked a bit like this:

To make target, based on my average sale value, I would need to sell two new contracts each day for a minimum of 48 weeks of the year or if you prefer, I needed to sell 480 contracts. I also knew that I would lose about 2% of those during the cooling off period and so to net the 480 I would need to sell 491 as a minimum. I was also very confident of the following:

- For each contract I would need to make direct contact with 10 people so that was 20 contacts per day.

- Of those 20 I would need to get 8 interested in a full presentation.

- 50% would get a quote and half would buy and I would make target.

- To get in front of the 20 I was sending out 50 letters every week and following them up with telephone calls and then making up the balance from the cashiers referring people to me. Each day I would work out how many I needed them to refer, inflate the figure and give the number to them as their daily target. At the end of each week I would supply cakes as a thank you for all their efforts. If you look after the numbers, the numbers will look after you!

I was working with a sales force quite recently in London; I had been called in by the owners to get them to the next level of sales success. I made it my business, amongst other things, to ensure that every salesperson in the team knew their own KPI to such a degree that they were able to tell me day on day how many calls they would need to make to get to their aspirational targets. I am pleased to say that they all managed to keep to 100% of the KPI and yes, at the end of the period the lowest performer was only 1.5% under their aspirational target.

All the others were over target. They were happy because they got the bonus and the firm smiled too as they beat their projections on net profit as a result of the sales performance. This was not the first time I have done this; it has happened many times before with a variety of businesses both in the UK and the US.

The background work will ensure you have that important consistency. From a personal point of view, when I was in sales at the sharp end, I made sure that my Mondays were always powerful days with great meetings organised. I did this, as there is nothing better than a great Monday, which then sets you up for the rest of the week.

"Help your positive attitude by always having a great Monday and Friday, Monday have some great meetings to go to and the same for Friday too!"

I also believe it is really important for morale to have a big finish to the week too. You can either do this by finishing on a strong appointment, or you can do what I used to do and make sure you have a good meeting but also spend time filling the diary for the following weeks and in particular the Monday's. There is nothing better than starting a weekend knowing that you have a full diary ahead of you.

Other ways you can plan to have consistent sales performance is to use all your time during the working day to advance your cause. Examples of the kind of things you can do include listening to motivational and educational recordings in your car or on the train while traveling. Make the commitment to learn something new each week, spend at least one evening in the week visiting an appropriate networking event in the local area.

Give yourself a week-by-week target, we've already mentioned the need for you to understand your KPI and so you'll know how many appointments you need to make, no excuses, pick up the phone and make that call. Spend time on your Friday filling in the gaps and compile your list of people to call next week. Do all these things and you can be assured that your sales performance will be excellent. Make your Monday a springboard into a great week and make your Friday a springboard for a great weekend with family and friends and a strong start for the following week.

Have a personal mission statement.

In many of my other books and presentations on running a business, I talk about the importance of your business having a clear Vision, Mission and Values. This is just as important for you as an individual business professional or someone who aspires to be a successful sales professional. Designing a mission statement for yourself is your opportunity to bring your professional and indeed personal goals into focus and make them more visible, the most successful people have a mission, or if you prefer a primary goal or purpose. More than that they are not just passionate about it but obsessive about it. Are you? If not, why not? Be obsessive about your future success, like all the other exceptional performers.

One of the ways I work toward achieving my goals is through visualisation. You might say I am obsessive about doing that to help me in my definite purpose. Visualisation is a really powerful tool, used extensively in sport and in my view nowhere near enough in business. You'd be amazed at the positive affect visualising the future can have on you; it really can impact on the overall outcome.

I have already mentioned how I used this technique when I used to play rugby every week. Part of my match day preparation was to spend some quiet time the night before the match and visualise the individual set plays and my role in them.

It didn't always go to plan but then life's like that, it did however have a significant effect on my attitude and performance. I used to do the same when I was in the armed forces on active service tours, I would visualise the patrol and my role in it before we set off, basing the visualisation on the briefing and all my training. Today I use the same technique to prepare for the presentations I give, the sales meetings I attend and the direction of my business. I even visualise my business plans!

Visualisation does not come easy, but I am convinced it makes the difference. You just have to put the effort in and make it a habit. To give it some substance begin with your personal mission, a set of goals and activities that will act as steppingstones on the way to achieving the mission. These will act as the foundation of the visualisation and the motivation we all need to maintain exceptional performance.

I am no psychologist, but this is how I think it works. The process of visualising the actions you are going to take or want to take wires your subconscious mind into the expectation that you are actually going to take those actions.

"It was Earl Nightingale who said you are what you think about.' How true that has turned out to be!"

It is more complex than this, but you can consider the mind to be made up of two parts, the conscious mind and the subconscious mind. We all think with our conscious or rational mind and whatever we think repeatedly sinks into our subconscious or creative mind. The subconscious mind has been likened to a computer. In other words, it cannot think on its own, it is not able to distinguish between good and bad, between true and false. It takes on face value, whatever is presented to it.

When the conscious mind presents the subconscious mind with the same thought repeatedly, it starts taking the thought seriously and sets about bringing it into existence. In laymen's terms, it means we are recreating all the images, sounds and feelings in our mind surrounding an activity in order to practise them in a perfect environment. Just like the small dojo where Morpheus and Neo fight in the Matrix movie.

It may sound hard or even unbelievable but let me prove to you that you can do it. Take a couple of minutes to close your eyes and imagine yourself going to the kitchen and getting a cup of coffee. Try to imagine every detail, even the smell of the coffee.

Were you able to imagine the cup of coffee? Maybe you were using your favourite cup, and that awesome coffee brand that you love. You may even want a cup of coffee right now. That's how visualisation works.

Don't worry if you didn't catch all the details, just like any other skill, you need to practise. However, it is worth the time it takes to learn it. Here are some well used examples of this technique working.

"On the subject of visualisation, you really must practise. Like anything the more you put in the more you'll get out!"

This first example was an experiment undertaken by Alan Richardson the Australian Psychologist. He took a group of basketball players, divided them in 3 groups and tested each player's ability to make free throws.

- The first group would practise 20 minutes every day.
- The second would only visualise themselves making free throws, but no real practise was allowed.
- The third one would not practise or visualise.

The results were astounding. There was significant improvement from the group that only visualised; they were almost as good as they guys who practised. Now we should take just a little time to talk about how to use Visualisation.

Visualisation is simple, but it requires you to practise often to get the best results. Just follow the steps and enjoy the process:

Relax: Take a couple of deep breaths, let go of all the tension, and close your eyes. It works even better if you find a quiet spot where nobody will bother you. I do it right before I go to sleep.

Start imagining the environment: Let's say you want to play guitar. Start by imagining your guitar, the shape, then the strings, the thickness of each string, until you have a clear and defined picture of your guitar.

Third person view: Now imagine yourself coming closer to the guitar look at your hands and slowly add detail to the image. Look at how you sit and hold the guitar, always trying to add as much detail as possible.

First person view: Feel the guitar in your hands, feel each string, focus on the sound that each string produces. Allow yourself to start playing, just as you would do in practise with the same exercises. Imagine yourself playing through the whole set without failing or stopping, just as if you were an expert.

Wrapping it up: Allow yourself to slowly come back. You completed your practise and the image slowly fades. When you feel ready, open your eyes again.

The steps above work because you are strengthening the paths for that skill in your brain. Your mind doesn't even notice the difference; so, practicing this way during those times where you are away from your practise environment can truly help you improve.

Start with a simple skill or task that you want to learn or change, like waking up earlier or eating slower. That way you can practise with something easier and strengthen your visualisation skills before tackling the big complex skills.

Remember, just visualising won't do the trick. You can't expect to be an expert by just visualising, but it's an amazing tool to improve your practise.

If you use visualisation alongside actual practise you will be able to improve faster than ever and soon you will be able to do all those things you want to do better and progress towards exceptional, sustainable results!

Enough I think of visualisation, we were talking about having a mission and using these visualisation techniques is a great way of making the mission or goals come to life. Now let's talk about constructing the mission itself. If you've never had to, or tried to, write a personal mission for yourself before here are a few hints that might help you.

Before I give you those hints, I just wanted to say that many years ago, when I was first told I should create my own mission statement, I ignored the advice. It all sounded a bit of a waste of time; surely something that simple could not make a difference to my future. Oh, how wrong could I have been. The action of creating a mission that is a challenge but doable, teamed with visualisation had a significant effect on me. I only wish I had done it sooner! Here then are a few tips to help you on your way:

- Write down what you're dedicated to.
- What is it you want to do for others?
- What do you want to get better at?
- What do you need to do to grow?
- How are you going to achieve all this?

"It may sound silly, but it works for me, I remind myself each day what my mission is. Not just in my head, I read it and then think about what I need to do today to advance the cause, you might want to try that too!"

From this you can design your own personal mission statement, don't just commit it to memory, write it down and keep it somewhere where you will see it on a regular basis. It doesn't matter if nobody else understands it, this is all about you. Then you need to visualise each step and what it feels and looks like to have made it to the end of that journey. You need to visualise the achievement day after day until you get there and you will get there, with the right effort!

The reason I ask you to write it down is because you are going to rely quite a bit on your subconscious mind to commit the activity to habit. This requires more than just thinking about it, the act of writing it down helps to bring this to your subconscious. It's like telling your subconscious, "This is important." Thinking about it now and again is just not going to be good enough.

It's serious but have fun

Life is too short.

Business is a serious thing, selling is a serious thing; living is a serious thing too. Having said that we shouldn't take ourselves too seriously, we should be enjoying life. The world revolves around humour and as a business or aspiring business professional you need to understand the power of humour. I am not saying you need to become a stand-up comedian, but you do need to understand that a little humour, delivered at the right time in the right way, to the right people, is a necessity for the exceptional business professional.

My advice to you is to become a student of humour and make this another skill to develop. It will assist you in becoming the best you can be. We spend much time working and interacting with our prospects, suppliers, colleagues and clients and therefore the better we can communicate and appeal to them the more successful we will be.

"Learn the art of subtle humour and timing, learn it from the professional comedians and practise it before you start using it during your presentations."

Humour is at the centre of the journey. I am not saying you have to get belly laughs from people, I am saying that if you can get your prospects and clients to have some fun and laugh you'll get far more sales than you would if you were serious the entire time! Life is too short to take it too seriously, if you can make people laugh, if you can influence them by having a good time, you can certainly get them to buy from you.

Humour builds rapport and relationships.

We all understand how important it is to have a good rapport before you can get the sales that you want. We also understand that when you have a good rapport, a good relationship will not be far behind. Getting someone to laugh is one of the quickest ways to build rapport. The other great thing about well-timed and delivered humour is it is infectious, when the prospect or client joins in you have yet another opportunity to learn more about them and build a deeper connection.

If you listen carefully to what they are saying when they are relaxed and having some fun, you can learn about their political views their philosophy of life and their prejudices. All of those details can be vitally important to you! They give you all the data you need to deliver to them all that they need. While it is good to understand the political views in some cases, please don't get dragged into political debates, that is to be avoided!

I use humour as often as I am able and is appropriate. I always use it when I am involved in my public speaking and workshops to ensure I build relationships with the audience quickly. I am not a stand up and I do not use traditional jokes, instead I just use subtle humour and illustrate important points with amusing anecdotal stories when and where appropriate. Like all things it is important to have a few guidelines for using humour, so here then are my top tips on the rules of engagement:

- When using humour, get your target to laugh early in the presentation. This helps to set the right tone for the remainder of the event.

- Never make jokes at the expense of others; you never can tell who knows whom. The last thing you need is your story being retold and getting told to the wrong people and damaging your valuable reputation.

- The best thing to do when using humour, or telling a joke, is use yourself as the subject or victim. This is good for two reasons, it shows you are human and don't take yourself too seriously and it is a very safe thing to do, no chance of upsetting anyone using yourself. Oh, unless you're presenting to a group and your Mum is in the audience!

- Not everyone will get your jokes, that's certainly true where I am concerned! It is often a good idea to try your stories or jokes out first before you deliver them to the audience.

- Never tell ethnic jokes, selling is about building relationships not hurting people. If you are going to tell an ethnic story, make sure it's about you not another ethnic group.

- As with every aspect of sales, take some time to listen first and if you get the hint that your humour is not going to work in this particular instance, then don't use it! That my friend is the real skill. Don't let your ego take over!

- One of my key rules is to use your own personal experience as the basis of your stories rather than repeating the stories from someone else. Remember, using humour builds rapport and making the subject yourself will build it more quickly and will show your human side, putting the prospect at their ease.

- Never retell the same story to the same person; if they heard it before they will not want to hear it again, it's only funny the first time.

- Learn the art of timing, do this by being a student of some of the best stand ups you know. That means you need to make some time to watch and learn from the experts.

- Understand your audience before you start. Make sure you use the right material; you don't want to offend your audience.

- Use the one liner and play on words to keep the prospect smiling.

- Avoid profanities, smut and politically incorrect language

Dare to be different

Create a differential.

If you can avoid being the same as the majority of the people out there, if you can create a differential and stand out from the crowd, your efforts combined with the selling skills will create greater success. The differential is important, but it is not the only thing to be considered; you should look to demonstrate the strength of your offering. You should also demonstrate, without doubt, that you are sincere and passionate about what you do. The most important aspect of what you are doing is providing the right solution for the people you're talking to. Some of the areas that you can concentrate on to create the differential might include the following:

- **Make sure that you have detailed knowledge of the prospect—Use the power of the internet, use the experience and knowledge of gatekeepers, clients and suppliers to give you all the background information you need to show the prospect that you really understand them and have regard for their needs. That means you need to make friends with gatekeepers not fear or disrespect them.**

- **Prepare with care—Take as much care as you can on every presentation you give. They are all equally important. Remember that preparation is key to your success. As part of the preparation, make sure you give thought and prepare for all possible objections that could be raised by the prospect or audience during your presentation.**

- **Have the discipline of timing—It was drummed into me during my years in the Army, always be ready for action five minutes before the allotted time. I've never forgotten that discipline and have taken it through to my business career. It is far better to arrive a few minutes early than it is to turn**

up late. I always feel arriving late shows a lack of planning and respect for the other persons time. Sometimes things happen and you can't avoid the late arrival. In these rare cases I always phone ahead and let them know, with as much notice as possible. It won't change you being late but at least it shows some respect.

- **Learn to be persistent—If you're going to be successful you need to be persistent in all your efforts. Not least in gathering all the important information you need to give a great presentation and do a great job overall. Persistency, in all aspects of the sale, is a really vital part of your differential and will make people think, 'Wow this person is good!' There is a difference between persistence and nuisance!**

- **You're a professional, so act like it—If you want to be taken seriously, if you want to make the serious money, then you need to be a professional and act professional all the time. Being professional doesn't mean you can't have some fun, it does mean take it seriously, always look and act the part. Make the prospect feel they are the most important person in the room.**

- **Don't be shy, get to the point—It is really refreshing to speak to someone who gets to the point and talks straight, you need to be one of those people. This doesn't mean be abrupt, be rude; it does mean say what you have to say. Say it with respect then shut up and let them talk, make notes, listen, observe but never interrupt, your turn will come around again. Be different, be memorable, for all the right reasons.**

"Speaking your mind does not mean you have to be rude or overbearing. Say what you need to say but always say it with respect!"

- **Show your confidence—You need to install confidence about you into your prospect, the more confident they are of you the greater the trust; the**

greater the trust the more sales you'll make. So, concentrate on building quality rapport and keep building. Use humour be certain of what you're saying and say it with confidence.

- **You—When it comes down to it, it's all about you, it's all about the confidence you have in yourself. Be positive, think positive, act positive and remember those famous words of Earl Nightingale; "You are what you think about." Be memorable and stand out from the crowd.**

When you start working on your confidence and developing your persona to be demonstrably different from the crowd, think about what you are doing, saying, the way you are acting, the way you dress and hold yourself. Think about the reputation you're building or want to build and ask these questions of yourself, for these questions you need to put yourself in the position of the prospect:

- Would I buy from me?
- Would I trust this person?
- Would I be motivated to take the right action?
- Would I be memorable for all the right reasons?

Putting all this into action is not easy and will take effort and patience. It won't always work for you and probably not for the first few times. That is why there are so few exceptional salespeople out there; most of us give up too easily or too soon.

There is a great story that Napoleon Hill uses in his books about the efforts one man went to, working hard to make his fortune in a gold mine. His initial success waned, and he gave up, sold the mine, his equipment and moved on. The guy that bought the equipment put some effort in and made a fortune from the same mine. The original man gave up far too soon only feet from a major strike.

Believe me all it takes is some effort, preparation, rehearsal and confidence that you can and should make a positive difference to the lives of those you meet. Don't give up, never give up.

You need to keep your eye on the goals you've set for yourself. Keep focused on the target, have those dreams and your mission always at the front of your mind. Show your passion, if you have no passion, get off the bus and find another bus to get on, the right one for you. Never let the people see you worry about things. Your aim is to get them to feel your belief.

Your belief in the product, yourself, your passion and your confidence. Above all **Never Quit!** I should point out that never quit means never stop trying to be the best. If something is not working and steering you toward failure, then stop and change what you are doing!

Have the right tools.

Make sure that you have all the right supporting tools and make sure they reflect the image you have or want to create. When you hand out your business cards, the message you want to leave behind is not 'hello, remember me I am just another one of the salespeople you met!' It is really important that if you create a persona that you maintain it after you've left the building here are just a few things you can do to improve your demonstrability after you've left the building:

"It is really important that anything you use as a sales tool is a good reflection of the image you want to create, if it's not don't use it!"

If you use business cards and most of us do, are they a reflection of the image you want to be remembered by? I am lucky because I run my own business and therefore have control over the corporate image. You may work for a business where you have no say on what the business cards look like. Don't worry, there is always more than one-way to address this. There's nothing wrong with you having your own card as well as the company one. The important thing is to have a business card that reflects the image you want to reflect. If you were the customer and someone gave you the business card you currently use would you be inspired to comment on it?

Don't think about your cards as being an expense think about them as being part of your image. Make them different enough that the person who has been given your card wants to show it to someone else!

Many of us use email, possibly more than we should do. The important thing is to make the effort to brand your email too. Think brand, think image, think consistency. Oh, and please do yourself a favour and take time to get a proper email address that related to you and the brand you are creating stop promoting suppliers with your email address and promote your brand instead. There is a big difference for example between chris474@gmail.com and chris@rainmakersclub.co.uk, don't you agree?

It will be a worthwhile investment in you and your image. If you look at all the truly successful people out there, you'll find that they have many things in common with each other and one of those things will be they are all obsessive about brand, image and reputation. That is a big clue for those aspiring to be successful. You need to be obsessive about your personal brand and reputation.

Ask more questions

The key to sales.

By now you'll understand that there isn't just one key to the door of sales but an entire bunch of keys and it's your job to have all the keys with you all the time, opening up the numerous doors in sequence. I think it would be true to say that two of the most important aspects of sales skills are being able to ask the right kind of question and then knowing when to shut up and just listen, really listen to each word. Observe and listen all the time!

If you ask the right question in the right way the prospect will tell you all you need to know to get the sale. All you need is to use your listening and observation skills and suddenly you'll have all you need to make the sale, getting the prospect to the point of making that decision.

I already know that while reading this you'll be thinking to yourself this is all so simple, that is true, it is painfully simple and yet so few people practise these simple and obvious activities and then sit there at the weekend wondering why things are not working out for them! Looking out the window for someone to blame, instead of looking in the mirror and taking responsibility.

I am not sure why we can't all do a great job as it is so simple but then again if we all did a great job the few would no longer look so exceptional! In my view so few do it right because the rest of us are making the same old moves, the same old mistakes, using the same old excuses and blaming anything other than our own lack of skill, preparation, attention, activity or whatever else it is we happen to be lacking. We are creatures of habit who like to follow the pack, all I am suggesting is you follow the Rainmakers pack instead. It is smaller but quite elite and wealthy in mind, body, soul and financially, which is the icing on the cake, here are some things you should consider even if you decide not to follow our community of Rainmakers:

- You won't get the sale if you're asking the wrong questions, or not asking the questions in an effective way.
- You won't get the sale if you're not listening and I mean really listening to what the prospect is telling you.
- You won't get the sale if you're interrupting the conversation making premature judgments about the prospect.
- You won't get the sale if you're assuming you already know the answer and so don't ask.
- You won't get the sale if you're failing to uncover the real needs of the prospect.
- You won't get the sale if you offer the wrong or an unsuitable solution.

An old friend of mine once told me that we were born with two ears and one mouth and that we should use them in that ratio, twice as much listening as talking. I know some who would say more time than that should be spent listening. There are those that say this may work for many products but ours is different and therefore we can't apply the same rules.

My answer is, that's just yet another lame excuse; What you're really saying is simply that you have yet to discover the right questions to get to the point where the prospect tells you all you need to know, rather than you spending your time telling them what you think they want to hear, or worse still telling them what you want them to say to you.

We have already covered the different question techniques earlier in the book, open and closed questions. As a rule of thumb in sales you should only use closed questions for the following reasons:

- To confirm a fact that only needs a yes or a no.
- To control the conversation or bring it back on subject.
- If you know the answer, yes or no is going to complete the sale.

Otherwise you should stick to the open questions that get the prospect talking and giving you all the data, you need to make the sale. Here are a few hints on how to design the right kind of question, to get the right kind of answer for the sale:

- Make sure the question is understandable, clear and concise. It can only generate an answer that needs no interpretation and has no double meaning.

- Make sure the question motivates the prospect to start thinking along a line that leads to their needs and your solution.

- Make sure the question promotes thoughts around your ideas and how they may fit with the need for a solution, your solution.

- Construct the question with care. You not only want to get the prospect thinking; you want to come across as smarter than the competition. This is not about being smarter than the prospect, even if you are!

- Make sure the question encourages the prospect to call on their own experience; this gives more credibility to their answer and makes them feel more comfortable.

- Make sure the question navigates the prospect towards the desired close, but only when the need has been accurately identified and confirmed.

- Construct the question so that it gets the prospect not only talking about their own business but also their needs.

- The question needs to extract the right information to make it easier for you to make the sale.

- The question needs to be posed in a positive light to set the tone of the meeting. People are more likely to buy when they are in a positive frame of mind.

- When you are asked something, use questions back to confirm their detailed requirements where appropriate, use this sparingly; you don't want to end up sounding like a politician.

- Don't forget to ask for the business, ask closing questions and when the time is right trying a trial close to encourage objections that might hold up the sale.

"The easiest way to get the business is to be well prepared, ask the right questions, identify the correct need and have the right solution. Then simply ask for the business!"

I think that closing questions should never be left to chance and therefore you should have a few prepared and well-rehearsed versions that you can pull out and use when the time is right. The right time will depend on the circumstances of the meeting you're in. Most salespeople that I know don't do this and many of them have a problem with their close ratio, I would say the message is clear! I know some really great people who do everything right apart from this. Don't get me wrong, they still make sales, but I am convinced if they gave more thought to closing questions, they could be so much better than they are right now.

I believe there is no such thing as the easy sale, even if you get to see a prospect and they just say to you I want one. They have probably done their research and looked into the business you're in. What they find will be a direct reflection of your efforts and the efforts of others around you who have helped to shape the reputation of the business. That is why no sale, no matter how they appear, come that easy. Behind all easy sales you will find hard working marketing at the heart. In many sales-oriented businesses, the marketing team don't get the credit they deserve and that is a whole new subject. However, back to the sale, it is possible to close a sale with a few well-placed questions. I don't think it is practical to say such a sale can be done with a specific number of questions, that will be dependent on the buying process, size and type of product. However, I do want to point you in the direction of asking the right questions all the time.

The right questions are the ones that take you a step closer to the sale with each one you ask. Here's an example of how you could structure questions to achieve that aim, think these through realign them to your situation and make them your own:

"Tell me when you select your widget what are the main criteria used?"

Let us say that the prospect mentions a few things like price, support and quality.

"Okay you mention quality, what exactly are you looking for in your price quality and support?"

This question will promote a thoughtful answer. Once answered you could follow up with other questions based on the answer. Once you have the answer you can ask another related question designed to tease out still further information and the true need of the prospect, like so:

"What is it that makes this so important to you, is it the most important thing?"

This question is designed to help you identify the true needs of the client so that you can better construct the presentation of the solution, in a way that will appeal to the prospect. Again, more questions can be used to help draw out as much data about the need as possible.

"If I could show you that we have the right quality widget and that the product will be in keeping with your image and reputation is there any reason why we would not be in the running to get your business?"

At this point you might have to answer a few objections or, you might be lucky enough to get a really positive answer. The prospect says that you are in the running, based on your answers and so your final question to close would be:

"Great, so how many would you like to start?"

In sales things don't always go to plan but I hope you can see from this simple example the importance of asking the right questions and making sure the questions you ask are asked for a specific purpose. That purpose should be to advance your sales presentation and get you closer to the close. I have said in this book on more than one occasion that it is really important to prepare and plan. Planning your questions, preparing for the presentation through practise is where all the smart money is. Here are a few hints you could use to start to formulate the right questions for you, your business and your product:

- What do you look for in . . .?
- What has been your experience of . . .?
- How would you go about . . .?
- How have you successfully used . . .?

- How would you determine . . .?
- What is the deciding factor . . .?
- Why is that a deciding factor . . .?
- What are your choice criteria . . .?
- What do you like about . . .?
- What one thing would you improve about . . .?
- Are there other factors . . .?
- What is your competition doing about . . .?
- How does your customer feel about . . .?

None of this is about the old-style hard selling. There is no backing the prospect into a corner, so that they have no option but to say yes and then later regret the sale. No, this is all about their needs and a solution that really is a true fit for them and a pleasure to be part of for all concerned in the process, this is professional sales.

Use powerful phrases.

Many sales coaches and sales trainers advocate the use of powerful phrases and statements that make you stand out from the crowd; this has its roots in marketing but is a very valuable tool for all salespeople. A word of warning though, these kinds of statements don't work particularly well if you don't have regard for all the other aspects of selling. It is pointless to have a great and powerful statement if you are unable to support it with great research, followed up with the right questions and the right solution for the prospect.

"If you want some help putting together some really powerful phrases, make friends with your marketers, or register with Rainmakersclub.co.uk and join the marketing groups."

In essence this all comes down to talking about the feature, its advantage and how it will benefit the prospect, always in this order or it will fail to make sense. Always deliver the FAB (Feature, Advantage, Benefit) with the prospect in mind and a language they understand. The success of such phrases comes from your own ability to be creative and to focus on the benefits and not too much on the actual product. It's not what the product is it is very much about what the product does and what that means to the prospect. A statement of this kind is used to let people know what it is your solution does for them specifically based on their needs.

Remember if you go out and buy a drill, what you really want is the hole it produces not the drill so concentrate on the hole rather than putting all your effort into selling the drill. The prospect wants the hole as their prime need, hit that first and the rest will follow.

A powerful statement or phrase is designed to motivate the prospect into action. It is designed to steer them into your buying process in the same way that marketing does, or at least should do. Your aim is to concentrate on the benefits; it will always be the benefits and how they relate to the true needs that will win the day for you. It will give you that sales buzz that comes when you know you have just supplied the client with exactly what they needed:

- Not the drill, sell the perfect hole the prospect is looking for.

- Not the printing, sell the perfect business card that will reflect the image the prospect wants to project when they are meeting people.

- Not the car, sell the lifestyle, the status, the environmental advantage.
- Not the life cover, sell the family security.

I think you get the point; these statements can be used in a number of ways to help with your sales, here are just a few ways you can benefit by using these on a regular basis:

- Gets your prospect thinking about what they want rather than being sold to by you.
- Builds your reputation and credibility so you stand taller than the others looking for the same business.
- Let's the prospect know what you do for them rather than about you or your product.
- Sets you apart from your direct and indirect competition.
- Creates curiosity so that the prospect wants to hear more about what you can offer them.
- Helps to create additional reasons to buy.
- Creates a very professional and positive image for the prospect.
- Will be memorable and creates a differential.
- Proves you are thinking about the prospect rather than product or need for a sale.
- Makes you come across as professional and caring rather than desperate to make the sale, even if you are!

How about an example of how you might describe, in a simple phrase, what you do that will make you stand out from the crowd?

> **Car Sales**—My business customers need to get to their meetings on time and stress free. On arrival at their destination they also need to create the right impression. After work they want to know they have a vehicle they can rely on. When my customers have important events to go to, they get into a car that delivers all they need including a compliment to their chosen lifestyle.

> **Temp Agency**—We provide you with quality emergency and temporary staff for your business to cover vital duties when someone is sick, absent or on their holidays, that way you lose no productivity or reduction of service to your customers.

I have heard many introductions in my time and to be fair most of them have not been that great. Here are just a couple of examples of really generic statements for general use, I hope from these you'll understand the benefit of having a few statements prepared and rehearsed ready for delivery at the first opportunity:

- Profits come from your productivity; we can help grow your sales by a significant amount. We could show you an improvement within 30 days. Let's talk.
- I don't know if I can help. However, if we spend a few moments together, over lunch perhaps, we can find out if I can. I will tell you so if I can and if not, I will tell you that too.

"It's good to have powerful and motivational phrases that get your prospects thinking in the right way. However, these are next to useless if you can't back them up with actions!"

Your elevator pitch

Break the ice when you're networking.

Networking is all about meeting new people and collecting more contacts that can deliver to you more sales leads, directly or indirectly. Simple, you'd think so, but it is amazing the number of people who I see going to networking events who seem to forget the main purpose of being there. They tend to stick to the people they know rather than risk talking to new people and perhaps have to face their big fear, rejection! The reality is there is very little rejection going on at networking. If you are rejected it is more likely to be because you haven't followed the rules, started selling too soon and concentrated on the product rather than the people!

When I question people, who contact me about improving their performance for lead generation and networking one of the most common issues is this fear of rejection. If you drill a bit further down what you'll discover is that in most cases this comes down, not to a real fear of being rejected but a lack of confidence in what it is they are going to say, to get things moving.

In some cases, it might even be partially to do with a lack of self-confidence. I have and continue to see so many salespeople or people selling who would rather get someone else to make the call or start the process, due to a complete lack of confidence. In most cases this lack of confidence could be solved with planning, preparation and practise! Some professions are worse than others and it seems to me that all they are lacking is a good opening pitch, often called the elevator pitch, and the confidence to deliver it. These are not just useful but essential for networking and should be used whenever you meet a new person in your role as an ambassador for your business and brand and in any event, you should want to create the right first impression.

The interesting thing is the people I meet who don't use these opening statements all have the same thing in common, that's right, they've done nothing about it. They are not confident because they have not planned what they will say in a given situation. They've not prepared anything and certainly not practised. Is it any wonder they stick to just the people they already know and make no effort to go to events and work the room!

Let me help you to put together a great elevator pitch. First let's make sure we have the objective clear in our minds. The objective is simple, we want to deliver about 30 seconds of good information about who we are what we do who we represent. We want to do this, as memorably and creatively as possible, without being too clever, which can also be a turn-off for the prospect. The other part of this and key to success is, once you have delivered your short message, it's time to ask questions, say a little about you and then ask as many questions as you need to get to the close. The close in most cases is permission to call or meet later for a detailed chat.

"It's a fact; those that do most of the listening are perceived as being more caring and better communicators. That is worth remembering when you're networking!"

The sort of questions you ask are the ones we've just covered in the last few pages, the ones that are going to gain the most useful data for you to identify this person as a viable prospect for sales or maybe introductions to future sales. Remember the important thing is to ask as many open questions as you can, to encourage a conversation and get the prospect talking as much as you can. Unless there is a specific reason, avoid closed yes or no questions. Also remember there is no point in telling them how you can help until you are aware of what kind of help, they may need. If you do this, you will just sound like every other salesperson in the room! Dare to be different and watch your fortunes rise. Maybe not overnight but slow and sure they will improve.

Before you run to the drawing board to start the design of your pitch with the really smart questions, take a time out to think about the things you would like to know as a result of the initial meeting at an event, what questions do you think you need to ask?

- What data are you looking for?
- What question will qualify the prospect?
- Will I need to ask more than one question?
- How can I get them thinking in the right way?
- How can I distance myself from the crowd?

Once you've thought this through compile a list of powerful questions that are going to make the prospect stop and think. Close the 30 second elevator pitch with a strong call to action; A closing line that is going to ensure the next planned contact for you. A 30 second pitch might look something like this:

Imagine you're at a networking event and somebody comes up to you and asks you, *"What do you do?"* Now is the time to deliver your prepared and much practised pitch, practised not to be parrot fashion but to be conversational and entertaining:

"I am the founder and chief revolutionary of the Rainmakers Club, a subscription-based community of small businesses all on a journey to exceptional and sustainable results, using our unique model of learn, share and develop. Our members get unlimited support and advice in return for a simple monthly membership fee. We focus on the one true purpose of every business and that is the creation of opportunity. Imagine the advantage this one simple model gives to the underserved small business market; we exist to create value and empower sustainable growth, building a business that works for you rather than you working for it."

Reading it off the page is not as good as hearing it delivered by the author. Be assured this is one of the opening statements I have used many times. Delivered with passion, it has worked for me. This pitch has led to multiple speaking engagements as well as multiple new members and training events! All from that one statement at a variety of networking event.

Make sure you deliver the lines with great passion and confidence if you deliver it in this way the person, you're speaking to can't help but be curious which is the ultimate aim.

At this point you should have the attention of your prospect and so it is time to ask the power questions you've already prepared for just such an occasion.

"I wonder how our community might be able to help your business and how you might be able to help them, perhaps we can meet and explore the possibilities?"

Keep asking questions until you get the information you need. Once you have the information follow it up with your closing statement, in most cases this will be enough. Here is another example of a question that takes you a step closer to a new relationship and maybe a new sale.

"I have helped many businesses to increase their sales by simply concentrating on individual performance and activities. If you have the right people, it is quite easy to turn them all into exceptional salespeople and create even more rain for your business. It works wonders for morale, let alone profits. Here's what I propose, lets meet for a quick morning coffee or maybe a breakfast have a chat and at the end of it if I can't help I will tell you so, if I can I will tell you that too, does that sound fair?"

I understand that this will only work if you are confident; I understand that you might get those that just place barriers in your way. That's life and it will always be the case. Consider this if you do nothing about it, you'll get nothing, if you try without preparing and practise you might get one or two hits, better than nothing, right?

If you plan, prepare, rehearse and practise you'll increase your hit rate, your choice! Do nothing and get nothing do something and get something or do it all and watch your leads increase. Me, I don't mind the rejection, because I know it takes three people to say no to me on average to get to the yes. I would rather do this and get one in four prospects to meet me than do nothing and watch those prospects either suffer due to lack of support or worse still go to a competitor who has the courage and confidence to ask! Actually, it's not just self-confidence; it is belief in the product and a true desire to help people too.

Now let's talk delivery.

"People are different so make sure you understand those differences and be prepared for them."

When delivering any pitch, you need to consider the difference in people, as we covered earlier in the book. Although the words you use may not change you have to be prepared to adopt different styles of delivery to suit the audience. As with most things in business and particularly sales, the best way to find out is to have a few questions up your sleeve, questions that will identify things that help you to refine the delivery of the close. Within your preparation you should include the following points that are relevant in all but the most exceptional circumstances:

- Brevity is always best, without missing the vital information.
- Get to the point but be creative in the manner it is communicated; you want to stand out from the crowd.
- Make sure what you say and the way you say it is memorable.
- Invest time in preparation and practise.
- Always have your questions and statements prepared, never leave it to chance.
- Make sure you gather as much information as possible to both qualify and understand how you can help, before you offer anything.
- Forget the product concentrate on the solution.
- Always finish with a close to commit the prospect to your required next action.

- Remember to have fun; business should be a joy not a task.

- When you've finished the delivery, move on to the next person, you can never have enough prospects.

I have learnt over the years, through victories and mistakes that you should only say what needs to be said to get the right message across to the prospect, no more and no less. Always deliver the message thinking of the prospect rather than yourself. So, talk you and you're not I and me. You will know when the commercial is successful because you'll suddenly have more meetings to go to. Be aware that success can only come from preparation, planning, practise and the right activity!

Referral gold

How to approach referrals.

First, I have to have my little rant about referrals and why so many people in business say they believe in the power of referrals and then do next to nothing about it. Despite the words it is clear they don't value the power of referral, spending next to no time at all doing anything about getting their own referral factory producing at full capacity! It makes no sense to me at all that so many people, in business, would ignore the opportunity to invest time in setting the foundations and then building a great referral system. Okay mini rant over, now down to business.

My first rule for getting great referrals is that you need to give before you get. If you give value first it is far easier to get a referral. I am always looking out for opportunities to refer people I know or meet along the way, to others that I know. Once you get the reputation of someone who will refer, you'll start getting the same back, people will refer to you. Maybe not from all, some people just don't get it, but not to worry, they're not destined to last too long. Concentrate your efforts on the right people, but always give first, it's a great way to work and a sure way of getting a great reputation. It feels good too, an added bonus!

"Always concentrate on being the first to give value. Give some value before you ask for anything!"

Right, so now that you have your referral how do you go about approaching them? Here are some basic hints and tips to help you on your way:

No speeding—There's no need to go too fast, take your time don't rush them or put them under pressure, you'll just come across as being desperate, or one of those high-pressure salespeople we all dislike. Make sure you obey the sales rules, only talk about their needs once you have discovered what they really are. Give value first and talk about them and their needs not you and your product.

Involve the introducer—Referrals will normally come from another person that you know and perhaps have done business with. In some circumstances it might be helpful to arrange the first meeting as a three-way affair, you the person who has made the referral and the person referred. Particularly if the person who made the referral is a current client with direct experience of your business. They will communicate all the positives and work as a living, breathing testimonial during the meeting.

Don't sell too soon—This is particularly true if you are having the three-way meeting. When you first meet up with the person who has been referred to you, the last thing you should be doing is talking product or trying to sell to them. At this point all you want to do is give them some value, build rapport and trust, to lower the barriers and get them to have confidence in you.

Always arrange a second meeting—This is particularly important if you were not on a one-to-one meeting, you'll certainly need to have a more private meeting whereupon you can get down to business. By the second meeting you'll have their confidence or at the very least the beginnings of trust and they will be ready to talk to you in greater detail, taking the relationship to the next level.

Never send everything you have through the mail—Avoid sending too much information to your prospect through the mail. Treat the mail like you would do the first meeting or the first telephone call. This is not where the sale is made it is simply one of your many sales tools. All you need to do is send enough to gain the interest and create some curiosity. Many people will ask you to send information as a way of saying no thank you. Learn to recognise these instances. Remember people will do this if you try to sell to soon in the relationship. People don't like to be sold to, but they do love to buy.

Don't forget the power of thank you—When you've been given a referral always take time to write a thank you note to the person who has referred to you. I also think it is a good idea to give them some feedback, once the meetings have taken place. Giving them a heads-up on progress will allow them to see the results of their efforts. This may even help in encouraging them to make more referrals. Although not all outcomes will go completely the way you want them to, make sure the feedback you give is always in a positive light to encourage future referrals too. Take the time to thank the actual introduction, keep it simple, keep it short and let them know you're looking forward to meeting up with them again.

Always under promise and over deliver—I hate it when somebody promises to do something for me and then doesn't deliver, I hate it even more when it is during a sales call and I am the customer. Make it one of your rules never to over promise and under deliver, just like we talked about earlier in the book!

"Imagine how much better your sales would be if each time you met someone you added them to your referral system! If each time you sold something you got two quality referrals, you'd be a top performer in your business."

My final point on referrals is, apply these rules and be creative during first contact. Be different, use your imagination and humour. Don't do what all the others do. Instead stand out and show them you're different for all the right reasons and then make them laugh, ask them to meet for coffee or lunch to have a chat.

Remember referrals are the easiest sale and you should invest significant time in getting your referral rates up. Do this by giving first; it's not by coincidence that most professional advisers (lawyers, accountants, financial advisers and business advisers) use referral as their main means of gaining clients.

Cold calling, is dead

It's all about hearts and minds.

I am always talking to people about sales and sales skills, often during my presentations on the subject I ask the audience what it is they would most like me to talk to them about. One of the more popular subjects the audience wants covered is cold calling, or how to get to a point where you no longer need to do any cold calling or prospecting.

There's a very easy answer to that question, I don't think true cold calling exists anymore and rightly so!

A cold call or maybe we should call it a cold approach, is an approach or call made by email, mail, in person or on the phone where you are going in completely cold, in other words your target knows nothing about you and you know nothing about your target. Now that's a cold call! The reality is there is no need for this in professional business and there is no excuse anymore for entertaining using it.

Cold calling has been replaced by research, social media and networking. I maintain that through these tools you can get to speak to whoever you need to, as long as you give it enough time and approach it in a truly professional manner. That means not trying to sell on first contact. Instead concentrate on building a relationship by winning hearts and minds.

Here is what I suggest has taken the place of the cold call journey, you can see from this that once contact has been established it's all about building the relationship and winning the hearts and minds of those you are talking to. In this alternative you will never be going in completely cold. You will know about the business and you will even know about some of the personalities too, thanks to social media and networking:

- We start the journey with basic research, usually on Google™ or some other search engine; we also look on one or more social media sites. This will confirm all the information you need to start the process of relationship building.
- Before any contact is made, make sure you have created a plan of action and done all the preparation ready for execution.
- My plan will involve a number of objectives leading up to the point where I plan to either get the sale, a referral or both. This is rarely the objective on the first few contacts. First contact is always about hearts and minds. Getting them to agree to a connection with a strong motivation for doing so. Next it is all about building that connection based on likeability and the identification of my experience or expertise. This helps them to have the confidence to move the relationship forward toward the ultimate objective of sale and or onward referral up the chain of command. At all times remembering to give value first. Here are my four top objectives:

  Objective 1: Build rapport and trust via giving value first.

  Objective 2: Gather the information needed to build the relationship and prepare for eventual presentation.

  Objective 3: Gain a business appointment with the decision maker (telephone or face to face).

  Objective 4: Continue to build rapport and value with decision maker.

You can see why with this system there no such thing as a cold call is anymore. You have a much better chance using this method to make more valuable connections and quality sales. All you have to do is concentrate on the people and not the product; all you have to do is win their hearts and minds, job done!

"Many failures occur in cold calling because the fundamental rules of sales are not followed. The caller spends too much time trying to sell and not enough building the relationship!"

Start strong stay strong.

We all know how important first impressions are in life. I would say in sales it is more important than in most other aspects of business. Your first contact with the prospect is very important from how your web presence looks and feels to how you answer calls emails and of course how you and your business look overall. It's so much more than that, when dealing with people in a sales environment. For the purpose of this book we want to concentrate on the human element. The things that will have an initial impact on the prospect maybe one, or all the following, depending on the circumstances of the meeting.

The first thing you say and how you say it; your expression and body language; the amount of sincerity you show; your passion; your creativity and what you are wearing, compared to the environment in which you find yourself. Yes, all of these will contribute toward how people will form their first impression of you.

If you're on the phone, which today is more likely than not, you really are going to need to have a great opening line, speak clearly, using appropriate language and a pleasant cadence, because that's all you've got. Making the right impression is most difficult on the phone and because a high proportion of first physical contact will take place on the phone here are my top tips for getting the most from the call:

- They can't see you, but you still need to smile when you talk, this will come across in your conversation and the tone of your voice, if you wake feeling like thunder, best to leave the phone alone!

- Always give the name of your company and don't say it too fast, make sure they hear you right it will save confusion or misunderstandings later.

- Make sure you state the purpose of the call as quickly as you can, perhaps it's best in the first two sentences. Honesty is best, no pulling of wool over eyes please, tell them it like it is!

- Brevity is key. Keep it as short as you can and still make sense. If it's not worth saying and adds nothing to the objective, then simply don't say it.

- Always bring help into the conversation, ask for it or offer it. I always find asking for help works best in cold calling.

- Introduce to them to the fact that you have some important information to share as part of the conversation, where possible and practical. If you don't have something important to say then get off the phone, better still don't pick it up to start with!

- If you can, use humour in the call, that doesn't mean tell jokes it just means be amusing to lighten the mood.

- Always close, don't leave them hanging. The close in this instance might be the next meeting or a first appointment; no matter what, always go for the close, that's the entire purpose of the call.

When embarking on a call by phone you might also want to prepare a few opening lines to help you get into the call. As always, the more you prepare the better, you'll perform and the better the results you'll get.

Some of the openings that were taught to me when I did my training, I still use today, they all have a light side to them and cannot be delivered without confidence, the kind of confidence that comes from practise and preparation. Here then are the four that were taught to me and that I seem to use them to the best effect:

- "I have some really exciting and important information that I want to share with your business."

- "I know we've not spoken much I am keen to talk to you as I have got some ideas, I would like to share with you."

- "I really needed to talk to your company as I have some information that I believe will have a real impact on your business . . ."

- "I am calling because I could really do with some help and I thought you might be the person to talk to . . ." (I love using this one)

It is important to say the right things in the right way when you're on a call and particularly the initial calls. So, I would say, by default, it's just as important to know what not to say on such a call. One of my pet hates when calling is to open with the typical line of, "Did you get the information I sent you?" Worse still "Can I speak to the person that deals with." Please make it stop!

The problem is it's the perfect get out of jail free card! The prospect simply has to say no and then continue with send it again and call another time. When the prospect does say no, you'll struggle to find something positive to say, most of the things that will come into your head will make you look less than you really are. You can't win using this if the prospect doesn't want to talk to you.

You'll probably find it better, if you're going to mention the information you sent by saying that you're calling about the information because it was the briefest of introductions and wasn't completely self-explanatory. Go on to say, therefore you wanted to talk it through with them. I would then make sure they were aware that this would only take a few moments. The call is still valuable even if they have not seen the material sent and it is much easier to use this approach when trying to start a sales conversation.

Don't just read all these great points, use them, make notes and start to prepare new opening lines for yourself and then practise their use. Remember practise makes perfect.

"Sales Calls are a great way to practise new approaches. Sales calls are a great way to practise without burning valuable leads!"

I treat sales calling as a chance to try out new techniques, new phrases and new approaches, almost as if it were a training ground.

Our brains are incredibly powerful tools and the thoughts that we have will and do directly affect how we feel about things. So, if you start off feeling negative about calling it will come across that way to the person on the other end of the phone. In addition, as if that was not enough, you'll talk yourself into a negative mood and into failure. Remember what we said earlier in the book, you are or become what you think about!

"I am aware that from time to time in this book I have repeated myself. That's because it's important. So again, I am asking you to understand the importance of maintaining a positive outlook and visualising your success not failure!"

Next time you're about to make those calls make sure you are prepared; I mean really prepared. Pre-plan and understand who your best targets are. Deliver the opening line with confidence and be practised, so you come across as a confident, knowledgeable, trustworthy, business professional. Cut out all the negative stuff, when you speak you don't need to apologise for interrupting or being unannounced, you just need to deliver the chosen powerful opening line, "I am looking for some help . . ."

Do your utmost to ignore the negative and remember that when you are told no, you're getting closer to the one that will say yes. In any event they are not saying no to you forever, just saying no to this particular offer you're making, at this particular time. Don't forget the importance of learning from those that tell you no! The more you can learn about why they said no the better you'll become at your job.

Be positive, don't complain, as a general principle people don't like to buy from people who are negative or complain. Make the commitment to discover your weaknesses and then one by one remove them. Find a sales coach, better still join the **Rainmakers Club** and continue your journey to be the best.

Selling is just talking

Make them the most important person in the room!

The initial opening will be the deciding factor on how far you get. If you're going to get any further, be aware that after each thing you say or do the prospect will be making the decision, to either listen intently to you or to ignore you and concentrate on something that is more important to them. Your mission is to make them the most important person in the room and inspire or motivate them to want to listen to you. The secret to this is nothing more than honesty. Don't try to tell them what you think they want to hear, find out what they want and then tell them the truth. The journey is simple logical and very effective if you stick to the rules.

- Explain things but say as few words as you can get away with. Remember two ears, one mouth, use them in that proportion.

- Ask thought provoking questions that get the prospect thinking about the right things for the meeting.

- Find all the facts; gather as much information as you are able.

- Say things in response that will establish credibility and trust in you.

- Qualify needs and decision-making powers.

- Always start with an objective and then steer towards it, don't leave without the next stage being made secure.

- Be positive even in difficult times. Learn to think on your feet, it helps with the development of your self-confidence and positive attitude!

- If you look at all the points, we've covered in the last few pages you'll begin to see the sales call model I'm suggesting you follow can be a real asset to your development and sales figures. Let's review those points again:

- Always remember to look and speak in way that reflects your image and values. Don't be something you are not; you'll just get found out. First impressions are all important in sales. What makes a good first impression will depend on the circumstances and the person you are in front of. Therefore, this is not an exact science, you'll just have to do the best you can with what you have, the more you put in the more you get out and improvement will come.

- Always get the prospect to think in terms of them using the product. Ask great questions that will demonstrate your knowledge and at the same time get them talking and thinking.

- Don't mess around too much, get to the point as quickly as you can, have respect for their time.

- When the prospect asks for specific information, don't navigate around it because you're not ready to talk about that particular subject, give them the answer they're looking for.

- Search for the real needs, you have to know these to make the sale. Think about using the following possibly relevant hot buttons:

    - Issues they have.

    - Their motivation, greed, vanity, fears.

- Be prepared to have more than one meeting, don't give up, all you'll do is hand the business to another person willing to work harder than you.

- Once you've given them a solution to a need that means something to them, they will buy, make sure it's from you by concentrating on them not you, show them you care, really care.

- Think about prevention, what issues and problems that mean something to them can your solution prevent, this will be a good motivator for any prospect.

- Always use testimonials, articles and anything else that will help you to gain their confidence in you and the product.

- Never fear the objections and rejections; these are all part of the process. The sale comes after these, providing you know how to handle them in the right way and to the satisfaction of the prospect.

- Know your Key Performance Indicators (KPI) and make sure you hit all your activity targets for each working day. Constant and consistent activity is the key to success.

Putting all these into practise will give you such an edge over the competition and you'll see a significant improvement in your sales performance and consistency. It will happen and happen fast if you just take the time to learn, prepare and above all practise. Nobody knows it all and you should never stop learning and seeking more knowledge.

"It will not be enough to just read this book and then put it in a draw or under the wobbly table leg! You need to put it into practise and change old habits for these new ones, only then will you start to see the success you feel you deserve."

Sales presentations

Rapport, it's all about rapport.

We've mentioned the importance of rapport a few times in the book already, now I want to explore this important subject in more detail, give you a better understanding of how to go about building it and what to avoid. I would suggest one of the quickest ways to establish rapport with your prospect is to find something you have in common with them. Once you've established this common ground the prospect will begin to like, trust and eventually buy from you and that's why building rapport is so important to you.

My preference is to find common ground outside as well as inside business. Outside for the icebreaker, inside to demonstrate synergy and expertise. From the start of the presentation you need to get to the point of common ground as quickly as you can, this is a great aid to building rapport. The usual overused platitudes can often come across as being insincere. It's okay to respond if one is thrown at you but don't be the one to start a long-winded exchange of platitudes, start by saying thanks for talking to me, here's what I want to talk about. Maybe say, I appreciate you giving me your time, here's what I want to share with you . . .

When you're building rapport, it is important to understand the amount of insight you can gain just by carefully listening to what is being said to you. Listening can tell you so much more than just the words being said. You should be able to tell within the first few words, what kind of mood the person you're talking to is in, also their personality type. Are they detail or big picture? Don't be afraid to acknowledge if the prospect sounds busy or distracted and offer to call back at a time that is better for them, this all helps to build that all important rapport, by showing your understanding of the situation. Sometimes you have to take your time to win the prize.

"I am a big fan of spending time finding out the personality type of the people I am talking to, so that I can adapt my presentation to fit their style. It is after all, all about them, not me!"

The more you learn about the prospect the better; it means you can start to include a personal touch into your meetings. This cannot be the case at first meeting, as it can come across as too much too soon. Doing it too soon can feel insincere, but you can build up to it with all subsequent meetings, to help develop an even deeper rapport.

What you can do on the first meeting is, start to understand the personality type, this enables you to adopt the right approach and prepare yourself for the kind of questions you'll be asked. It might be worth looking at an example or two:

If the prospect is a big picture person, then you'll adapt your pitch to give all the headlines and the outcome and then only fill in the detail that is specifically asked for. If you were to concentrate on the finer detail at this point, you would start to frustrate them and run the risk of losing the sale.

Another example would be the exact opposite, a detail-oriented person is going to want to know about all the fine print and get frustrated if you just talk in big picture terms, the result is the same, you'll run the risk of losing the sale.

The key, whatever the circumstances, is not to pitch before you have established the rapport. You'll win the sale by winning the hearts and minds of the prospects. Don't ever forget, people love to talk about themselves, their experiences and the things they like, that's the key to the door. Let's face it a person is more likely to want to buy from a friend than they are a salesperson.

If you follow these simple guidelines and bring all the tips together; if you understand, the prospect will not buy unless they have confidence in you and your product, then you are set fair to create significant success in sales. Here's a few ideas to build your prospects confidence:

- Always be prepared, no excuses, just good solid preparation before the meeting.
- Make your sales presentations interactive; involve them as much as possible without losing control. Let them feel part of the process.
- Use testimonials and articles about you, your business and your product to support what you're saying.
- Use a live testimonial by letting the prospect talk directly to someone who has bought from you and experienced the delivery of your promise.
- Use testimonials, but don't bombard them, take it slow, remember your winning hearts and minds.
- Always make a point to talk about what happens after the sale, you'll be there to help, not just ride off into the sunset.
- Make sure you mention the desire to have a long-term relationship with them, not just a quick fix.
- Be there because you really want to help, not because you really need the commission.
- Make the effort to get some video testimonials, they can be used at point of sale and are incredibly powerful. Never go to a meeting without your Smart-Phone, so when you get the chance you can add another clip of another satisfied customer.

The price is not an issue you need to be concerned about, unless you have failed to build rapport and confidence. If you have won, the hearts and minds then all things are in your favour and you'll be able to handle that common objection of price. I will deal with objections later in the book. I will just say if the question of price does come up early or late in the sales process, you should concentrate on the value it brings not the cost. The sooner you communicate the value the better.

"The more time during the presentation you spend on demonstrating the value to the client the less likely it is that price will be an issue when you close the sale."

Build their confidence to get the sale.

There's no good or bad time to build the confidence your prospect needs to buy from you. This is something that should be happening from first contact and continue for the life of the relationship. When talking to a brand-new prospect, the quicker you can build their confidence in you, the quicker you'll get to the sale and those vital referrals. In most cases you're going to know when you've achieved the level of confidence you need for the sale. When you master this, good things start to happen, you'll get your calls returned, for example, a sure sign that you have won their confidence.

Things to avoid.

I am sure you won't be surprised to hear that I have some pet hates, where sales skills are concerned, things that I believe should not be said during a sales presentation, words that might get the prospect thinking, or feeling that you might be insincere in some things that you say. These feelings will erode the trust you've worked so hard to develop. I know I am not alone in this opinion and I have had many an interesting conversation with other sales experts who feel exactly the same way. So, let's try to avoid using these words and phrases:

"To be honest . . ." Come on; does this mean that you weren't being honest before? That's the impression it gives me!

"Frankly . . ." Why would you need to say this unless you're being insincere or have been insincere? Shouldn't you always be frank in what you say?

"To be frank . . ." So, before you said that you were telling stories, not being truthful?

"Honestly . . ." If you have to use this, you're almost accusing the prospect of not trusting you, or worse still you're about to tell a whopper!

"I mean that . . ." You probably don't mean that, particularly if you have to say you do!

"If I can show you a way . . ." watch out here comes a textbook close that everyone just out of school uses!

"Are you prepared to order today?" Far too obvious and there are a hundred better ways of saying this without turning the prospect off.

Starting a telephone call to someone you don't know with, **"How are you today?"** The immediate reaction is what are you trying to sell me!

"Can I help you?" Please leave this for the million and one retail assistants who can't think of something more interesting to say!

Try not to spout or preach about how good you are, or your ethics are. Instead just concentrate on doing a great job, look after the prospect's needs, think about them. Do it for them and be honest, the rest will take care of itself. The trick is not to tell people what or who you are let your actions do the talking; let others do the talking for you. You just do a great job for all the people you meet or connect with along the way.

If you can, get them involved.

It is often a great idea to get your prospect involved in the presentation, making it interactive. If the circumstances are right you can get your prospect involved in a number of ways, just don't put them in harm's way. If you do decide to get them involved make sure it is in keeping with the circumstances and relevant to their needs, not yours! I have heard some sales coaches say they think it's a good idea, if you're doing a formal presentation to a group, to get the prospect involved in the actual set up of your equipment. I'm not sure I agree with that, it doesn't really fit with my belief that you should be making them feel like the most important person in the room.

I do think it is a good idea that you start the presentation asking them what they would like to get out of it and then add that to the agenda. To do this you need to have the knowledge and confidence in yourself and product to field all questions. I will tell you this is not for the faint hearted but can be very fruitful in group presentations. It is a great way to demonstrate your expertise to the audience, building their confidence in you.

You should make the formal presentation as entertaining and interactive as you can to get the prospect more involved in the process. Particularly where product demonstrations are involved. If you can, use more of their senses, and maybe even have more than one speaker, you'll get a better response, get them using their voice, sight, hearing and their tactile senses and you'll win them over more effectively than if you just ask them to watch and listen to just one speaker, sitting as if they were in a classroom.

"Make your presentations memorable, like many other things do not underestimate the importance of planning and preparation. When dealing with group presentations, always invest time in rehearsals."

You can also heighten their involvement by asking questions designed to get them thinking as if they are already using, or already owning the solutions you have in mind. One quite effective way to do this is to ask some open questions that will get the prospect thinking in this way, some examples include:

- How would you see yourself using this product?
- If you were using this, how and when would you use it the most?
- Taking into account your specific requirements, how would you see this working in your environment?
- What are the features you like the best about this?
- In your view what do you feel will be the best features for you?

A few tips on using visual aids.

Some of the rules we use in public speaking are just as relevant to formal sales presentations as they are to presenting to large audiences. Here are my top tips on using visual aids like PowerPoint™ in your sales presentations.

- Don't overcrowd the slides; a good rule of thumb is to keep to one subject on a slide. It's okay to have more than one slide on a subject but not wise to have more than one subject on the same slide.

- You already know my views on the use of humour, so just to make the point again, it's okay to use humour on one or two slides within the presentation as long as you follow the basic rules already mentioned earlier in the book.

- Use the slide to reinforce what you are saying not the other way around. Don't just read what is on the slide, all you'll do is lose the interest of the people you're presenting to, they can read much faster than you can talk and so they will be ahead of you and just get bored!

- You should never have to apologise for the content or quality of a slide. Never use a slide unless it's one you have built or designed and then there will never be a need to say sorry, because they'll be great, because you have checked and double-checked and rehearsed with them. Simply put, if you're not 100% happy with them, don't use them.

- Keep your slides simple, including the transitions, the more complex you make them the you increase the chances of something going wrong with your presentation, simple is best.

- Be creative and avoid using the same old clipart that all the others are using, instead be different, be creative and stand out from the crowd.

- Unless you're really sold on it, I would really avoid the busy slide backgrounds. In all my presentations I prefer to use a simple white background, unless I have someone to do me a really great design that is not a distraction from the content on the slide, just keep it clean and simple, it's the content you want to promote not the design.

"Less is more where your slides are concerned. Keep them clean, keep them simple and concentrate on the content, not the flashy design and transitions. Only use sound if you have a great sound system and it adds to the drama!"

- If you need or want to brand your slides, make sure the branding is not a distraction from the content of the slide. With my plain white background, I also use a small version of my logo to go in the corner of each slide I use.

- If you can, include a testimonial or two into the presentation, toward the end is best and use anecdotes to illustrate your key points. Telling a story is so much more powerful than facts and figures, I think.

All you need to know about objections

Tell me the real problem.

I think it would be true, in most cases, to say that an objection raised by a prospect is their way of letting you know they haven't had all the information they need to make the decision to buy from you, right now. At this point maybe all they need is some more information, a greater motivation to buy and some good old-fashioned reassurance from you. They just need to be clear on value, suitability and to know without doubt that this is the right thing for them to do.

During my workshops and presentations on sales skills, I will always point out to the audience, there are only a very few real objections a person can raise. If you take the time to explore the full range of real reasons for raising objections and take time to be prepared for all the possibilities, you can significantly improve your sales performance.

Prepare yourselves for a shock! Sometimes the prospect will not tell you the whole truth. At least not right away. The reason for this might be because they don't want to risk offending you or making you feel bad, perhaps they are embarrassed by, or don't want to tell you the truth. Maybe they think to hide the real reason and tell a white lie is easier than the truth, so they just say something to try to get rid of you.

1. We don't have (or have spent) the budget.

2. I can't afford it.

3. I have to talk this over with my partner (Manager, Director, Lawyer, Spouse, Girlfriend, Boyfriend etc.).

4. I need more time, or I need to think about it.

5. I am not ready to buy today.

6. Can you come back to me in a few months; the time will be better then?

7. This level of quality is not important to me.

8. I want to think about it.

9. Business is a bit slow right now.

10. I let our consultants handle this kind of decision.

11. We have a policy of getting a number of quotes before we make a decision.

I believe that in most, if not all, cases the following are the only real objections, learn to handle these well and as second nature, then sit back and watch your sales performance soar, it will all come down to practise and confidence in what you're saying.

As with many things in sales, the secret is to drill right down as far as you're able to get to the real objection. I said earlier there are a finite number of objections, here then are the objections we all come across, regardless of what product we are selling:

- The prospect doesn't have the money, or maybe they're just too tight to spend what's required.

- They don't have the credit to be able to spend.

- They are not able decide to or unable to decide on their own.

- Maybe they don't have the authority to spend without additional approval.

- They believe they can get a better deal elsewhere and so are holding out for more quotes.

- They have already made a decision to follow an alternate path.
- The prospect already knows someone in the industry whom they're committed to do business with.
- They don't want to change vendors at this time.
- They want to take a look around to see what else is available.
- This is not a high priority at this time and therefore they don't want to spend time on making a buying decision.
- The prospect either doesn't need or thinks they don't need the solution you're offering.
- The prospect believes the price is too high, or knows the price is too high.
- The prospect lacks confidence in your product.
- Maybe they don't like you or the company or lack confidence in you or the company.

Getting to the real objections should be your top priority followed by handling the objection to continue with the sale. If you fail to get to the real objections, you'll end up dealing with the 'red herring' and then be left to ponder why, despite your best efforts, you were unable to get the sale.

"In most cases, I truly believe all objections can be handled before the event by just mastering the sales process covered in this book!"

When you get to the real objection you then need to qualify it and ensure it is the only one before you begin the process of handling it or them. The best way to do this is simply to acknowledge the objection and then ask a simple question. Let's assume the objection identified is price, you'd simply ask:

"Apart from the price is there anything else that would prevent you from going ahead?"

Keep asking this question until you get to the point where there are no more objections. Now you have to handle them.

As a rule, salespeople who don't handle the objections probably lack some knowledge and confidence. There's only one way to become proficient at handling objections and that is simply preparation and practise. You'll need to make sure you have a detailed knowledge of the technical side of the product you're selling. Make sure you have all the right sales tools to hand and that you know your subject, in this way your confidence will be high and objection handling will be a pleasure, giving you and the client the satisfaction you both desire.

Why do we get objections?

Objections, for the most part, are simply the prospect letting you know they need more information. The number of objections you face can be reduced simply by making sure you cover everything in the right amount of detail for the prospect. Do this by taking into account their personality type. During your presentation, if you cover everything to the satisfaction of the prospect, there should be very few, or better still, no objections, apart from the usual price related questions, which are not always true objections.

We get objections because there are doubts in the mind of the prospect, or perhaps unanswered questions. In some cases, theses doubts are created by the salesperson. If you're not listening to the prospect or talking too much filling the silence, you can easily over sell and begin to create these doubts in the mind of the prospect. Get into the habit of saying the important stuff and then shut up, let them speak, you listen!

It might be the prospect is just looking for more clarification on some aspects of the pitch you're making, or maybe they just want a better deal than the one you are offering. They might even need the approval of someone else to buy. This would be an indication that you had failed to correctly qualify the prospect, either by not asking the right questions early on, or perhaps you didn't listen to what they were saying.

There are key things that you need to cover in the presentation and if you miss them you can guarantee you'll get objections, so here are a few things you need to avoid improving your chances of a successful sale:

- Lack of qualification, you've not discovered if they can make the decision or not. Result? Objections.

- If you've failed to correctly identify the prospects true need. Result? Objections.

- If you've failed to establish the true value of the product to the prospect. Result? Objections.

- If you've not taken the time to build a good rapport with the prospect before you've made your pitch to them. Result? Objections.

- If you have no rapport, then it is likely that you will also not be trusted by the prospect. Result? Objections.

- Maybe it was just a really weak presentation and therefore the prospect has not been inspired to buy from you. Result? Objections.

- The most common is you've failed to anticipate the obvious objections and therefore not covered them off during your presentation. Result? Objections.

In essence the very best way to overcome the objections you could face is to cover all the bases before the close. Even the very best salespeople will still get objections from time to time, so the rule is to be fully prepared for them and practise your technique. Make sure you take time to research the most common objections you'll come across and then prepare for them before the event. Talk to other salespeople in your network of connections and find out the objections they experience the most, to help you prepare.

"As a rule of thumb, objections are a great indicator of how well you are doing with your sales presentations. The fewer objections the better you're doing. The more you get, well it's a good bet that you've missed something during the sales process that was important."

When you've put together your tactics for dealing with the objections make time to practise until they become second nature, natural sounding and conversational. Never and I mean never, operate outside your own values, maintain your integrity and in turn your reputation.

Listen to the objection with great care.

Listen with care to the objection, if the prospect repeats the same objection to you there's a fair chance it's the real thing. Don't jump in too soon; give your prospect a chance to talk it through completely before you talk, unless you're asking more questions to gather more detail about the objection.

Some sales experts will tell you at this stage you should agree with whatever the prospect is saying and then later when they've had their say you'll get your chance to give your side of the argument. I have to say I don't subscribe to this point of view. I think to do this is to break one of the golden rules; the one that states you must always be sincere. Far better, I believe, to use empathy at this point, tell the prospect, you can see it from their perspective, because you can, but that you'd like the opportunity to share with them the way you see it.

If during this process you feel the client might be stalling, by giving you an objection that's not their real concern, you'll need to get them to acknowledge the fact. Here are just a few ways you can get this to happen:

Say to them. "Don't you really mean?"

Perhaps you prefer to be more direct in which case you could just say. "Your saying (Insert objection) but I think you really mean . . ."

Another alternative is to try saying, "Many people have said the same but after some discussion most of them agreed that they really meant . . ."

Don't assume there's just the one objection.

As I had said earlier you must never assume the first objection, you're given is the only one the prospect has. When you've been given the first objection and you're satisfied you have the detail right and it's a real objection, before you handle it, you need to be asking the key question:

"Apart from [insert objection] is there anything else that would stop you from going ahead?"

Then if need be asking again in a slightly different way just to make sure.

"So, you're saying if it wasn't for the [insert all objections] you would go ahead?"

Alternatively, you could say:

"So, if I can satisfy you on all these points, you're saying there is nothing to stop us doing a deal?"

This example acts not only as a check to make sure there are no other objections but also as a trial close to test your prospects commitment.

"Using statements that acknowledge you want to deal with the objections to your prospects satisfaction but at the same time test their commitment to the sale is a really good idea at this point in the process!"

I think the best way to do this is to ask in a way that requires the prospect to think about buying the product and see what they have to say. For example, if the only objection was related to the price you might say:

"If I get the price or the terms to a point where you're satisfied would that be enough for you to make a decision?"

Like the other example above this is a great way of getting the commitment before you have dealt with the actual objection. This gives you a chance to test the prospects commitment to do business with you, are they serious or just making excuses?

Before you can give a really good close you will have to make sure you answer the objection in full. If for some reason you're not able to do that right now, then try saying something like this:

"I will need to gather this information for you, once I have put it all together and you have the evidence in front of you would you be prepared to make up your mind?"

You can see this is difficult to say no to and gives you a chance to re-group and sets you up for the next meeting.

Another part of this is to use statements that assume the sale will go ahead once you have solved the objection. The best way to achieve this is to ask questions that get answers that will confirm the sale, here are a couple of good examples that have worked for me in the not too distant past:

"I am sure we can do this, that being the case I assume we have a deal?"

You could even say:

"If I could do this for you would we have a deal?"

Use positive statements leading to the close.

The use of positive statements that lead to a close is a very successful technique that I have used on many occasions, but it is also one that I feel is under used by others. Here are a few more statements you can use to set the tone for handling the objection and steering the prospect toward the close:

"I understand how you feel, others in your situation have felt the same way at first but then they found that . . ."

Using positive examples of other people's experiences in conjunction with testimonials is a really powerful tool in objection handling and I urge you to try these. Remember practise makes perfect and mistakes are good as long as you're learning from them and not repeating them. If you have not used this technique before try using it to handle objections during a cold call. Just don't give up on the first attempt. Use the cold calls as your training ground.

"Others have felt the same way as you. If I can demonstrate to you that this is not the case would you be prepared to make up your own mind?"

With this one this is the ideal time to consider using testimonials that support your standpoint. This is just one of the reasons it is so important to collect testimonials for every circumstance as often as you are able.

Once you've handled the objections you can use more questions to steer you and the prospect further toward the close, questions like:

- "When should we start this for?"
- "When would you like it delivered?"
- "Which is the best day to deliver?"
- "Which is the best day to take the payment?"
- Where and when do you want it delivered?"

Can you prevent objections?

It is possible but difficult, which is why so few even try, it takes confidence, preparation and loads of practise. I am certain you can reduce significantly the chances for objections to be raised by ensuring your sales presentation is covering all the bases. This requires you to know your market, understand the range of objections you're likely to come across and cover them early in the process, or when it is practical, or logical to do so. This is easier than it may appear to you, all you need to do is follow the process described in this book and follow these useful hints:

- Gather all the right information at the start of the presentation and fully qualify the prospect.

- Cover Features, Advantages and Benefits in detail, after you have established the right level of rapport, identified and agreed the needs of the client and agreed on the solution.

- Talk in detail about cost and payment plans based on your knowledge of their financial position gained during the questions at the start of the process.

- Make time to fully understand your prospects business and the market they are in. Start this process before you even meet, with basic research using search engines, websites and social media.

- Depending on your skills and experience you will be able to reduce or prevent objections. Take these actions to reduce them and make the ones that do surface that much easier to work with.

- First you need to identify all the possible objections through research and other methods. One of the most valuable things you can do is talk to your fellow salespeople and perhaps some customers. Don't forget your own experience. Find out what the top ten objections are, with those in your market and those you would most like to do business with.

- Design some suitable scripts to handle each of the top ten objections. Make sure you include a closing question for each of the scripts.

- Design or collect sales aids that will help to overcome the objections such as testimonials case histories and data to illustrate performance and value.

- As much as we all hate to role-play, this valuable tool should be used to practise the scripts and the use of the sales aids effectively.

- During the process of role-play, you can amend and improve the scripts based upon the responses you get from the recipients.

- Then it is time to try them out on prospects, to refine the delivery. Remember practise makes perfect. This also gives you the opportunity to fine-tune your handling techniques.

"Use a combination of verbal and visual aids to help you handle the full range of possible objections. Practice your pitch and make it passionate and conversational."

Once you have this ready to go, the job is not over. I would suggest you review the content of the sales aids on a regular basis, to keep them up to date with changes to the product or market trends. If you include the new scripts and knowledge into your presentation, when you get to the end of the pitch there will be no objections to handle!

More tools to use.

Collect real life stories from your clients, past and present, the challenges they have experienced, and the positive outcomes achieved, as a result of their interaction with you. These can then be used as part of the objection handling process where you can use empathy and say to the client:

"I understand how you feel, I know another business who felt the same way and they found that . . ."

You can also use testimonials, letters or better still video testimonials these will all go toward demonstrating to the prospect why they should be dealing with you to help them with the solution being discussed.

Use easy to understand data, they say a picture paints a thousand words, so where you are able, use visual aids. I like to use comparison charts that show the competition, price, performance and any other useful comparisons to assist in illustrating the points I am raising. This can be very powerful, but you need to ensure you're comparing apples with apples, make it fair, you want to maintain your credibility and reputation.

Always use your own experience as one of your main tools for handling the objections, use phrases like:

"My experience has shown . . ."

Above all make sure you're fully prepared and practised for this vital part of the sales process. If you can anticipate the objection you can prevent them from occurring. This will put you at the very top of the game. To do this, like all things in business, requires confidence, the confidence that comes from planning, preparation and good old-fashioned practise.

Selling really starts once the objection is raised.

We already know that in many cases the first thing you hear is not always the real objection. The key skill for an exceptional salesperson is to be able to get past the stalling techniques and get to the heart of the real objections raised. Here is a list, you'll recognise it, as will most people, because no matter what the product or service these the objections are, we all hear day in day out. These objections are used to delay making a decision, mainly because people don't like being sold to! So often what is being said is not the real objection but a smoke screen, assuming you have done your job right:

- I want to think about it.
- It costs too much.
- I need to talk it over with others.
- I'm quite happy with what I have.
- We have no budget left for this year.
- Call me back in six months.

If you take a look at these, you can begin to see that they will all in some way relate to value. That is a huge clue to what you have to do to get over the objections. We know that suitability is an important factor but when you've demonstrated the suitability it will all come down to value.

Sometimes these are true objections, but I would say that most of the time they are either a stall or simply not the truth! In my view the key to handling objections, other than having the confidence to do so, lies in the following; interestingly the following points, when you get it right, are the biggest asset I know to building that all-important confidence we speak of:

- Your knowledge and application of all the skills associated with selling.
- Your detailed knowledge of the product.
- How much you know and understand about the prospect you're talking to.
- How creative you are in your thinking.
- Your mental attitude.
- Your sincerity, really wanting to help, not just trying to get the sale.
- How persistent you are, in the right way, at the right time. Rome wasn't built in a day.

Your first step should always to be to get all the objections out into the open and then to handle them. Make sure you've uncovered the true objection. For the next few pages I want to share some ideas on how to handle the objections on the list we have just gone through.

It costs too much.

What does this really mean, that is the question? You have to understand the meaning to handle this objection. The thing is there are a number of potential meanings and you have to find out the real reason for the prospect telling you, it costs too much, or it's too expensive. The true objection could be one of the following:

- The prospect can't afford it.
- The prospect could get the same product elsewhere and or cheaper.
- Maybe the prospect is thinking, "I just don't want to buy this from you."
- Perhaps it's the company, or maybe even both!
- It could be they don't understand the cost or don't see the true value of the product against the cost.
- Perhaps they are just not convinced of the need and want to know more.

In my experience a little under 50% of the price related objections will result in a no sale because the objection is not dealt with sufficiently, so that gives you many opportunities to get more sales despite the objection. That is why you need to make sure your objection handling skills are up to speed and well-practised. The first thing you need to do is to consider digging deeper into the objection, try these techniques:

- Engage in a conversation that can prove the affordability of the product, for example, "In reality what this product can do for you will cost less in comparison than if you were to continue on your current course."

- Question in more detail, to find a level that is affordable, "What are you willing to pay?" "What can you afford?"

- Find out how far off their budget you are, "How much over what you can afford is this price?"

- Show them a window to the future, "You're worried about spend today when you should be considering the value this will bring to you over its lifetime."

I would like you to pause for a moment and consider the following question. How many of those examples relate to situations that could have been avoided earlier in the process?

The answer to that is, most of them! That is why I maintain most objections can be avoided if you are doing the job right.

"We will all experience objections from time to time, but you really can significantly reduce the number by simply doing your job right!"

In many of the sales presentations I have done, where price was an issue, I have taken the following action to manage the objection:

"Other than the cost is there anything else that would stop you buying from me now?"

I do this because I want all the objections out on the table, so I know exactly what I am dealing with and make it more personal by referring to me, rather us or the company. If we assume the only issue is the price of the product then the conversation will progress something like this:

"If the price was lower, would you buy from me right now?"

The prospect says yes:

"So, you're saying other than price, there is no reason we can't do business?"

A point not to be forgotten is, if the prospect wants your product enough, they're not going to let price stop them from buying from you. All you need to do is show them a way they can buy, given their current circumstances.

I need to talk it over with others.

I used to hate hearing these words, "I need to talk it over with others," or words similar to this, mainly because it was a strong indication that I had done something wrong or missed something earlier in the sales process. In most cases it would be a combination of lack of enough research and insufficient qualifying of the person I was presenting to. That said, despite my hate for hearing this, it's not the end of the world and you can get around this if you try.

Here's what you need to do, first make sure you learn the lesson and take more care in your qualification next time. Now you have to take four steps, these are:

- Despite them not being able to make the decision you still want to get their personal approval, they're bound to have a say, even if it's just an opinion. Win their hearts and minds to keep them onside, the pitch is not over yet; you might need their support.

- Make sure you have a good rapport and relationship with the person you're talking to and if appropriate include as many of their team members as you are able to during the process. No matter how superficial the connections might be, these will all help you when the decision maker starts to ask around for opinions about you and or what you have on offer. Remember all things being equal people buy from people and mostly people they like. When you talk to them use the terms us and we.

- Make sure, when you find out the prospect, you're talking to is not the decision or sole decision maker, you get a meeting with all of them together. It won't just save time; it will empower them. There is a feeling of strength in numbers and therefore they will be more likely to tell you the truth, which after all is what you want.

- If you have to, make the entire presentation again to those who've not seen it then that's what you'll have to do. Far better though to save time and effort and get them all together first and that means you have to have all the right information about the decision process as early as you can in the relationship. At first contact gatekeepers can be a great help in achieving this. Win their hearts and minds and they will help you with the information you need to progress.

Another thing I believe is good practise in these circumstances is to ensure you have at least won over the person you are initially talking to, before you move onto the next person. The reason I say this is because they can become a great help to get all the people involved into the room for the full presentation. To find out how far you've got with this aim simply ask this question.

"If it were just down to you to make the decision on this would you be going ahead?"

If they say no this gives me another opportunity to see if there are any other objections hanging around that have not come to the surface yet. Then it's time to handle them and then perhaps pose the question again, before gaining their assistance to progress things.

"We can't win all the time and so accept that you'll not win the sale on every occasion, this should not stop you from remaining on good positive terms and ask for referrals."

If there were no movement forward at this point, I would still not completely give up. I am not suggesting I would make a nuisance of myself and each instance should be assessed on its own merits. I am saying if you've won hearts and minds you can still go a little further. The prospect is saying no but may still have some faith in the offering; it's just not the right time for them.

So, take it a little further and get them into the mindset of making referrals by saying something like this:

"So, given that you would go ahead under different circumstances, you do see the value of this solution?"

I hope they would say yes to this. In which case I would continue with:

"Do you think others in similar circumstances would also see the possible benefit from. . .?"

Again, the hope is the answer would be a yes. Now we are able to prime the prospect for some referrals.

Like so many things in life, prevention is so much better than cure, so make sure you take your time at the beginning of the sales process and ask the right questions. In this case questions that will qualify who, how and when decisions to buy are made, this will save you no end of time. The sooner you find out the real situation the sooner you can progress in a way most suitable for the circumstances.

I'm quite happy with what I have.

The prospect may be very happy with their current supplier, but it may not always be that way. They may not know about all the features advantages and benefits available through you. Your task is to ensure you put that right early on in the presentation. Concentrate on your differential or some other item that would win over the prospect and make them consider you instead of or as well as the current supplier. On many occasions I have managed to get a trail with a limited deal that once proven is adopted completely over the existing supplier.

To overcome the objection (I'm quite happy with what I have) you're going to need to know what it really is the prospect is saying, how many of the reasons listed below are you going to have to deal with to handle this objection fully? It's vital to find out first before you attempt to handle the objection. If you don't find the real reasons all your efforts will be wasted:

- Are they getting a better price or great value proposition that you cannot match?
- The quality of your service or the product or maybe both compared to the existing supplier?
- Perhaps there is an existing strong relationship or history that helps the current supplier.
- Maybe the prospect has no other knowledge of who or what is available and therefore buys because it is easier.
- Maybe the delivery times work best for the prospect with the existing supplier.
- Has the decision been made based on a previous trusted referral and they want to stay out of respect for that relationship?
- Has buying from this supplier become a bit of a habit?

Once you've discovered what the details are, you can start to think about how you will be able to best deal with the real objections. You'll already know how to handle the price and quality issues. Where you are up against the habitual purchase or a strong relationship, you're just going to have to show great patience and tenacity and over time build rapport, build the relationship and slowly win them over.

I have to say again, though, it is far better to have done your job well at the beginning of the process than have to deal with this level of objection at the late stages of the close!

We have no budget left for the year.

In my experience this objection is one of the most frequently used by a prospect, the reason for this is quite simply because it's the simplest and most difficult objections to handle and often the truth. This is also the one that most salespeople will fear the most. I believe for the professional practised salesperson this is no more difficult to mitigate or prepare for than any other possible objection.

You do this by simply asking the right questions at the right time, confirming the ability to afford early in the process. This is only an insurmountable objection in a small number of cases, because there are so many options you can use to mitigate the issue, here are just a few examples:

- Your product can probably span other budget areas where there is some wiggle room; this is an option where the prospect is sold on the value to them (which should always be the case).

- If you get the right motivation and you are talking at a high enough level, you can get them to make an exception or vary the agreed budget to make room for the purchase.

- Maybe they just said this to get rid of you!

- Now and again it might even be the truth, but most businesses make provision for additional spend and budgets are a guide not an exact figure, so it all comes down to motivation.

Dealing with this kind of objection, like so many others, will require you to ask more questions to get to the real reason. You might like to try questions like:

"Let me tell you about the payment plans we can offer you..."

"If this solution solves your issues is there any reason why you can't make changes to the budget to get this included?"

"Who would have the power to exceed the current budget to include this?"

Another option might be to ask:

"When would be a good time to set up a further meeting with you and the others that can make this purchase an exception?"

Another way of handling this would be to ask the prospect the following questions leading to a future commitment:

"If the budget wasn't all used up, would you be buying this product from me?"

Assuming the prospect is going to say yes to this, you follow it up with the following question:

"When is your next budget meeting?"

At this point you're going to find out the date of the next meeting and your objective is to get as much information as you can, about how the budgets are decided and what you have to do to get onto the list of new spend. Information you're looking for includes the type of proposal you may need to submit any due dates and the preferred format for the proposal.

"When you're asked to submit proposals for a future purchase or budget for your offering, always arrange it so you can follow up the submission in person. In most cases this will improve your chances of success."

You'll also want to influence the means of delivery, far better to deliver it in person giving you another opportunity to present the solution and take full responsibility for the information given and how it's delivered. It is a good idea to try to include the person you have built a relationship with so that they are onside for the meeting and feel involved. This will encourage them to be more of an advocate than they would if they were sitting on the sideline.

If you have the authority and you're talking to the main decision maker, you could also suggest the prospect buys now and is invoiced now but the payment is not due until the start of the new budget period or after budget approval, if they feel confident the purchase could be included in a special out of budget payment.

The 'no budget' objection has to be one of the most difficult ones to deal with, because quite simply you never know if this is the true objection or not. One thing is certain, if you are submitting a proposal on the back of the no budget objection, you need to make sure it is not just presented to the decision makers on time but error free and with all the terms and conditions prepared and in order! I would also make sure that you follow the sales rules, make it all about them and all about solutions and all about value.

Call me back in six months.

In my experience this objection is just the prospect being as polite as they can to you and what they are really saying to you is, "No thanks." In other words, this will rarely be the real objection and if you really want to continue with the battle for the sale, which all good sales people would want to do, then you need to get to the real reason and try your best to deal with that.

Like so many of the objections you'll experience, this is a really good indication that you've not done something right earlier on in the sales process. I think this is worth looking at in more detail, but first back to this six-month thing.

You could ask more questions to get further into the subject of why you have to wait for six months before the prospect is willing to buy. An example of a question you could ask might be:

"What will be different in six months?"

or perhaps:

"Is there a particular reason for wanting me to get back to you in six months?"

You might even ask:

"What is preventing you from taking action today?"

If you believe in complete candour, then perhaps you should consider facing this head on and asking:

"Are you really saying no?"

On the other hand, if you want to continue trying for the sale, you could continue along one or more of the following lines:

- Ask the prospect, "Do you see yourself buying in six months?"
- Try to find out who else is involved, "How will the decision be made?"
- Maybe ask the prospect (make sure you have authority first), "Could you buy now and pay in stages?"
- If relevant show the prospect what the delay will cost them or what they could gain in the six months.

- Ask them if they have considered the cost of delay.

- Show the difference between the cash spend now and the value of the sale, the return on investment (ROI).

Getting regular objections? Look at your own performance for clues.

I truly believe that if you are getting to the closing stages of your sales presentation and having to handle a selection of objections, the issue is all about you and your performance during the preceding steps in the sales process! If you've covered all the bases and taken your time to ask all the right questions and gather all the right information then almost, if not, all objections will have been taken out of the mind of the prospect.

If this were not the case you would have called an end to the meeting early, saving you time, or giving you more time to spend with those that are serious about buying. I believe that objections will happen for one of the following prime reasons:

- You've failed to establish the right level of rapport with the client and therefore, trust or prospect confidence in you will be too low for them to commit.

- Perhaps you've not correctly identified the needs of the client, in other words you've not asked enough questions to establish the need and started to sell the solution too soon.

- Maybe the features, advantages and benefits have not been covered in enough detail to demonstrate the true value of the product.

- It could also be that you have failed to motivate the prospect to want to buy, maybe there's just not enough desire to buy.

- It could also be that you've not established a sense of urgency for the purchase right now.

Now if you feel that you've covered all these aspects then perhaps there is a deeper reason for the objections, perhaps it's related to one or more of the following:

- Maybe the person to whom you're presenting is not the true or only decision maker.

- Maybe, just maybe the prospect has not told you the truth about ability to afford and has no money.
- Perhaps the prospect just doesn't like you, your company or your product.
- It could be the client feels the price is just too high, or they just don't understand the value proposition.
- It might be they have a contact, a friend who they can buy from on more beneficial terms, or just because they prefer to buy from a long-standing friend rather than you.

"I can't put enough emphasis on the importance of really understanding the sales process and doing all you can to cover all your bases before you get to the close! This doesn't mean you'll always get it right; it does mean you'll know how to handle it!"

There is only one antidote for this and that is to make sure you understand the full sales process. Do your research and ask multiple questions that will tease out all the important information that will enable you to cover all the bases. This way the objections never see the light of day and you save much time and effort. The key to this is practise. Practice after all really does make perfect!

All you need to know about closing

The ultimate close.

In my view the ultimate close is the one where you have to say nothing at all. After you've built rapport, got to know all about the prospect, identified their needs, presented the solution, answered any questions, what is the best possible outcome? It has to be when the prospect asks you how they can make the purchase! That has to be the perfect outcome, the perfect sale! The more prepared and practised you are on all the elements before the close, the better your performance throughout the process and therefore, the more likely it is that you'll satisfy all the requirements of a sale.

In the ideal world if the prospect fails to meet the criteria for a purchase they would never get as far as the close. The close is reserved for only those where it is a suitable course of action to take. That means no objections, no wasted time and that's what we all want in the perfect world.

It's my opinion, based on my own experience in sales, that all things being covered in the presentation, with all the right answers, the prospect will be motivated and want to continue and discuss the terms of the purchase because by now they will want to buy from you, they will be asking you, rather than you asking them!

"Visualise being that good that when you get to the end of your presentation, they ask you for the sale!"

Why do so many fear the close?

On my travels talking about sales and sales development, one of the constant challenges I face is getting salespeople to understand, they are never going to be exceptional at this vital skill until they've got their heads in the right place. Closing the sale is one of those parts of the process where it is so important to have the right mental attitude.

I believe one of the main reasons closing seems to be the part of the sales process that many hate is simply because they take the rejection of their offer as a personal rejection, which is rarely the case. If you ask for the sale and the prospect declines, it will be because they don't have enough information, or perhaps the deal is not right for them for some reason. It's nothing personal, if you've followed all the rules!

If you've taken the time to follow the process and done it well, you'll never get to the point of closing, if they are not in the market. Just doing the job right reduces the chances of them saying no significantly. If, however they do say no you'd do well to remember they are not rejecting you just the offer that's been made. This rejection is also not forever, the deal is just not right for them right now. With that in mind what is there to fear? This is not a personal rejection. Take it on the chin, learn from any mistakes and carry on with the journey.

When you are told 'no,' always remember to find out why and see what you can learn for the future. Closing is why you started the conversation, so forget your misplaced emotion and finish the job, ask for the business, if they haven't already beaten you to it.

Make sure you recognise the buying signals.

As a professional salesperson you need to recognise the buying signals the prospect will deliver to you throughout the sales presentation, here are the top signals you'll come across, make sure you never miss them:

Questions about delivery, availability or time— *"When can I have it by? Is this in stock? How much notice do you need?"*

Questions on price, rates or even affordability or deposits— *"How much does it cost? What are the ongoing costs? Can I afford this?"*

Questions about your business expressed in a positive way— *"How long have you been with the business?"*

Asking you to go over details again— *"Can you repeat what you said before about. . ?"* **Talking about their current or past supplier and problems they may have experienced**— *"We had issues with service levels."*

Questions about key features and quality— *"What is the capacity, what else will it do for me?"*

Questions about warranty periods and support staff expertise— *"Will your people be able to answer our questions, how long will you support the product?"*

Questions about what other things your company is involved with— *"What other products or services do you supply?"*

Questions about who will be responsible for the relationship post sale— *"Who will be our main contact, or answer queries?"*

Asking to see the demonstration again, or wanting to see parts of the presentation again— *"Can I look at the samples again?"*

Asking questions about your other customers, or for testimonials— *"Who are some of your current clients, can we talk to them?"*

They might just make noises of affirmation during your presentation—*"That's interesting, that would fit with our direction."*

Your ability to recognise and then deal with these buying signals is key and really can be the difference between sales failure and sales success.

Avoid yes or no answers at the close.

If you are in the process of closing the deal, I think it is wise to avoid using yes or no answers. I think it's far better to answer the question more fully, or even pose a question that seeks confirmation as part of the response. I think this is the right thing to do as it will ensure you maintain some control over the process, this makes it easier to navigate the prospect toward the purpose of the meeting, the close.

People are often tempted at the point of close to give the obvious and short answer to questions, believing their job is done. I would say you should certainly give an answer, but it should work toward the goal of closing the sale. If the prospect asks you if the product comes in blue as well as red, you'd be tempted to say, "yes." If they want to know if you can deliver by next month, you'd be tempted to say, "yes" again. If the prospect asks you the time for delivery, again you would be tempted to just give the simplest of answers, for example "we can usually deliver in two weeks."

"Ensure your progress toward the sale by gaining confirmation of the intent to buy at the same time as answering their question."

Although the answers are not wrong, I'm don't believe they give you the best chance to get the eventual close you look for. Instead you should try using the prospects question to get closer to the close and the confirmation of the sale. So your answer should give them the information they are looking for but also gain further confirmation that the prospect wants to buy from you. Here are some examples to illustrate the point:

- "Does the product come in blue as well as red?" Your answer might be, "Yes it does would you prefer it in blue?"

- "What are the delivery times, could you deliver next month?" Your answer would be, "Is next month when you'd need the equipment by, is there a particular date you prefer?"

- "How soon could you get someone to take on the task, could you do it within the week?" Your answer would be, "Is next week when you need to make a start?"

Being able to create the right response when you're in front of the prospect requires you to be able to think on your feet, think creatively and deliver the response that takes the prospect further down the road of closing. Above all, always be prepared and make sure you practise, practise and then practise some more.

How to ask closing questions.

No matter how great your presentation has been up to this point, unless you are asking for the business, or better still the prospect is asking you, the entire meeting has been for no real purpose, you and the prospect will be left hanging. The important thing is to make sure one of you closes the sale. Once you've asked the ultimate closing question, shut up and wait for the answer.

My advice to sales teams I've helped to develop has never yet let me, or them down. The advice on closing is simple, logical and works:

- The close should start from the moment the meeting has started, sometimes before that, through marketing and research. The most important thing to remember is you need to sow the seeds early. Tell the prospect the purpose and objective to the meeting from the very start.

- Next, remember to ask for the business when you hear the first real positive buying signal. The key? During the presentation your mission is to eliminate the opportunities for the prospect to say 'no' to your closing questions. You do this by ensuring you've covered all the bases and reduced the chances of objections or the prospect saying no at the crucial moment. Prospects that are really not interested should be discovered long before you get to the close.

Much of your success in closing will come from the questions you ask. The type of question will be dependent on the product you are selling to them. Here are just a few examples of the kind of questions you could ask:

"Would you like these in blue or red?"

"How many of these do you want in the darker colour?"

"Is the beginning or end of the month best for delivery?"

"When would you like us to start?"

"Are you paying by Debit or Credit card?"

You can see that these simple examples give the prospect a choice and at the same time eliminate the chances of them saying no to you. You let them decide but limit the choice to a positive outcome.

There are examples of questions you can ask that do give the prospect the opportunity to tell you no but before you use these you need to be sure they have real interest in your product, for example:

"Would you like me to book you in for the installation next Monday?"

As you can see this gives the prospect the chance to say no to you even if that is unlikely. If the prospect does you can come back with:

"When would be the best time for the installation?"

As with most things in sales and indeed business the best way to ask these questions is to do it in a sincere and friendly manner. Please don't push or use pressure, that is a sure way to lose the sale. Just ask and then shut up, silence is very powerful. Keeping quite can be difficult for salespeople, who seem to believe that all silence needs to be filled with their voice. Ten-seconds of silence is too much for them and seems more like a minute than ten short seconds. When I was first asked to practise using long pauses I found it very uncomfortable to start with. You'll need to take my word for two things, one how powerful it is and second how much shorter the breaks are than you imagine.

I believe, like so many others, one of the best ways to get the sale is to get the prospect thinking as if they already own the product and then to simply ask for the business. I heard a speaker on sales once liken this view to selling a puppy. He said the best way to sell the puppy is to let the prospective buyer hold it. Then offer to let them keep him for the day. You try and get the puppy back off them the next day! I think you'll get my point. Here are some more realistic examples to consider:

- Use the copier for a day before the sale.

- Try this at home before you buy.
- 30-day free trial before you buy (I'm always using this one).
- Get your first issue free.
- Take it for a test drive.
- If you owned this satellite package what would tonight's viewing look like?

These are all closes that follow the same principle as the puppy sale. You're always going to say that your product is great, this is a way of getting them to see for themselves how good it is by touching it, trying it, or perhaps visualising its use and subsequent effect on them.

I appreciate this is not possible in all types of sale, but it is worth remembering the principle and keeping it in your toolbox. You'll notice the 30-day free trial is used extensively in cloud technologies and Social Media, as well as many other online offerings.

Let the prospect chase you for a change!

There are occasions when it might be a good idea to let the prospect chase you rather than you constantly chasing them! It might be that from time to time, like all of us, you chase too hard. You may come across too eager to get the sale and don't give the prospect the room they need to make the decision to buy. This is a skill that takes practise, don't use it until you have all the other skills in place and can perform them all proficiently.

"Many people in sales can come across as too desperate and people don't like to be pushed. That's why letting the prospect do some of the chasing can be a great idea, you need to use it with care! This is not an excuse to be lazy!"

This technique is frowned upon in some circles as being too old school. Let me tell you this, it does work when used in the right place at the right time. I think there are many reasons why it works, and it seems to me in a world where an increasing number of direct sales are trying to be made by call centres, this technique, old school or not, is a breath of fresh air and does get results. The main reason it works is because people don't like to be sold to, but they love to buy, so let them buy! Here are two good occasions to use this technique:

- If the client shows just a little interest but not enough to make you think they will buy right now, talk to them about not buying right now, if you've done your homework you increase significantly the chances of them chasing you to get the sale done.
- Again, the client might be showing some, but not much interest, talk to them about the product being possibly more than they can afford, or maybe phrase it as being a higher investment than the average person is willing to pay. Make the inference that it may be a little too advanced for their current situation. However, remember this is a risky strategy and one that should be used with care and be well practised. This technique should only be used by those who have the skill levels and confidence to do this without offending the prospect. If you get it wrong, learn, practise and try again.

When I have used this technique, I have used phrases that are quite soft and not offensive but still have the desired effect, for example I might say something like; This is a great product but might be more than you need right now. Clearly the use of this is dependent on the circumstances and the product.

How soon should you close the sale?

I am often asked, when should you close the sale? The most obvious answer and strictly speaking the correct answer is when the prospect is ready to buy. The reality is that many people in sales are so preoccupied with talking and completing all the things they have been taught to say, they think the close comes only when they've finished what they have to say, or should that be what they have been told to say. The true answer is somewhat different to this but nonetheless far simpler than most would imagine.

You should start to close the sale before you even meet or speak to the potential client. If you're really smart the close starts with the marketing activity. Good marketing makes the sale easier, exceptional marketing almost makes it redundant and turns a salesperson into more of an order taker! Much of your sales success will be determined by your attitude toward the task.

If you approach the sale with the right attitude, a positive one, you'll find you achieve far better results than if you are approaching the task with a negative one. That's why I say you should start the process of closing before you speak to the prospect and regardless of the level of marketing activity you should always start with you and your attitude.

"Talking about having the right attitude, I can't remember a time when I went into a sales meeting not expecting to get the sale. I am certain this attitude gained me more successes than entering the meeting expecting the worst!"

I always go into a sales situation with the expectation that I will get the sale; I've convinced myself to that outcome before I even start. Having that attitude is transmitted through my language, pace, tone, passion, body language and the way in which I treat the prospect. At the first opportunity I will tell the prospect quite directly what my objectives are going to be, often with a smattering of good humour. By doing this I find my meetings always seem to get off to a great start.

So, what are these objectives? Well, first I make it clear to the prospect that I am there to help in any way I can. Second, I am seeking to begin a long-term relationship and finally that I want the process to be enjoyable for us both, life's too short not to have some fun along the way.

I'm sure that another positive side effect of telling the prospect about your objective is it gives them a feeling of ease and makes building rapport and information exchange far easier, the close has already started to happen. Telling the prospect what you are looking for at first contact and then closing the sale promptly when you get the first true buying signal, is the right thing to do, providing you have covered all the bases.

I guess what I am saying is, where selling is concerned you don't have to leave the best till last. In sales the best part of the process is or should be the close. We should get the close done instantly it becomes possible. Always go to meetings or make those calls with the attitude of a winner not a loser. If you feel the call you are making is highly speculative, then that will be because you haven't put the early hard miles in, like for example the research and ensuring you talk to the right people. I can see no point in wasting yours and their time, talking to the wrong people; that makes no sense at all, unless you're using it as a training exercise with cold calls to assess new material!

Understand the product from the user's perspective.

I have said earlier in this book how important it is to understand your product, not so you can show off to the prospect with your expansive technical knowledge but to make sure you can competently answer questions about the product when called upon to do so. Well, there's another great reason to have this expert knowledge of your product and to fully understand how the product is being used on the job. With this level of knowledge, you're able to explain to the client how they can profit from its use. Now I know this sounds simple and very obvious, you'd be amazed how many people don't have the level of knowledge, to really understand how the product is used at the sharp end.

If you're not sure, you should invest some time in finding out, watch the product being used, ask the people using the product for observations. Find out what they like about and just as importantly find out what they dislike about it. The more you understand about how the product is being used in the real world and how the people that use it feel about it, the more you can talk to your prospect about the true value of the product from their perspective.

The more you understand the better your communication to them during the presentation. This will help them to really buy into the features, advantages and benefits. The result of that? They will be more likely to buy without being asked and that is the perfect sale, when the clients will close themselves based on your information and experience.

Sales aids and tools

Enhance your performance.

I believe the use of sales aids and tools can really enhance your performance and your reputation with your prospects and clients alike. They are perfect for illustrating important points, particularly if you have to do a number of follow-ups before you get the sale. These aids and tools include some of the everyday items you use in business each working day such as email, telephone, leaflets and other related literature, electronic or hard copy. There are some quite effective and very obvious tools you can add to your list for use in sales that will help to enhance your performance above your current levels, for example:

- A supply of branded cards or note pads that you can use to handwrite messages to your prospects or clients, this is a good personal touch and will help to build rapport by demonstrating that you care and value them. In the world of email and text, personal handwritten notes are not just unusual but also highly valued.

- I've talked earlier in this book about the power and value of client testimonials. As part of your sales toolkit have a series of well-presented and branded client testimonials that you can leave with your prospect.

- Make a collection of supporting articles that can illustrate the benefits of your product, or perhaps demonstrate practical examples of its use.

- I also like to use video clips in support of the product and its application. These are already very important and have started to take over from printed testimonials in popularity.

- Small, useful or novelty gifts also work well, branded phone covers, USB sticks, pens, mugs, branded post-it notes, tee-shirts all have their place and use in your sales toolkit.

- Giving more than expected is also of great value, for example the unexpected thank you call or invite to lunch of drinks after hours.

- Don't forget the all-important FAB sheets (Features Advantages & Benefits), I like to have a fully branded set of prints that document with high colour the features, advantages and benefits of the product I am selling.

- Other things you should consider include graphs and facts about the market and use of your product, perhaps figures on the profits or savings that can be made, from real life examples.

Who works in sales? We all do!

Sales, we're all in sales from cradle to grave.

It's true! We are all selling in one way or another all the time and some of us are better than others at getting the close we desire on a regular basis. The interesting thing is, when we first came into the world, we were all approximately equal and all started selling from that moment. The best salespeople are new-born babies because they always get the close, they are looking for! You could argue selling is part of our DNA and is the original and oldest profession!

"Can you imagine how great your sales figures would be if you were as tenacious as young children trying to get their way? Just avoid laying on your back, kicking your legs and screaming, that would be bad!"

Think about it and you'll know it's the truth. Young kids who want more chocolate or the latest game don't know how to give up, they will just keep asking and asking until they get the close. Then we grow up and for some strange reason we seem to forget how tenacious we need to be to get the sale. Our close ratio goes from somewhere in the high nineties down to maybe the low forties, just because we forgot about tenacity and motivating the person to see it your way. I wonder how much you'd be earning right now if you were still closing in the high nineties?

Some sales experts will tell you that on average it takes up to seven contacts or touch points to get the sale. These touch points include the sales presentation, the objections, every aspect of the journey. Now we have to consider what it takes to get to that point as often as you're able. Is there some great secret, or some age-old wisdom I can share with you? The answer is no. Simply put all you need to do is remember what it was you did as a child when you wanted that chocolate, yep, it's that simple, persistence, plain ordinary persistence, that's the secret. Please don't make the mistake of thinking persistence is the same as pressure sales techniques. Persistence is about not giving up, even when faced with challenges, persistence is not about relentless inappropriate sales pressure and certainly not about flogging a dead horse. It is underpinned as is everything in sales with knowledge and relationships, having courage and having a genuine desire to help.

Even if you are not in a sales position, each conversation you have starts with you expecting a certain outcome and you will do all you can to get that outcome (within reason). When you want a day off, when you want a raise, when you want to meet your buddies at a different bar before the game, you will do your best to close the conversation with the desired outcome! How does that differ from sales? When you get right down to the nuts and bolts is doesn't. We are all selling, all the time, all our lives, so why not be great at it?

Should I leave a message, or call back?

This is a question that I used to ponder over quite a bit when I worked for the bank. Years of experience and trying different techniques resulted in what I'm going to share with you now. First, I would in most cases leave a message but now I do more, I never just leave the message. I use my imagination and knowledge of the prospect to find other ways to directly communicate with them. I have a few simple guidelines to start; I have used these for some time and developed them to suit my personality. You could do the same, think them through, develop them, make the your own:

1. Learn how to get around automated phone systems to get closer to the sale.

2. Design a message that creates interest, compelling the recipient to return the call; in the same way you would deliver an elevator pitch. In other words, create some curiosity, and therefore the desire to call back.

3. Selling, is best treated as a competitive game, always play to win!

4. More on the creation of curiosity, be creative in your thinking make sure people remember you, be professional, be different, remember the mission, which is not always the endgame sometimes that has to be achieved in logical stages.

5. Never be unprepared and always take time to practise. Think before you speak. So, don't pick up the phone unless you know what you're going to say.

It is worth taking some time to learn how to deal with the telephone procedures of some of the bigger organisations that can sometimes be difficult to get past a series of gatekeepers; here are some of the things I use from time to time. Success depends on the person on the other end of the phone, but these tips can improve your odds. It's interesting that most of the companies using multiple gatekeepers, paradoxically, will agree they would not want to turn their back on possible opportunities, solutions or innovations that could help them develop. They say that, yet the systems in use may well prevent these possibilities getting through the gatekeeper maze. All the more reason to find a way around them, or leave a really good message that stands out from the crowd, for all the right reasons, follow these hints to help improve your results:

- Build rapport with the person that answers the phone, it doesn't need to be too deep just show them you're a sincere person, assuming you are, if not we have a problem! Once you have their attention tell them you don't want voicemail and would really appreciate knowing how to contact your target direct. If you have won them over, you may well get the mobile number or be given some other shortcut. It's got to be worth a try. The key is treating them with respect and appealing to their natural desire to give help when asked, particularly to people they like the sound of. Candour is key here.

- Find someone in administration that can help you to gain information about the diary or movements of the person you want to connect with, so you can book a call or appointment that will suit them the best. The helps to warm things up, the warmer it gets the easier the progress toward the sales presentation.

- You could always go all the way and get someone in the building to make an appointment with the person you need to talk to for you. I use this all the time and I can tell you it works! Perhaps the easiest way to do this is to connect with someone from the company on social media, this takes time, don't rush it and have a sincere desire to help. Better still the person you really want to talk to for the sale. Then when you call you can ask for them by name. You can send them a message and gain their agreement for a call or a meeting.

- For bigger organisations it might even be worth getting through to the PR department, after all it's their job to give out information! Show them what's in it for them. For example, illustrate how much potential value there could be if a deal was done. The usual warning though, don't try to sell to them too hard! People hate to be sold to, people like to talk about themselves, that's a clue, start by thinking about them, give value first, compliment them on some of their work. You'll be familiar with some as a result of your research before the call!

- Go networking locally and find a champion either in or associated with the persons business. The hope being they will introduce you to them. The best way to make this happen is to give value first. So, refer someone to them, make it quality and then ask for your introduction. That is why networking is so important.

On balance I do believe it's best to leave a message but are you going to get a return call? In many cases the answer is going to be no. Why? Because in most cases the recipient cannot see the value in returning the call and that is another big clue for you. Make sure you leave a message that will either create some curiosity or encourage the expectation of some value from returning the call. That is why it is so very important to invest time in research, finding out as much as you can about the business and or the people so that you are able to create the right kind of motivation.

"Don't start selling too soon, you can't sell without knowing the needs, hold back and concentrate on them not you and your product!"

One key point to remember is never leave your pitch or part of your pitch as the voicemail, this will be a waste of yours and their time and will certainly not encourage a return call. Here are a few more ideas that you might want to experiment with and see what works best for you:

- Be minimalistic and just leave your name and number and a brief hook, in a very business-like manner.

- You could try using humour but take this route with care, we're not all born comics and without practise you could fall flat on your face, don't use politics, religion or creed, don't tell jokes.

- Use a direct style and let the prospect know you wanted to send them some important data and needed to check their email details or address details as well as explain what and why you are sending it.

- Use curiosity some might describe this as dangling the carrot. Alternatively, just ask thought provoking and proactive questions to encourage a conversation that helps you to discover more about the possible motivations to buy.

Another key point is if you're making a series of calls and you are using a combination of methods, do make sure you take notes to refer to later, this could save a few red faces and in any event is just good practise. The last thing you want to be doing is referring to the wrong set of circumstances during a second or third call!

If you're considering a voicemail system for your own business make your selection with care, it's not about what the sales guy tells you, it's how it makes your customers or prospects feel when they get in touch with you. Think about how you feel when you get stuck in a voicemail maze.

I guess you could say that I'm a little old fashioned or perhaps it's just that I am in sales and therefore feel people are better to talk to than machines. In the ideal world the phone would be answered by a machine called a human and they would decide whom I should talk to and when it was a good time to be put through, as well as relay messages to the right people, like I said I'm probably a little old fashioned. I would suggest however that the human touch will soon be the method that is seen as special rather than the machine. That's not to say automated systems don't work for customer service calls (incoming),

you need look no further than the Apple automated customer service system for Internet sales and support, it really is something else!

In my own office I use a very simple automated system to direct the call generically to either sales, existing clients or accounts. Guess which option gets the most use? Of course, sales!

When it comes to leaving messages here's my take, ask yourself if you got this message would you return the call? If your answer is no, don't leave that message, record a better one. It is probably best to prepare something and then practise it a few times before using it, first impressions are so very important!

What if they won't agree to an appointment?

Assuming you've got through and you don't have to leave a message but for some reason you're not getting the appointment what could be the problem? Maybe you did get the appointment and they either didn't show or perhaps cancelled at the last moment, not giving you the opportunity to reappoint. What could be the reasons behind this, everything happens for a reason! Maybe it was something to do with one or more of the points listed below? These come from my own experience and the experience of other sales professionals who have done their apprenticeship and learnt the lessons:

- Maybe during your call, or in your message, you've failed to establish enough interest or curiosity to motivate them to make the appointment or to see it through.

- Perhaps they just couldn't see what was in it for them, where the value was for them.

- Perhaps you've not given them enough to recognise the need and how you might be able to help.

- You may have said the wrong thing or failed to establish any trust or rapport during your initial contact.

- Maybe the prospect has the wrong opinion of you or your company.

- Maybe you have used another person to make the call and they have not taken as much care, as you would have done.

The ways around this are quite obvious when you think about it, they are also very simple to put in place, try whichever one of these fits the circumstances:

1. Use your ever-growing contact database, you know the one you are building day by day while you network and meet new people! Use it to find a contact that knows the person you're trying to make the appointment with. Ask them if they can call your contact and smooth the way for you to get in front of them.

Perhaps they will even be willing to find out the real reason this person doesn't want to talk to you.

2. You might want to try sending them an email of local testimonials from people they might know or recognise and a short note with some suggested times and dates for a meeting.

3. Try winning hearts and minds with something unexpected, like a small branded gift. You can really melt the ice with this kind of innovation and unusual gesture.

4. One of my favourites, when there's a gatekeeper in the process too, is to spend as much time winning them over as you can (you don't want to fake it, so be sincere). Once you have them on side, the contact with the prospect becomes that much easier, particularly if you take time to find out about the prospect from the person who knows them so much better than you.

5. Find out where they go, if they network, and be there too. Make contact through this medium and you might make much better progress than you expect but remember don't act like a bull in china shop, take it easy, win their trust first, by building rapport. This doesn't need to be just a networking event it can be any gathering where contact of the right kind can be made, even a sporting event can work. Find out where they go and then go there. Be subtle and take care, nobody likes a stalker! Remember it's about them not you. This method of contact of course includes social media too!

6. Send them a letter that doesn't talk about the product or the solution, you need to identify and establish the need before you can do that. In this letter concentrate on showing expertise ask thought provoking questions and sell the idea of an appointment. I also use blogs for this. Blogs and other social media platforms are a great way to generate leads by demonstrating your expertise.

7. Wherever you can do your own sales calls that way you can really concentrate on building first-hand relationships.

The main thing is to be a bit different, be a bit creative, be a bit courageous and take a chance. Don't be afraid of making the occasional mistake, don't be afraid of rejection. They are not saying no to you or your product forever, they are just saying no at this moment. What you should be afraid of is not taking action and not learning the lessons that will improve your performance in the future. Lack of improvement, lack of persistence will simply hand the opportunities to your competition.

When things go bad

Things do go wrong, even for good people!

It's true things do go bad sometimes, despite your best efforts. It's just as true that in every group of people you'll encounter there is always good and bad and sometimes, until you experience their actions, it can be difficult to see the difference on first contact. Sales is no exception, in years gone by you could argue, sales had more than its fair share of the bad. When sales was not seen as a profession to be proud of, a profession in its own right, it did have a tendency to attract the wrong people, the ones that only cared about themselves and the money they could earn, rather than the people whose lives they were affecting. I am sad to say that is still the case today with some firms. The best way to judge is, if it looks too easy or sounds too good to be true then it probably is!

Right now, though, I want to talk about when sales go bad, when this happens and it does and it will happen to you too, it's not always because you did a bad job. Sometimes these things just happen that way. What we are interested in is reducing the chances of it going bad by doing a great job. I guess the first thing I want to say here is things will go bad when you start to relax too much and take your eye off the ball. The most common reason for taking your eye of the ball is ego due to previous successes. Don't let your ego fool you into thinking you can get away with not preparing for every sale you set out to make!

"Don't let successes go to your head, don't let your ego take control. In sales you have to work hard, prepare and practise. The world is full of mediocre salespeople who think they are the greatest because their ego's and mothers tell them they are!

When I look back over my career in sales I can clearly see where the errors were made. The key to success is to learn from your mistakes but it has to be said that far better than learning from your mistakes is to learn from others, therefore avoid making as many. Sadly, for some reason we don't like to do that, and many seem to believe that learning from your own is far more effective! Here then, as a means of assisting you to learn from others, namely me, are some of the howlers I made in the early part of my sales career. I hope these help you to avoid the same mistakes!

Jumping to conclusions before you meet the prospect

In my early days there were a number of occasions where I would make the wrong decision about a prospect, before I had even taken the time to talk to them. I would do this based on some really quite superficial criteria. I can even remember on one occasion deciding not to follow a lead up because the area in which they lived was not one that I thought much of and judged that they were not right for the product I was selling. I could not have been more wrong. Eventually I learnt that lesson but not before I lost potential business to a competitor.

So, the rule should be never to prejudge a person based on their location, looks, dress, the way they talk, or even if you think they can afford to buy what you have to offer. Like me you will waste many great opportunities in this way. I am not saying you have to ignore your instincts, but I am saying do your research, gather evidence and then decide on the action you should take. The opposite is not true, the buyer or potential buyer will make a judgment based on first contact. You should always have that at the front of your mind, so make sure you sound, look and act right, all the time.

Not researching and qualifying your prospect.

If you don't ask the right questions, or worse still ask no questions at all, your sale is bound to be on a collision course with failure. It is vital to any sale that you take time to discover, by qualification, that you're talking to the right person to give you the outcome you're looking for and to discover what your prospect wants and needs before you go too far into the sales process.

Don't talk, listen!

Most sales professionals will tell you listening is a vital skill in the sales journey. However, the reality in many cases is somewhat different. For some reason many salespeople seem to hate silence and feel compelled to fill the gaps with more conversation. I know we have already covered this, but it is worth saying again, it really is that important! At the extreme salespeople will even jump in with possible answers or even answer the question for the client, just so they can keep the momentum of their onslaught. They concentrate on the selling process instead of listening. On many occasions I have seen a prospect ask for the sale and the salesperson was so wrapped up in the process they didn't hear it and kept going, guess the result? They lost the sale. I am sad to say that I have done this once or twice too in the early days. My fortunes changed once I really learnt the lesson!

You're not the most important person in the room!

A cardinal sin that will make any sale go bad is to be condescending, talking down to a prospect, making them feel like you consider them to be lesser than yourself. Always, always treat your prospect with respect. In any circumstance in sales the client or prospect is always the most important person in the room!

Address their needs not yours.

Listen to what they want and act on that. Don't listen and then ignore them presenting a different solution to the one they need. If you can't help them, have the integrity to tell them so. Your job is simple you're there to address their needs not yours.

Don't let your sales target pressure the prospect.

If you're prospect really does need time to think about it, don't be tempted to pressure them to make the decision now for fear of not making target. If you're not making target it's not their fault, you need to look much closer to home. The other thing to avoid, which will always end in a bad sale, is putting the prospect under pressure to buy now, simply because you're afraid if they don't buy now, they'll find a better alternative. If you feel this way you clearly have failed to build the relationship, or your advice is not in the best interest of the prospect, or you don't have confidence in your own product. If that is the case, you might need to think about your future or the future of the product!

Split personalities don't win sales.

Don't be good cop at the beginning of the sales process and then bad cop when it's time to close. You'll lose their confidence and loose the sale for sure. Sales will always turn bad if you send mixed messages.

Don't say it if you don't mean it.

A sure way to lose the sale is to show a lack of sincerity or worse still show false sincerity. Don't do it, don't say it unless you mean it. I would go still further and say to you, if you're only in it for the commission you might want to consider a new career. In my experience the best of the best in sales have a passion for the product and a passion for the people. They have a genuine desire to help and the commission is a highly valued reward for their passion to help, not their reason for selling.

The wrong attitude.

This can really kill the sale. Your attitude should never be based on you feeling like you are doing them a favour. Don't go to a meeting thinking you might fail. You should go with the belief you're going to win. Imagine being a sports person who takes part in the games with the belief they're going to lose!

I guess from this we can say the best way to ensure things don't go bad with our sales is to follow the basic guidelines of good sales; here are my top tips for getting it right:

- Make sure you really understand the needs of the prospect before you start presenting a solution (your product).
- Now that you know the needs, does the solution really hit the mark?
- Make sure you employ active listening techniques, maintain plenty of eye contact and let them know you're really listening to them.

- Take notes, confirm details and ask questions that refine your understanding and encourage the prospect to give you the full picture.

- Are you really being sincere, do you really care and are you showing it?

Now here are some things you should avoid at all costs:

- Never use high-pressure tactics on your prospects, remember people really do hate to be sold to but always enjoy the experience of buying.

- Never assume the prospect doesn't recognise those oh so old and oh so predictable sales techniques, instead build rapport and trust.

- Never hide the facts. Don't invent spin to avoid or handle objections.

Why we fail

What makes a sales career fail?

The first thing I want to say is we are all responsible for our own successes and failures and to a certain extent our future too. With that in mind you'll not be surprised when I say that in my view most of the sales careers I see fail come down to the wrong attitude. If you think like a winner, you're more likely to act like a winner and if you act like a winner, guess what happens next? Yes, that's right you'll start to win more than you lose.

During my time in business I have come across a reoccurring theme to the characteristics that seem to go hand in glove with sales and indeed business failure:

1. **Low self-confidence—I think it would be correct to say that the number one characteristic I have and still to this day come across is a lack of self-confidence when it comes to selling. Ultimately you are what you think about. If you think you can't then it's fair to say you won't. If you think you can, I can say with some certainty you'll lose less, try harder, have more fun, be more successful and happier. With a positive attitude you'll also be able to accept the occasional loss, none of us can win them all! Those with the right attitude see the loss as part of the essential journey to the win, they take solace in their numbers, knowing you need to get past the no to get to the yes.**

2. **Lack of belief in your product—Another common fault is a lack of belief in the product. If you don't truly believe in the product or the service you're providing to your clients, it will show, and it will have a negative effect on your sales success. Selling is not just a job to earn a commission and if it is, you're destined never to be an exceptional salesperson. So, when you're**

looking for a job, make sure the product captures your imagination and your heart, make sure your motivation is the people not the commission.

3. **Not having a goal to aim for—If you don't have a goal or a set of goals and you fail to plan and execute that plan, you will see your sales career begin to fail. Take a look around and you'll find all the salespeople who have sustained exceptional results have goals and have plans how to achieve them. More than that they then make significant and sustained efforts to make those goals a reality, through activity. If you need further evidence just go, ask them. Listen, your vision of the future and your plan to get you there are key, fail to plan and you will fail.**

4. **Not maintaining your positive attitude—Your attitude is a key component in your success. If you let your motivation slip, you'll see your sales do the same. Remember you are what you think about. Make sure your glass is always half full not half empty!**

5. **Rejection is not about you—Don't let rejection get you down. Remember when they say no they are saying no to the product right now, not forever and unless you're in the wrong job, or have upset them they're not saying no to you.**

6. **Failing to know your product—You don't need to share all your knowledge all the time, but you do need to know all you can and use that information when called upon to do so. If you don't know your product inside and out, confidence will suffer and in turn sales will suffer.**

7. **Failing to know your prospect before you sell—Sales failure will certainly come if you don't take the time to learn about your prospect, invest time into building rapport and trust. It's the rapport and trust that makes the sales world go around.**

8. **Not taking time to invest in you—We can never know everything and sometimes we forget things. Invest in yourself. Take part in training and coaching. Having a mentor will also help in the prevention of sales failure. You never stop learning. Make sure the mentor you choose has done it and done it recently. Use Rainmakersclub.co.uk to connect with your next mentor!**

9. **Failure to really listen to the prospect—The prospect is going to tell you everything you need to know to make the sale. Too many salespeople become preoccupied with their own knowledge or the end game than to take time and**

really listen to what the prospect has to say. This invariably leads to sales failure. Learning to listen is vital, learning to ask the right questions to unlock the information you need is important in the prevention of sales failure.

10. **Failing to overcome the objections—To prevent sales failure all objections must be dealt with to the full satisfaction of the prospect. Understanding the objection and dealing with it, making it clear to the prospect that you understand, can make the difference between sales success and sales failure. Take time to learn the most popular objections, prepare and practise your responses, become expert in dealing with them.**

11. **Not dealing with change—Change is a constant in business and in sales, things always change. If you were not able to deal with change and accept it, working with it to gain the best possible outcome, I would say eventual sales failure is assured.**

12. **Not being a people person—If you're not a real people person, you'll find it difficult to succeed in sales. Selling is all about people not about products and so it's essential you like people, that means having a genuine interest in them and their well-being over the possibility of earning a commission.**

13. **Too driven by commission—You're destined to fail in sales with no long-term future if you are only in it for the commission, rather than for the buzz of the sale and a job well done. The commission is a welcome reward of a job well done.**

14. **Over promise and under deliver—If you build a reputation of promising much and delivering less than expected, your failure will be assured. Far better to under promise and then over deliver.**

15. **Not understanding the nature of luck—If you sit back and wait for your luck to change you can be assured of sales failure. Luck comes from hard work and the harder you work the more luck you'll begin to experience.**

16. **Lacking in persistence—If you're willing to give up the chase after the first no you receive, or the first obstacle placed in your way, if you're not persistent in your work, then failure will surely follow.**

17. **Lack of the right activity—If you're not putting in the right activity and if you're not working to your own KPI then sales failure will not be far behind.**

Your competition

Don't pick fights

No matter how you might feel about your competitors, don't get caught talking about them in anything less than positive terms, again mentioned earlier in the book but important enough to be repeated. If you bad mouth them, you'll only make yourself look vindictive and cheap. On the other hand, you need to be realistic in your outlook when it comes to the competition. Business is a jungle and it's all about survival of the fittest.

Don't make the mistake of thinking your competition won't do, behind the scenes, all they can to beat you to the prize, just like you would to them! To come in first you need to be smart and you need to work hard, harder than anyone else. People around you will start to call you lucky but you'll know the truth! Anyone that tells you, you need to work smart not hard is wrong! You need to do both!

Follow these simple guides when it comes to talking about the competition: Never say anything bad about them, keep to this undertaking even if your prospect is saying bad things about them. Instead praise them as a worthy competitor and afford them the same respect as you would any other person or organisation. As an alternative you should simply illustrate how you are different and how this will benefit the prospect.

Make a point of discussing both your strengths and differential. If you can use testimonials that illustrate why you were chosen over the competition. It's really worth having a plan and overtly seek testimonials for this kind to use in sales situations. Never underestimate the strength of well-positioned testimonials.

"If I am pulled into commenting about the competition, I simply say, I know these guys, we all have our part to play in the market. This keeps you clean and safe with reputation intact"

Above all I would say it's vital to maintain your values, ethics and professionalism, all the time, even if it means taking a few cheap shots from the competition, bite your tongue and stick to these guides. As a result, you'll come across as a professional and likable business and that my friend will lead to many wins for you and in turn your customers, past present and future.

I can think of a recent example, just after we had launched the Rainmakers Club a national networking organisation showed a total lack of understanding of the importance of these rules and indeed a total lack of understanding of what we were all about. Consequently, one of the directors, a very short man from Texas, embarked on a campaign that on the face of it was confrontational and potentially damaging to us.

Our reaction was obvious and clear, we maintained our distance, declined to comment but remained true to our brand values and invited him and others who supported his view to be our guest at one of our educational events. I explained to him that this way when he commented on us, he could do it from a position of direct experience rather than gossip. Sadly, he declined the offer. But what was notable was the number of their membership who disliked their stance and became part of our community. Stating that his actions said more about him and his business than it did us.

There are always exceptions to the rule, and you'll find most of the competition are fine with you, they may even help you and swap business opportunities with you, this is certainly the case within the Rainmakers Club community. With this in mind the most important thing for you is to understand your competition, know where they are in the market and who their main customers are.

It should go without saying you should know if they are taking your clients and on what basis they achieve this. Above all the most valuable thing to know about the competition is what their next step is going to be, that will give you real power!

I would also make sure I had samples of all their marketing material to ensure I had a good solid understanding or their strategies and tactics for sales and marketing. I also think it's a good idea to do the occasional mystery shop on those competitors either closest to you or the ones that create the greatest true competition. You could argue that your competition is anyone who has the capacity to take the customers budget, the one they would have spent with you, that is the true competition.

This level of knowledge will also help you to identify potential weaknesses in your own business and new strategic and tactical ideas to give you back or create an even greater edge. When you discover areas where you are weak against the competition, fix it as quickly as you are able. If you're working for someone, make sure you communicate your findings to the right people. This will have two major advantages; it will make sure you can compete, and it will get you noticed by your company as a serious player, making you more valuable to them, now that can't be bad.

Customer service

All customers deserve your respect.

In essence there are only three things you really need to know about customer service, and they are:

- If you don't get it right, the customer will let you know by voting with their feet and that will just benefit your competition.
- Customer service is not the exclusive domain of the customer service department.
- Understand that it starts with marketing and continues with you at point of sale and all you have to do is treat people the way you'd want to be treated, yes it really is that simple.

There is no secret to great customer service. It's simply an understanding that the relationship building doesn't stop once the prospect says yes and becomes a customer. This is just the beginning of building an enduring relationship. I personally can't understand those companies that don't spend time developing this essential skill. Why would you spend all that time and effort building the prospects confidence in you, the product and the company only to ruin it all by not having customer service follow-up? After all your easiest sale is to an existing client!

Here are just a few hints from the thousands of things you could do to develop good customer service. These, I believe are the key ones that will get you the greatest results by taking them on board, avoiding the bad and implementing the good.

First let's look at some things that can put your relationship at significant risk:

- Concentrate on commission, product or profit over the person, quality and good service, will damage your success.
- Letting your ego take over, feeling that you are more important than the customer, will damage your success.
- Becoming complacent, due to the success you've experienced or the growth of your business, will damage your success.
- Developing your business with the introduction of departments without teamwork, accountability and clear responsibility, will damage your success.
- Not investing in a culture of ongoing coaching and regular training will damage your success.
- Committing the sin of not really listening to the customer and I mean really listening. Never try to anticipate what they are about to say, let them say it. If you don't you will lose sales and customers.
- Complacency and not paying attention to the competition and the customer and in so doing, losing them to each other.
- Worst of all, perhaps, the over promise followed by the under-deliver or just plain lying to the customer.

During my career, I can think of many occasions where I've had direct experience of all of these examples. I am sad to say that even after learning the lessons, I know I've fallen off the wagon and committed one or two of them again! Learning from mistakes is essential but first you have to recognise that they are mistakes. Then and most important of all, you need to have a very real desire not to make that mistake again and take overt actions to avoid these sins of salesmanship and customer service.

These important relationships can be very complicated as all inter-personal relationships are and it is very easy to make the occasional mistake. Mistakes are good as long as you and your business learn from them. Like many others in my line of work I don't believe that satisfactory customer service is good enough. Back in the day it might have been but customer expectations these days are so much higher. Being satisfactory will no longer cut it if you desire to be an exceptional business. To be fair I know nobody in business that sets out to be anything else but so few make the grade, few still take the right action consistently, that is why there is such a wide gap between the successful salespeople and all the rest!

"Learning from your mistakes is a very positive outcome but an even better one is learning from the mistakes of others. To do this you need to leave your ego at the door!"

It's my belief that all customer service should be planned and executed at 100% each time, every time. If you're building your business, building your reputation, the truth is how the customer views you is all that matters. No matter what you might say about yourself, what they say is the only true reality worth consideration. You will make mistakes from time to time, just remember from these mistakes' lessons should be taken and improvements made immediately.

Take time to make the customer feel like the most important person in the arrangement and remember that in many cases problems you face are chances to create beneficial conclusions for you the business and the customer. Just like sales, customer service is all about listening and learning how to ask the right questions at the right time. Ask open questions to gather the information you need and closed to control the conversation and fill in the knowledge gaps. So, what can you do to improve your listening skills?

Improve your listening skills

The first thing you can improve on is not interrupting, let the customer have their say and let them know you're paying attention to them, after all they are the most important person, right? When you ask questions, when you've finished talking keep quiet and let the customer talk, ignore the temptation to fill the silence with more chatter, the customer probably just needs some thinking time.

You should always avoid prejudging the situation or the person, if you do fall into this trap, it will distort what you hear and change the way in which you would deal with the situation. As the customer starts to explain their point of view, avoid the temptation to second-guess what they're going to say and jump in before they have finished getting their point across. Make sure you hear the entire story before you respond. Even if you truly do know what they are going to say, don't interrupt, as this will give the impression, you're not interested in them! Take all the facts into account before you speak again and when you do, offer potential solutions.

Another great skill is not just listening but reading the person, their mood and attitudes. In some cases, it's what they don't say that can be important or perhaps what they imply. Take time to improve your interpretation skills and learn the art of the silent communication of body language.

Take your time, think before you speak, think between points raised and made. Listen and digest what has been said, really understand it before you open your mouth to talk again. In my view the best way to demonstrate you're really listening is to simply take the right action as a result of the communication. I know this all sounds very simple and that is because it really is that simple, like so many other things in sales and in business. Don't forget the power of short silences too. When you respond do so with a thoughtful look and a short silence to demonstrate your consideration, this goes a long way to winning over the hearts and minds of your customers; because it shows you care and allows you to engage your brain before opening your mouth!

Customer service as part of the sales process

Earlier in the book we looked at the sales process and you'll remember the last phase of the process we called consolidation. In essence this is all part of the customer service journey. The greater the experience you create for the customer at point of sale and beyond, the greater the level of loyalty and the greater the volume of referrals and repeat business you'll receive.

It is my belief that good customer service should, like sales, be a skill that everyone throughout the business should practise. More than that, it should be ingrained into the very fabric of the business as part of the overall culture and core values demonstrated by all. What then should this culture and core values look like for the business that is serious about customer service?

I would say it should be dedicated to customer satisfaction and this dedication should be demonstrated by all staff, regardless of position or experience. The business as a whole should demonstrate a sense of urgency when it comes to dealing with customer issues, now! Not tomorrow!

Accountability and responsibility are another key value for customer service. No passing the buck, just deal with it. Never get caught saying something and then not doing it. Make sure you always fulfil the promises you've made. When you're talking to the customer or dealing with their issues make sure you always use empathy for their situation and point of view, explain your position with care and respect.

"Showing empathy means telling the client you can see it from their point of view, then ask if you can explain your view, softly, passionately and with care."

Another really valuable trait to encourage throughout the business is that of flexibility and a desire to go beyond the expectations of the customer. It is also good to encourage, in all staff, the capability and desire to not just take some responsibility but to also make decisions and not procrastinate.

Really good customer service requires consistency and delivery of the promise, on time, every time and that requires commitment from all staff. Just one more reason why we should select our people with great care and invest in regular training and a culture of coaching.

Do more than expected!

Some years ago, I was running a business with a national sales force of nearly 300 people, it was a task full of challenges. With well over 1 million in sales each month customer service was key. Here are just a few of the ideas I implemented in the business to help in the development of exceptional customer service:

- Early in the process I realised the importance of keeping the senior management involved in the coalface, where understanding the customers' needs and the journey, we were creating for them was most visible. Having top management make occasional sales calls with other team members was all part of this process; the credit of the sale always went to the person responsible for the area, not the manager! In this way we could always deliver timely coaching where and when it was required.

- I also included a policy that any customer complaint had to be dealt with using a consistent process with consistent standards and timing. Making the customer feel really important in the process was also key. To do this we would always get senior management involved in the complaint handling system, as well as the original salesperson. This was so the customer making the complaint did not get the feeling that the fox was guarding the chicken coop.

Customer complaints can generate sales.

At first glance this may seem a strange statement to make but believe me this really can happen. What starts out as a complaint, handled really well can result in an unexpected sale! This will not happen often, but it does happen. Regardless of this you should always want to do the best for your clients, if you don't look after them someone else will.

I don't buy into the belief that the customer is always right; I think the customer is right some of the time. I do however believe that we, as the expert have a duty to educate inform and coach the customer so that they are able to make a fully informed decision. The better informed they are the less likely you are to get a complaint and the more knowledgeable your customers become.

No matter how good we may be, customers are still going to make the occasional complaints and when this happens, we need to be doing all we can to put the issues right quickly, efficiently and commercially, while still giving the customer the all-important personal touch. The personal touch will do something that for me is vital; it will help you win their hearts and minds. If you have their hearts and minds, you'll in turn get their loyalty and trust, followed by sales, referrals and repeat business.

Take full responsibility for handling the complaint and remember the customer might be frustrated or angry and you need to avoid reacting in the same way back at them. Be the calming influence, show compassion and empathy and remember hearts and minds. You also remember the customer wants solutions and solutions now, not later. Here are some really useful steps you can take:

- Make sure as early in the process as possible you let them know you understand how they feel.

- You also need to show them empathy. If you can share some similar experiences with them and tell them how that made you feel this will start the process of wining them over.

- Use active listening, make sure you get them to tell you everything, don't interrupt, let them get it all out in the open. It is okay to ask questions, to make sure you have the full picture and all the information.

- Be sincere, don't argue or get angry with them. Make sure they know when you agree with them. If you don't use diplomacy. Say something like "I understand how you feel, I do see it slightly differently, can I explain?" Can you see how this is less confrontational than saying I don't agree with you?

- Make notes at the time of the conversation and use the notes to confirm the details back to the customer.

- As with sales, find some common ground and build rapport.

- Use sales skills to present the solution and get the customer to buy into the solution.

- Once the situation has been resolved make a follow up call to show you really do care.

- Above all learn from the situation and share the information to help prevent a repeat of the same issue again.

"People, all people, have a tendency to always see things from their own perspective. You need to see it from every angle and find winning solutions for all involved."

The better you handle the situation the greater the benefits will be for you. It is your responsibility to do all you can to make sure the customer gets their point across. Customers will often know what it is they want to say but may not be great communicators or will let their emotions get the better of them. You need to be able to help them and use your skills to interpret and seek confirmation from them. How well the situation is resolved is entirely in your control.

Just for leaders

Run sales meetings that inspire and motivate.

Sales meetings for your sales staff are a vital tool in maintaining and developing their performance and your communication with them. These meetings are also a vital link between what the company wants from the team and what actually happens in the trenches. It's at these meetings that all that marketing activity can begin to be converted into cash through motivated and inspired salespeople who will, in turn, generate more sales and happy customers.

A word of warning never have a meeting for the sake of having a meeting! They should be scheduled, planned, prepared and executed to a formal agenda that will ensure expectations are met and managed.

The sales meeting should be a forum for reporting, reviewing and coaching the performance of your team, or delivering your performance results to your boss and learning how and where you could improve your game. The overall purpose should be the coaching, training, problem solving and above all encouragement to take the sales performance to the next level.

I have been to and heard about, many sales meetings that clearly don't cut it and clearly don't give the participants any real value. In some cases, they were just an excuse for the bosses to flex their muscles and the sales guys to wax lyrical about that ever-elusive big deal that's just around the corner. If you want to have really good, really valued sales meetings then here are my top tips. No apologies for saying the same things I always say, it's just there's only one-way to do it and that happens to be the right way. For what it's worth, I think this is the right way:

- Have a clear agenda with plenty of positive examples of success and solutions capable of solving any team or individual weaknesses you are aware of based on review and real metrics.

- Don't spend too much time on administration save that for another time.

- If you do have to discuss problem areas or weaknesses, make sure you give notice to all attendees, so they can take some time to think about the content and contribute. Make sure you have solutions ready, don't leave people focused just on the problem without a solution. At the same time encourage alternate solutions from the participants. This will make for a much better meeting.

- Make people feel good, concentrate on hearts and minds, do this with awards, congratulations, competitions and success stories, use plenty of praise. Don't limit praise to just your star players, spread it around, just make sure it is justified and sincere. Improvement is good, so praise it too.

- Include something in each meeting to help develop skills, maybe rotate the presentation of this to a different salesperson for each meeting. This will serve to enhance individual skills and promote more team spirit.

- Help the team to earn more money through coaching on sales subjects like objections, or areas of general weakness and include those who are strong so they can share their expert view.

- Occasionally invite someone from the outside to give valuable alternate perspectives, invite an engineer, or production person, maybe even a client.

- My personal preference is to have the meeting early in the week and early in the morning, with pastries and great coffee. It makes for a good start to the day and the week.

- Keep things on track. For those who turn up late make them pay a donation to charity as penance, always start on time and always finish on time, no matter what stage you get to. This is where preparation and planning come to the fore.

- If you need to reprimand, do it in private, save the negative for behind closed doors. Giving praise in public is fine and a good thing to do to help motivate others. Never make public praise a chance to have a dig at others, never!

Writing & Listening

Writing and sales.

We've all received sales letters, you come home from work and there they all are on the mat or in your inbox demanding your attention along with the inevitable bills and spam. Have you ever noticed that most sales communications look the same, even before you get them out of the envelope or open the email! I usually don't even bother to open most of them. I can tell just by looking at them they are nothing more than overt sales letters.

Remember the rules of selling and particularly the rule which states; people hate to be sold to, but they love to buy. You should consider this when you're thinking about the content of your next sales letter.

There are some letters that I will open, and these are the ones that stand out from the crowd. The ones that do seem to work, are the ones that give value first and don't sell right away, these also often appear and feel personal too. You can do this by using a handwriting font and ensuring they are fully personalised. With emails you can replicate the personal style using cloud or internal email system. These days you can even do this with email systems built into your website. If you're using traditional mail you can print envelopes to look like they have been handwritten, better still hand write the salutation and the envelope.

Please don't forget the mail you send out will initially be judged on the way it looks, you'll be judged on the reputation of your business, on how you sound and on what you say. You'll also be judged on what you write and the way you write it. Be innovative and people will think that's who you are. If you're creative they'll think that of you too, guess what they'll think if your letter is uninspiring and predictable sales fluff?

I've met many a salesperson in my time that have a real problem putting words on paper or screen. It's not so much that they don't know what to say more that they haven't thought it through and considered what it feels like to be a prospect. Here are my top tips on writing sale letters emails and blogs for sales or lead generation:

- Don't use smoke and mirrors, state the objective of the letter early, get to the point but make it noteworthy, think of it as the headline in a newspaper that's going to make the reader want to know more.

- The best way to write a great letter, email or blog is to really understand your target market so you can tell them what they want to hear in a way they want to hear it.

- Try to keep the words to a minimum without losing the impact and creativeness. Try to use short paragraphs to emphasis the important points.

- When you've written it don't just send or post it. Take a break. Go back to it and reread it, then edit it where needed. Do this a few times, taking out words that aren't needed and when you can make no more changes, it's time to send or post it.

- As a rule of thumb, you should keep it as short without losing the purpose.

- Don't over complicate and only write in their language, avoid superfluous jargon.

- Use some design in your letter; make it look interesting, use bullets and lists for emphasis.

- Use **bold** to bring out your most important points.

- Don't sell too much, keep it clean and follow the rules of selling.

- Never use the letter or email as a pitch, use it as one of a combination of sales tools, use it to demonstrate your expertise and quality.

- Add something to create a differential, maybe a supporting article or some testimonials that are relevant to the subject.

- Personalise the content as much as you can, the better you do this the greater the chances they'll do business with you.

- We all use technology these days and so make part of your differential some handwritten sections or a font that looks like handwritten, what used to be commonplace but is now so rare it has now become special.

- For smaller runs sign the letter yourself and handwrite the salutation. When using email use a signature image where you can. Use a friendly colour like blue.

- Don't push too hard for the business, nobody likes to be pushed too hard.

- To really emphasise the point try using a P.S. at the end to make the point again.

If you follow these guides you will see more success. Before you send the communication out, ask yourself, were you really thinking about the people, rather than the product or service, are you giving value and demonstrating your expertise?

"Like most things writing well takes practise, you can probably tell from this book that I need some! Don't give up you will get better, concentrate on the people not the product, you'll do fine!"

Listening the most important part of communication.

Remember the story about the university study to find the best communicator in a room full of students. They voted on each other while being observed? Remember the person voted, as the best communicator was the one who had done the least talking and the most listening. I would argue listening is the most important of all the elements of communication. When I say this to people they always nod with agreement and yet very few organisations take the time to train on listening skills. Here's a thought, just because all those of us blessed with hearing say we listen, it doesn't mean we actually listen!

Think of it this way it's no different to being taught the skill of observation. You could be forgiven for thinking that as long as you have 20/20 vision, you'd not need to be taught observation. Wrong! I remember thinking the same thing when I first attended the class on observation after I joined the infantry. It didn't take long for me understand that seeing is not observing. In just the same way hearing is not the same as listening. Hearing can be filed in your brain as a background noise or the most important thing going on right now. In selling it needs to be the latter.

I want to look at the keys to listening, I think the first step has to be to recognise that even when we think we are listening sometimes we're not. Often instead we're distracting ourselves by our preordained opinion on the subject under discussion, or too busy thinking of what we want to say next. In many cases we are doing both, particularly in sales and almost as commonly in leadership. If you want to see bad listening skills in action look at politicians from different parties talking to each other. Nobody listens, they are too busy looking for a gap to say what they want to say, usually a cheap shot! Ops let's not get political or personal, it's against the sales rules!

Listening with clear intent.

Start by understanding two key issues. First always listen with the clear intent to understand what's being said. The next thing is to start listening with the intention of responding as a result of listening to what's being said, not what you have already decided to say.

Have a think about this listening thing. Think about the way in which you listen to people, not how you think you should listen but actually how you do it in practise right now. For example, do you do something else too, when people are taking to you? Is your mind somewhere else or do you give them your undivided attention?

Many of us would say that's not the case, when in fact we are not really listening, more likely we are waiting for the gap to make our comments. Sometimes we think we know the answer before the other person has finished talking and so we simply wait for the gap so we can have our say! This has already been mentioned before and so you already know this is not the way to do it, but did you really take it in?

Perhaps you're one of those people who will start to listen but then stops, when you know what you want to say. In extreme cases not only will you stop listening but interrupt the person to get your point out on the table. Just think for a moment how that would make you feel if were happening to you? Do you also stop listening if the person starts to say something you don't really want to hear? I am sad to say that this is something that I have done in the past. I am getting better but now and again my passion gets the better of me and I fall off the wagon. Sorry where you saying something?

Why do some people not listen?

Why is it that some of us just can't listen as well as we should? Some of the common reasons include not wishing to hear what you believe the person in front of you is going to say. Other really common reasons for people not listening include:

The person talking is too familiar to you and therefore you take them for granted. Perhaps you've other things on your mind that are acting as a distraction.

Most common though is a preoccupation with the things you want to say rather than paying attention to the person in front of you.

If any of those habits, that's all they are, sound like you then to improve your fortune in sales, break the old habits and replace them with a new desire to really listen and engage with the people you meet. After all sales are all about people, right?

"The three most likely places for bad listening to take place are in sales, in relationships and where egos are out of control!"

Listening, the rules.

Start the process of becoming much better at sales, much better at relationships and business by simply follow these simple and obvious rules of listening.

- First leave your ego at the door.

- Don't interrupt; your turn will come in good time.
- Ask questions to find out more. Once you've asked the questions keep quiet and let them talk.
- Don't prejudge, if you do, this will taint how you interpret what's said to you.
- Listen from a neutral position, no matter how difficult that might be for you.
- Where possible use eye contact and verbal affirmations to demonstrate you're listening.
- Never jump in with opinion or solutions until you've heard the entire story.
- Take as much notice to what is not said as you do to what is said.
- Ask smart questions to ensure you have all the information and fully understand the situation.
- Demonstrate you understand what has been said to you by taking affirmative actions, use positive body language and inflections in your voice.
- When it's your turn to talk think solutions, don't be tempted to just enhance or add to the problems stated.
- Avoid the distractions. Concentrate on the prospect and what they have to say and what they want.

There are many things we can do to be better listeners but by far the best thing we can do is simply learn to keep quite while they're talking. Concentrate on what they are saying to you. Don't underestimate the power of your silence and the amount you can learn by letting people talk while you just listen.

It's really amazing how much you can find out just by keeping quiet and really listening, and you will learn the most by asking smart questions and then shutting up and listening. Without doubt the better your questions and the more you listen the more sales you'll get. That's true simply because the more you know the better you can pitch the solution.

The secret is to listen with the single and clear intention to understand what is being said to you, rather than with the intention of merely responding.

Also remember, never argue, or offend the prospect. Never think or act as if you're defeated. Try to make friends at all costs, use empathy and get on the same side of the fence as the prospect, above all never tell a lie.

Trade Shows

Some basic rules for successful trade shows.

These kinds of shows can be a fantastic source of leads and a great place to build your contact database. I think that all salespeople should exploit these shows as often as they are able. See and be seen, learn about the competition, the market, the future and build contacts.

Just have a think about how long it would take you to get in front of the hundreds of people you could meet at a show. Think about having them all under the same roof on the same day all with the same intention, to buy, sell and network, what a great opportunity for you.

If you're going to exhibit then make sure you've prepared well and have all you need to make it a success, remembering the amount you have to pay to make your mark. If you don't have the budget to look good as an exhibitor, then go as a guest. I personally think you need to invest in some good quality graphics and get your message right!

"Exhibitions are great places to network and generate leads. If you're going to take part and have a stand, make sure you have the budget to make it a good one!"

What I have observed, at many shows I have attended, is the tendency for those tasked with operating the stands to rely far too much on their stand to attract the right traffic and nowhere near enough on the personal touch. I am not saying they won't get people on their stand; I am saying if they were more proactive the traffic and lead generation would be significantly better, all it takes is a little more effort.

When I have been on stands, I have even gone as far as to go around to all the other stands and invite them to come over in their break to share some nibbles and exciting news, I can tell you, it works!

When you have a show or exhibition on in your local town, you need to be taking full advantage of it. At what other time would you be able to see so many potential and existing customers in the same area at the same time? This is your time for prospecting, catching up, relationship building and selling. As with most things there are some basic rules and ideas you should consider following to help you with a successful outcome, these are:

Get the right motivation—Make sure you are fully motivated before you go to the show. I have found the best way to do this is to simply remind yourself of the figures! At the last show I went to before I started writing this book there were 150 businesses taking part with stands and the organisers were expecting a footfall of well over 2,500 throughout the day. I knew it was not possible to see all those people, but I also knew I could certainly talk to many of them throughout the day and as a result generate new connections, new interest, new leads, new sales and a few quality referrals too!

Just think about it, if I was lucky enough (that means worked hard enough) to talk briefly to 15% of the footfall during the duration of the event, that would be 375 people. In my normal working day, I would struggle to talk to more than say 15 people. So how long would it take me to talk to 375? The answer is 25 working days or if you prefer five weeks! Now for me that is a huge motivation. The rub is most people would also feel the same way but when they got to the event, they would wait for people to come to them rather than go find people to talk to.

Remember the 7 P's—Prior preparation and planning prevents poor performance! Modesty prevented me from including one of the P's, but you've got the message. A trade show has got to be one of the most cost-effective sales opportunities you'll come across during any given working year and as such deserves your attention.

So, leave nothing to chance and invest time in planning and preparation. Make sure you have refined and rehearsed your pitch. Make sure all your marketing material and product information is up to date, accurate and easy to follow. Make sure you are ready to handle objections. Have your powerful questions and answers ready and make sure you have done your homework and researched as many of the people that are expected to be there as you are able to. All this preparation and planning will certainly pay off and will certainly give you the edge, making the investment of being there very worthwhile!

Visualise the plan—Don't just plan for the sake of it, before you leave your office for the event make sure you know the plan and have spent time visualising it so it is at the forefront of your mind throughout the duration of the event, be it hours or days.

Make it easier to execute by setting very specific goals, not generic ones but very focused, for example specific people to meet and talk to with specific outcomes. Make it challenging but not impossible; this will help to maintain high levels of motivation and activity.

Stay in the middle of it all—If the event requires you to be away from home, then make sure you book a room early and be as close to the venue as you can possibly be. If there are parties or any other form of gathering pre, during or post the event, do what you can to gain an invite to them so that you can continue to connect and build relationships. Please note I am saying continue to connect not sell!

Get there early—If you have to travel to get there think about arriving the day before, so you have time to rest and be fresh for the start. Of course, if you were exhibiting you would probably need to do this anyway. Don't be tempted to overindulge, leave that to others and watch them suffer later in the day while you are still fresh and up for the challenge.

As well as getting there early to ensure you are well rested I also like to get to the venue, early on the day, so that I can watch people arriving and plan my approach, as well as take advantage of the lower footfall to wander around and get a feel for the geography. I also often stay late too, so that I can squeeze every last opportunity out of the investment made.

Network during the set-up phase—If you're exhibiting, this is easy, not so if you're a guest. However, that does not mean you can't still do this. On more than one occasion I have managed to gain entry before the event, giving me a chance to meet with a specific person, I have even ended up helping them with the set up too! My main message is making sure you get maximum exposure and put in maximum effort to get the very best return on your time or cash investment.

Make a VIP goal for the day—If you're anything like me you'll have a list of people in business you would like to meet up with and do some business. It's a good idea to find out from the organisers of the event if any of your targets are going to be at the event and then to build a list of those people who are going to be your priorities for the day. Make it your goal to connect with them during the event.

You don't have to make this too complicated, don't sell to them simply make it your goal to meet with them, affect the introduction and talk to them briefly. Of course, if you get the chance to take it further then please do so.

"Making a list of people you particularly want to connect with on the day is a really good idea. I always seem to work more efficiently when I have a planned goal."

Seek out a few existing customers—As with networking you should invest some time into the people you already know. I would suggest you spend more time with new prospects but look after your existing people too. At events I like to make a goal for this too. I think this is a throwback to my Army days, where everything needed to be planned and executed according to the mission so that objectives could be reached. I do flexibility too and understand sometimes plans have to change but the mission stays the same!

I like to connect with a number appropriate to the number of days the event is set over. An example is for a two-day event I would set a goal of 10 and then do my best to take some if not all of them out for dinner with each other and in so doing create a mini networking group.

Teamwork is good—If more than one person from your business is going to be attending the event it is a good idea to work as a team and gain even more reach. Before you start, make sure each individual has a series of goals and share them with each other before the event to avoid confusion, cross over and enable cooperation in achieving the stated goals.

Choose your seat with care—Many events also have breakout areas and seminars. If you're going to attend some of these and your purpose is not just to learn something but to connect, take time to find out where your targets are going to be and be there too. It is not always possible but if you get there early and watch who else arrives you can start a conversation and maybe even sit with them to further improve the relationship you are trying to build. When you meet up with customers and prospects, ask them if and what seminars they will be attending and then be there too.

My personal favourite be a guest speaker—This is my personal favourite because speaking and writing are two of my passions. I appreciate that standing up and talking is not every one's cup of tea, but it really is only a matter of practise. Being able to stand up in front of an audience and demonstrate your expertise in an appropriate subject is a great way of generating leads. Make sure you pick a subject that is going to attract the right kind of people for you and then concentrate on giving them value based on your knowledge, opinion and expertise.

Always expect the unexpected—Often opportunities arise where you least expect them. The key is to always be prepared to face them head on. At events of this sort you will be rubbing shoulders with decision makers so be prepared and stand out from the crowd for all the right reasons.

Be open to opportunity all the time—At these events in every corner there will be chances for you to shine. Don't merge into the background and then again don't stand out for the wrong reasons. Instead find the right balance, a reflection of the reputation and brand values you want to be remembered for. At every opportunity you need to be looking to talk to as many people as possible. Look at badges and initiate the conversation; you never know when you might bump into your next major customer!

Your aim is to meet people, do it quickly—Everyone at the event is going to want to meet as many people as they can, so be as brief as you can and only linger when you know you have their real attention. To do this you need to be able to qualify people very quickly and accurately. You can do this by having a great pitch and powerful qualifying questions. Confirmation that they are willing to meet and talk to you later is good enough at this stage.

Never, never, prejudge—You can never tell who might turn up. The guy in the jeans with a carrier bag might be a CEO so always be aware always be respectful and listen and watch for clues, all the time!

Brevity is key at these events—Time is of the essence and so your opening pitch should be no more than about 60 seconds, take time to design a great pitch and then invest time in making it second nature, flowing and above all interesting for the listener. This is why preparation and practise are so very important before the event.

Get to the point—You need to get to the point quickly and when you tell the people what you do, make sure you do it in such a way they can see how you can help them with their needs.

Show your human side and have some fun—Be enthusiastic and have fun, there is nothing wrong in using well placed non-offensive humour, business should be fun. The best subject for some humour is often yourself and never your prospect!

Balance that handshake—Nobody likes a limp handshake and you don't want to be crushing your prospects hand either. Have a good clean firm handshake. Don't offer a submissive handshake (palm upwards) nor a dominant one (palm down), instead keep it straight, palm vertical with the ground.

Avoid spending too much time with people you work with—This is a disadvantage to you and them and simply wastes the time you could be spending with new prospects. You can always catch up with your friends once the event is done.

Always look to establish a prospect need—This is important, simply because you can't possibly sell anything until you know what the person you are talking to needs!

Gain information through good questions—The secret is not to say too much too soon but to get the information you need through good questions that generate the right information for your purposes. The only purpose should be to embark on the journey of establishing rapport and perhaps the need. Once done this will allow you to give your information to the prospect in a meaningful way for them. The true art of sales is knowing what to say and when to say it for maximum affect.

Let them see how you solve problems—Most people at these events are not going to remember what you do or have said unless the way it's delivered will show them how what you do helps them solve their problems and that is worth remembering.

Assess their level of interest—You're not going to sell now but you need to remember how interested they were because if things go to plan, you'll have a number of people to follow up on. My first sales manager taught me to note down on their business card my assessment on their level of interest. I still use that today when I go to events. I use a code that is unique to me and nobody else would understand. These days I use my phone not the card!

A tip on note taking—In the old days I used the back of the prospects business card. Things have changed and technology is far more efficient and so now I use my Smartphone for notes. The key is to do it immediately after the encounter so that you don't forget important details. The longer you leave it the more opportunities you put at risk. It is also worth using some kind of memorable shorthand to save you time.

Your aim is to pin them down to the next action—The golden rule is to never let a keen prospect go without first agreeing to the next action. The agreement to a meeting is always a good option, make it nonaggressive, ask to meet over a cup of coffee.

Be remembered—Do, say or give something that will be remembered, better still use a combination that will ensure you are remembered. Those that have met me will always remember my business card because I have made it so different and have done for some time. Not the same design but the same idea of creating curiosity and being memorable.

When it's time to go, it's time to go—You have many people to see and many opportunities worth your attention, so when you have what you need, say thank you, shake hands and move on to the next person.

Make your handouts memorable too—If you're going to use a handout of some description make that memorable too and make it valuable, giving value first will help to get you remembered and place you higher on their list of people to reconnect with later.

Review and adapt—Things don't always go to plan and so the ability to think on your feet, take a time out and adapt your plan is all important, remember the mission and go for it.

Don't overindulge, better still just don't indulge—The last thing you want to do is drink too much and make a fool of yourself, stay sober stay at the top of your game.

You can still have a good time—Don't push or be pushed keep it natural and have some fun, just like life.

Extend your contacts—Ask for a list of the attendees and contact the ones you did not connect with during the event. Tell them you wanted to chat but ran out of time and would like to arrange a meeting. Do this as soon after the event as possible, while they are still in networking mode. Be charming be sincere and do a great job.

Networking

It's easy and yet most people don't have a plan.

Let me start by asking you a few questions, I want you to sit back and give them some real thought because I believe networking, when done well, can open doors you haven't even dreamed of. The investment in networking is well worth the effort but the effort needs to be centred on the following proportions, 20% maintaining existing relationships and 80% making and developing new connections. Here are a few questions for you to consider:

1. How do you use networking to help with the development of your business and or career?

2. Do you spend enough time each week networking on and offline?

3. Have you set a target for weekly networking activity based on your own business target and needs?

Let me explain question 3 in a little more detail. I know that to reach my own personal sales target I need to be connecting with at least 20 new people each week. Most of these will come from networking and referral. I therefore need to ensure I put the activity in week on week to help me make target for new sales.

"When you look at the most successful people, behind the scenes you will find they always have a plan. Networking, on and offline, is very valuable and so make sure you always have a plan of attack!"

Networking can be an exceptionally valuable tool for your business and even if you don't have targets you should still use networking, it can be great fun and at the same time help with the development of leads, brand and reputation. Here are just a few of the things networking can do for you:

- It helps you to meet and become known by people who can help you build your business and your career.
- It helps to create some momentum for you and your business.
- It will generate new business and new friends.
- Networking helps to start building long term enduring relationships.
- It can be the most valuable source of quality referrals.

I am guessing, that like most people and indeed like me your main objectives for networking are going to be:

- Developing more useful business connections.
- Generating more sales leads leading to more sales.
- Improving your learning and sharing experiences.
- Getting more involved in the community to enhance brand and reputation.

To be a real success in networking, like so many other things in business, it is best to have a plan. To help you on your way here are the questions I ask myself when I go through my annual planning session at the beginning of each New Year, you may want to use this too:

- This year who do I want to meet to improve my business and sales figures?
- Where have I been networking and how is it working for me?
- If it is not working, am I using it the way it was intended to be used?
- Where should I be networking to achieve my objectives?
- Where do my customers currently network and other businesses that I would like to be customers of mine?
- Who do I know that is better than me at this? Will they help me?

If you get the answers to all those questions, you'll be well on the way to having a really good plan of action for your networking going forward. Planning is one thing, doing is something quite different, as someone once said, talk is cheap! You can make a real difference to your life and your performance by being one of those people that makes plans to guide them and then acts on them.

This is not planning for the sake of planning; it is to initiate the right actions at the right time. All it really takes is the will, the desire, the motivation to get up and do it! Only you can make that happen, coaching, mentoring, training, self-help are all good but when it comes right down to it the real results are all down to you and your activity, without the activity nothing changes!

Networking, on or offline, is all about connecting.

No matter what you think about networking, it has gone from being a positive activity to a necessary tool for business. With the arrival of Social Media in business, a global fashion, it's something you need to be part of. What do I mean by this? Simple, a few short years ago networking was all about businesspeople meeting up at a hotel and swapping cards and pitches with each other. It soon developed into more organised events and clubs for education and referral. Soon this overflowed onto the web so that conversations could continue, and relationships developed still further. Most recently networking had spread to the general public too and has been re-invented and branded as Social Media!

Networking like Social Media is an essential business tool and is all about connections, content and conversations. Connections drive content that create conversations that encourage connections, and so it goes on!

If you doubt the power of networking, I have two real examples for you both relate to me and to be fair I am nowhere near the best networker I know. The best networker I know happens to be a member of the same global networking organisation I am part of. If you needed proof how good he is, join the Rainmakers Club and see how long it takes him to connect with you!

Back to the examples, I went online and connected with some new people. It took me three posts to get to a point where we were having a good exchange of views. I just want to add these were not businesspeople I had met or had knowledge of before. Our icebreaker was we were on the same site and so had a shared interest. One of these people subsequently invited me to write an article for their magazine. Another unrelated person read the article and invited me to their office.

When I got to the office, they referred to the article (which would never have been written if it had not been for the networking) and asked if I would be a guest speaker for a few hours at a sales conference. To cut the story down, the conversation continued for some hours and I ended up meeting the entire board. I agreed to do the talk but pointed out why this was not the best idea and we could do much better than that to inspire more sales. I ended up working with them on the development of their sales team and strategies for just over a year for a six-figure number and in that year increased their turnover in sales by a number that was worth significantly more than the fee! Everyone was a winner from the individual salespeople, to the business and me!

On another occasion I went to a physical meeting and got involved in a chat about Social Media, as a result of that I was invited to attend again and be a guest speaker. After the speaking slot I was invited by one of the audience to do an after dinner spot at a London event on the same subject. In that audience was the senior partner of a London firm and they approached me to not only be a guest speaker at their annual conference but to also help with their strategies.

Both of these examples would not have happened without networking on and offline! Networking does however have some fundamental rules that should be followed. Most of these rules have come from that networker I previously referred to on my Rainmakers Club site and so I can take no credit for them, even if I have for the last few years made them my own:

- Always plan how you are going to participate at the event or online. Who would you like to connect with; whom do you want to read your material? If it is a physical event prepare a pitch and any supporting marketing material, you might want to give away.

- I always try to arrive a little early at physical events so I can monitor who is arriving. I do this because my aim is usually to meet as many new people as I am able in the time given.

- Take time to review the list of people online and their basic profile, or for physical events, walk the room a couple of times, that will pay off later when you start to have conversations. This will also give you a better understanding of whom you want to connect with because in most cases quality is better than quantity.

- Make sure you have your 30-second commercial or your opening sentence introducing yourself well prepared. Get to the point, don't sell but create some curiosity.

- Concentrate on being happy, positive, interested and passionate.

- Say or write the person's name in your conversation at least twice, this will help you remember them, and it is also pleasing for them to see or hear you using their name.

- If after contacting you discover the person it not a good prospect for your objectives then don't waste yours or their time, move on politely but always consider the reciprocal referral opportunities.

- If you are at a physical event, eat early or don't eat because it makes it more difficult to mingle and you can blow it with an accident. You only get one chance to make a first impression. Here's a good reason why I say this: I was at an event only a few months ago and a very dishevelled man, who clearly took no pride in himself was mingling, trying to sell financial services with tomato sauce on his tie, shirt and chin. If he had followed this rule, he might have had more luck!

- Whenever I go to physical networking events, I make it a rule not to drink and you should too! Celebrate afterwards the successes you gain from being sober.

- Don't smoke, the smell will put people off and while you're outside having a puff you could be missing out on the opportunity of a lifetime!

- At physical events try to stay until the end. The reason is simple the longer you stay the more connections you can make and the further down the road of results you can travel.

- Possibly the most important rule, have some fun and be entertaining, people like to be with people who are happy and fun!

People I meet who tell me they don't go to networking events or connect online because it is a waste of time, either don't get it or they're not doing it right. People who do go and don't end up with the results they are looking for are just not doing it right. The solution is simply asking for help from someone who gets it and does it right. I promise you, after a little effort on your part you will see the results.

Choosing the right platforms and events is also important. If you need help, ask your top five customers where they go and go there as your start point. Ask you online community where they go and ask if they can take you as a guest. The main thing is to get out there and go with the right attitude and objectives.

Don't overlook other events too; sporting, culture and entertainment events all have their role to play in networking for business. Just don't try to sell, just try to connect, selling comes later, after the relationship is built and the trust is present.

Work that room!

When you attend the more traditional physical events there are some things you can do to increase your productivity while working the room. Here are some ideas I have picked up along the way, most of them have come from others I have watched and learned from, when I first started out and was desperate to be more productive and successful at networking.

These ideas need to be used in conjunction with the tips you have already read about earlier. They work best together, or at least they do for me. Give them a try and see how you get on. Please also share your successes with me, I will be happy to hear from you. I would say the most important thing to commit to habit is making sure you spend more time on new contacts than you do on existing. I am not saying ignore those you already know, just that you should not be spending all your time with them. Get a balance that works for you and that is going to achieve your objectives overall or for that particular event.

"Getting the best from your online and physical networking is all about finding the right balance, a balance between confidence and ego. That means not too much ego but a good helping of confidence!"

So here then are a few subtle things you can, along with getting the balance right, do to improve your networking at physical events, these are things that I was taught and with practise have worked for me:

- Work on your self-confidence, as you practise and gain more experience so your confidence will grow. Once you have the confidence you need to work on controlling it along with your ego. We all need to have some ego but again it needs to be kept under control!

- Before you give any additional information, after you opening elevator pitch, ask the other person what they do and listen to them with care. Make it all about them rather than you. Even though this may go against your natural instincts. Making it about them will create the relationship so much quicker than if it's all about you! Once you have established this basic rapport then move on to find other points of mutual interest.

- Use your business card as a means of judging their true interest in you. Offer them your card they will often then return the compliment, which gives you an opportunity to offer to meet and swap notes on opportunities. You may even offer to send them some information, which you will follow up on. If they are reluctant to give you their card, ask for it using the phrase "I would like to send you some information." I think at this stage if they are still reluctant to cooperate, you will probably find it tough to get a meeting with them and you need to keep working on them. You will have to decide if that should be now or later. Their mood and body language will tell you all you need to know.

- If you get to the point where you feel progress has been made, now is as good a time as any to close them down to a next positive action. For me this would be to get them to agree to a meeting over coffee. I won't sell them on anything else other than arranging that meeting with them.

- When you have achieved what you set out to or discovered this is not the right time for them, don't hang about, politely finish the encounter and move on to the next person.

- If you feel your confidence ebbing away due to a few rejections, to be fair at network meetings rejections are quite rare, simply intersperse the encounters with people you already know. Just remember not to stay with them too long; this is about new connections more than existing ones. You already know these and know they will see you and listen to you as and when you ask but they are useful for pepping you up when needed.

- In the past when I have gone to events with a colleague, I have found the temptation to stay with them far too great and so I started to bring a little competition into the room. We would simply have a sporting bet on who would gain the most qualified leads or booked meetings by the end of the event. This had the desired affect and rather than spending time together we would separate and work the room, neither of us wanted to be second!

- Practice making what you say interesting and brief. Most people in business like brevity, even the great talkers, as it gives them more time to mingle too!

- Avoid negative conversations and don't get drawn into talking bad about anyone in your community. You never know who might overhear you and whom they might know.

- Always be polite, not a doormat but polite, show restraint and respect. Don't forget the incredible power of saying please and thank you.

- Concentrate on the kind of problems you can solve rather than facts and figures about you and your product. It's all about winning confidence, winning hearts and minds.

- If you can get involved in the running of the networking clubs you join, that is a great idea, if you have the time. People like to mix with and do business with people they see as leaders.

- Don't forget that most, if not all, the people at events will want to be selling, that is one but only one of the reasons I don't try to sell but build relationships at these events, another reason, you've heard many times before but that doesn't make it any less true and that is because people don't like to be sold to.

With so many events how do you choose the right ones to attend?

I have been networking for a few years now and the proof that it works is all around for us to see. One of the results of this success is the number of local to you networking events that appear in the calendar every week. While I was writing this part of the book, I reviewed my local area on the Internet and found over 35 events within the next 10 working days all within one hour of my office. So how do you decide which ones to go to and which ones to miss?

In the early days I would do my best to get to as many as I could. The only downside to that is the cost and amount of time it takes. I also found that I was not able to give value first to those that I met, there were just too many of them. I soon learnt the importance of being selective and making smart choices and so I made up some simple guides on how to choose the events week on week to attend:

- Unless it is a mastermind group, I will only attend an event that is frequented by my current preferred targets.

- Unless it is a mastermind group, I will only attend events that I know I can get to meet new people to expand my connections.

- Unless it is a mastermind, breakfast or a lunch group, I will only attend events where there is an understanding of the power of referral.

Building Rapport never stops.

Even if you are talking with someone you are already connected to you should always be working on the development of your rapport with them. If you already know the person and you have a business agenda you wish to present or talk to them about, get it done as quickly as you can. If they are talking to another person you don't know at the right time in that conversation, ask them for an introduction. If the introduction leads to anything make sure you keep to the rules, keep your promises and take time to say thank you to your original contact. Always try to return the compliment by making a referral to them.

Building rapport with someone you have not met before is simple really, once you understand they need to feel like you are taking them seriously and don't just want to sell to them! The key to this is to get them to talk to you, so you can find a few things out about them before you start your 30-second commercial.

If you ask a couple of well-placed questions to start the process and listen intently to the answers, you will gain insight and be able to find common ground. This will give you a really good base on which to continue to build rapport and possibly modify your pitch to be more suitable to their circumstances. Make sure you ask open questions to gain the maximum out of them and use active listening to ensure you take in all the important facts. At the same time, make them feel important; make them understand you really do care!

Finding out a little personal information is also a good way of establishing common ground. Once discovered make it part of the conversation and then bring it back to your preferred next action. In my case, this would usually be a meet up for coffee to explore business opportunities.

A word of warning, if you are a taker no amount of rapport building will give you any longevity in networking, you need to be a giver too. My preferred route is to always strive to give value first; it's a great way of being taken seriously.

When you attend networking meetings please remember it takes time to gain trust. For the first few meetings it's probably a good idea to just take a watching brief and learn about the meetings and how they work before launching yourself into working the room.

Giving value first is really key, don't push too hard, that is not the way to gain success in networking. When you are giving, don't measure what you get back, just stick to the plan and trust the dynamics, the more you give the more you will get.

They don't all need to buy from you to create success.

Networking is certainly about generating more leads and in turn more sales but that does not mean you have to sell your product to all the people you connect with. Be seen as the leader, be seen as the expert, be seen as a person who creates value and the rest will look after itself. As with most things in sales this is all about activity, the right activity.

"Being seen as the expert is a good way to give value. A good way is by taking on some guest speaking roles and maybe even writing a blog or two. Circulate them at the events asking people to go online and join the conversation. As the author you will be seen as a centre of influence."

Also recognise that a connection can lead to multiple referrals, which in many ways is so much better than just a one-off sale. If you really connect at the right level, you can have a never-ending stream of referrals from people who really trust and like you.

Don't expect to get instant results; the relationships need to mature to give you the real benefits. So, work hard, follow the rules and stay the course, the results will follow, in that you can trust.

The brave new world

People have changed the way they buy, and we need to change too.

There is no doubt people have changed the way they buy and the more technology takes over the more we change our habits. Lines are blurring and marketing takes an increasingly active role in the front line of sales. Today the smart businesses understand that everyone working in and on the business has a sales role and that all communication is a form of sales. For the most part, gone are the days of the high-pressure sales professional. There are still a few out there but their days are well and truly numbered. Today it is all about consultative selling and information.

The new (well now not so new) breed of sales professionals is more versed in people and that has become their emphasis more than product. Having said that they still know 100% about their product but choose not to use it as a hammer to crack the nut. They use it as a tool. Using it from time to time when the circumstances are right. The new breed relies on their knowledge and skill with people and the product, not with pure old school sales skills. Those skills are still important just not as important as they were. People still do business with people, but information and the Internet now play a much larger role. That is why giving value first and being the expert, being online, is so important to your sales success.

With the new breed there is no manipulation but bucket loads of knowledge and truth. If you want to join the growing number of new generation business savvy people, who will tell you they are not salespeople in the traditional sense of the word, they are people who want to help. They will tell you they are just passionate about helping people and passionate about their product and what it can do for people. If you want to join that number, who are turning out to be the most successful sales people in their respective businesses, then you need to do some self-assessment and adopt some new habits:

Don't say whatever it takes to get the sale, don't overcook the capabilities or suitability of your product, instead simply tell the truth.

Be seen as the expert not the salesperson. Being seen as the expert rather than the salesperson will lower barriers and create more trust in what you are saying, use social media to get your message out there.

Don't be pushy, instead be nothing but helpful all the time.

Sell through experience, don't push all the time, better still don't push at all, use your experience and knowledge to demonstrate what really works.

Total knowledge of the product means you never make stuff up and always have all the prospect is going to need to make a fully informed decision.

Problem identification, with knowledge and experienced based sales you'll be able to identify a potential issue and do something to prevent it.

If you are in sales and you have read those last few points and think you are not there yet, then you have a slightly different priority right now and that is to gain all the knowledge and share experiences with others who may know better to bring you up to speed quickly. Invest some time in you and plug those gaps and watch as your fortunes change. Be the success you know you can be, all it takes is your commitment, the right attitude and the right activity. Join **the Rainmakers Club** and start learning, sharing and developing.

Numbers

It all comes down to numbers!

Since as far back as I can remember, everything for me has always come down to the numbers. Numbers hold the key to success not just mine, not just yours but everyone's! Let me explain what I mean.

When I first started to play rugby at school, I wasn't that good, but I wanted to be. So, unlike some of the players on the team I had to train hard and practise my skills all the time. At first it didn't seem to make a great deal of difference but the more I practised the better I became. The same thing happened in the Army, when I first joined, I was not that good a shot and that's not a good thing to say if your chosen career in the Army is as an infantry soldier.

With a little help from my section commander and loads of practise on the indoor range after hours, I gained the experience and skill. By the time I joined my unit I was qualified to wear the cross rifles emblem of a sharpshooter. I didn't stop there, I continued the journey and qualified as a sniper too! It all came down to the numbers, the higher the number of my practise sessions the better the results became.

"Know your own numbers so you can plan for success. Know how many contacts you need to make to gain an appointment, how many appointments to get a sale and how many sales to reach your own income targets."

When I started my first sales job my trainer drummed it into me that it was all about the numbers and understanding my personal performance figures. Once you understand the metrics you are able to control and predict your performance and it will all come down to concentrating on the right activities. If you are not getting enough sales then, assuming you have a great product and pricing strategy, the problem will be found in your numbers. Talk to more people; make more appointments and hey-presto more sales!

I know how many people I need to talk to, to gain the right number of appointments, to convert the right number into sales, to hit my own personal objectives. If you're not already doing this yourself now would be a great time to start. All you need to know is this:

- What is the average cash value of a sale to you?
- How much cash do you need or want to make in a given period?
- How many prospects do you need to see before you get a sale?
- How many sales do you need to make in any given period?

If you start to keep some records, you'll soon understand the numbers and then you concentrate on maintaining the right attitude but at the same time the right level of activity. I can say that in all but a very few cases salespeople who are not making it are simply not putting enough activity into their working day. Perhaps concentrating on the wrong kind of work! If you don't want to do this or feel that you can't, then you really need to have a chat with yourself, you may be in the wrong job!

Things that will affect the numbers!

The numbers are a constant, they will vary from person to person and will only change as your performance gets better or worse. The key is to either be consistently good or improving. This can be achieved in the following ways:

- Never stop working on your attitude, the maintenance of that positive mental attitude is key to getting the numbers right.

- Make sure you understand your own personal goals; it's never good enough to simply turn up.

- Help to keep on top of new opportunities by networking and help to maintain your confidence.

- Never stop learning; never let your ego make you think you know it all. Seek new learning all the time.

- Know all you can about your product and have all the right tools in your bag all the time.

- Always do what you say you're going to do and follow everything up, never let your clients or prospects find you wanting.

- Have bucket loads of self-discipline. We all fall off the wagon from time to time but fight it and have the discipline to keep going when most around you would give up.

- Don't forget the numbers they are the key to your success, live the numbers.

- Remember that the more sales call's you make the luckier you're going to get, like so many things in business it's all about the activity.

- Some will read this book to learn more on the subject of sales success, the key is there is no secret it's all about, people, product, attitude, work and numbers, it always was and always will be.

- Knowing how to sell, knowing your product, having the gift is great, but none of these things will help you if you're not seeing enough people. Activity, activity, activity, practise, practise and then practise some more!

- If your sales are not going in the right direction, all you need do is check your numbers and you'll find all the answers you're looking for.

- If your role is a salesperson for the business then try to stick to some disciplined sales activity, you should try the model I used when I was working for the bank, I kept to that in most of my subsequent businesses too! The times I didn't keep to the model that works for me and many others I know, were the times I was closest to failing:

- Talk to at least 10 new prospects each day.

- Make at least 10 new appointments per week.

- Make your follow up calls.

- Make one hot presentation in the morning and one in the afternoon.

- Have a lunch or breakfast each week with your customers, I tried to do this at least twice a week.

- Attend at least one networking event a week.

- Keep good records to monitor your own performance.

When I was at the bank this resulted in at least two sales each day and that brought me in at the top end of the league table in my first ever job after the Army. As a CEO for the first time these numbers allowed me to take a £250,000 turnover and transform it into £13,000,000. Later the same numbers allowed me to build three very successful international sales teams for other people.

And Finally

The numbers all come down to you!

Sales, consultative sales, when done well, when done with the right attitude, for the right company, with the right product, can create for you true independence but in the final analysis it all comes down to you!

If selling is a challenge for you, then get some great training. If you can sell but won't sell, get another job or change your habits! If you think your poor performance is down to those around you, think again, exceptional salespeople don't play the blame game; they just ignore the distractions and get on with making sales. They don't do it for the money, or at least not for that alone but because they like the buzz, the feeling of doing a great job for their customers! Maybe the problem is the remuneration package, if it is, don't waste time, you are a professional businessperson and the key is to sell more.

Ultimately your business success will come down to your sales success, and that's going to be all about you and your attitude. I have heard many a business or sales guru stand in front of audiences of developing businesspeople with promises of doubling their income. For many this may appear to be pie in the sky, the reality is you could do that if you follow the rules, put the effort in all the time and remember these last few points I want to make:

Make sure you have a positive mental attitude and keep it. If you need some help with that read Napoleon Hill or Earl Nightingale. The key is to believe in you and not let all the others bring you down. Some people just like moaning about things and there is nothing they would like better than to bring everyone else down to their level. Remember your goals, your objectives, keep positive and work toward them in all that you do.

The next thing to get right is your goals, as these will help you maintain the right attitude for sales success. Do you remember that old saying, which points out the best way to eat an elephant, is in small bites? Think of your ultimate aim as being the elephant. Think of the small bites you will need to take to keep the whole thing manageable as your short-term goals. Don't just plan them in your mind, commit them to paper and review your progress on a regular basis. Constantly ask yourself; what can I do to improve these results or achieve this or these goals quicker?

Be one of those people who know they don't know everything and commit to learning and improving your knowledge and skills as an ongoing feature of your business and personal culture and values.

If you don't network or use Social Media, I am going to ask you to be open minded about the power of these activities. Not just for developing new contacts and eventually sales leads and more sales but to help you in your learning and development. To really feel the benefit, you're going to have to leave your ego outside the door! Understand that none of us know it all and there is always room for new learning. Join **the Rainmakers Club** that will be a great start!

Start to think and act like a leader. Even if you are not in a traditional leadership position, you still need to think and act like a leader (a good leader that is, so don't corrupt yourself and leave that ego outside the door). Each time you make a sale you do it through your leadership ability. Add to your list of must have skills or development the subject of leadership. Start today by adopting some of the great habits covered in this book!

Put yourself in the centre of things. Get involved in your local community and build a great reputation. Remember it's not all about you, make it about others and help. I will just say if you operate in this way you, like me, will soon understand that it's not just about building the right reputation, it will make you feel good about your life too! Start your own program of self-development and let us help you to create exceptional and sustainable results.

Understand the prospects you are going to talk to before you have your meeting. Use the power of the web, particularly their own website, search engines and social media and learn as much about them their product and their market as you can before the event.

Make sure you live by your personal value and be memorable in all that you do. Be creative in your thinking, don't follow the crowd but at the same time don't be too out there. The key is a healthy balance. To be truly successful you will need to have the courage to really go for your dreams. Let your passion and motivation to do a great job, motivate others. If you can do all that, I think you will be remembered. I also think you'll be considered by many to be well above average compared to the masses.

Sell because you want to help others. I am not saying is it is wrong to want to earn good money or to be motivated by the money you can earn by being one of the best. In reality most great salespeople are motivated by money to some degree and I would doubt those very much that say they are not. The key is that within the personal values of most of the top salespeople you'll find a very real and true passion for helping others. It is the buzz of doing a great job that continues to motivate them, even through the touch times. There is much to be said about getting business for others, just like the many BNI members will tell you 'Givers gain.' I just don't see why you should have to pay money to do that, do it as a natural part of your day and not just for those who are in your paid for club.

Possibly one of the hardest things to do is to remain focused all the time. We will all have our off days but if you learn to maintain that positive outlook, more often than not you will experience more success. Please don't let all those negative people around you bring you down to their level, oh and they will try! Once down there it can be difficult to get back. Always start and end your day at the top of your game and in so doing watch your game improve.

Relationships it's all about relationships. Salespeople who emphasise the importance and desire to establish long term relationships with value, always seem to fare better than those that simply concentrate on the next sale or the next commission. The saying, make a sale earn a commission make a friend build a career, is still as true today as it was when my first sales trainer told me this, all those years ago. When you concentrate on the people and not the product, sincerity, integrity and value are all by-products of that people centric approach.

Work hard, never stop learning and make sure you have some fun doing it. Life, work, being in business is supposed to be fun too. The strange thing is the more you learn the harder you work the more fun you have. It is no coincidence that those you see around you failing never look happy and never seem to be putting as much effort in as you and certainly don't appear to be having much fun. There is a link between activity, results and happiness!

You will not close all your deals. If you do all the things we talk about in this book you won't suddenly become successful. But, if you follow the tips and hints and make them your own, you will see improvement in your figures and you'll probably feel better about your future too. The true success, the exceptional results will come from your ability to build and maintain the right mental attitude and concentrate on the right activity and the right work habits all the time. Don't worry about falling off the wagon from time to time; just make sure you get back on it again, straight away!

Well, I think that's about it for Making Rain, there is enough in this book to get you started if you're just staring out, enough to remind you if you are slightly off your game and enough to help you develop into more than you are right now.

No matter where you go from here there is one thing you can be completely sure about and that is your future and your success is all in your own hands. Don't waste time playing the blame game when things don't work out. Remember you have control of your destiny it's just a question of how much you want it. If you see others around you having more success than you, it's a fair bet if you drill right down to the root cause you'll find it comes down to attitude and activity. So, let's go and develop your personal work habits making you even more valuable to your business!

Don't let those negative people drag you down.

The world is full of negative people who like to drag everyone down to their level; they are the human version of Marvin the paranoid android from Hitchhikers Guide to the Galaxy.

Negative people tend to live in a downward spiral, where nothing is ever right or good. You and you alone have the choice! Make that choice now—choose not to let anyone tell you that you can't or won't. You make the choice to be a success—surround yourself with the right people and positive habits to avoid the spiral.

This is my hope for you and there is nothing stopping you, apart from yourself, it's not easy and consistent effort is key. As I have always been told: "Remember, people will try to rain on your parade—and they will, because they don't have one of their own!"

"Don't let the negative spiral get in the way. You have control of your destiny, use it!"

A personal message to you.

I want to finish with a personal message to you. I have been selling all my life, I just didn't recognise it until I started to take myself more seriously in business. Once you understand that all communication is selling and all selling is communication, you'll start to want to be better and more successful at this must have skill. As you get better, you'll also begin to recognise that great businesses focus on sustainable and exceptional results and these results all depend on communication. I should say great communication.

So learn the skills of selling in this book and adopt the habits mentioned within these pages to. If you do, you'll be well on the way to being the best you can be for yourself, your family, your business or any business you work with. Reading the book was the easy part. Now you need to separate yourself from the rest by doing the tough bit—putting it into practise.

Join ***the Rainmakers Club*** *to take full advantage of more material and online help. Join to connect with others, set up and join conversations, start your own discussions and support groups to help you and others to bridge the gap. I am on the site so do connect with me and join the group that is in support of this book. Or you can call me, if you want a nudge to get you going! Enough said, let's go!*

All the very best

About the Author

Chris Batten is a published writer, speaker, mentor, founder of the Rainmakers Club and serial entrepreneur. He spent many years in the armed forces, where he successfully completed six tours of duty and achieved many qualifications that, he maintains gave him the confidence to try anything, but had no real practical application outside the Army, other than the leadership, communication skills and confidence to give it a go!

If pushed, he will invite you to pull up a 'sandbag', to listen to stories of daring-do! When he was a soldier. It had a huge effect on his life and is something he admits to being immensely proud of. It continues to be a big influence over who he is today. It was in the Army that he built the most enduring friendships many of which continue to this very day. These days he will tell you he gets his adrenaline fix from being an active Crew member and Helmsman for his local Lifeboat.

At the age of 34 Chris started his tumultuous journey into the world of business, starting straight after his last active service tour. His first role was in sales with a major UK bank.

This found him operating out of several branches in Norfolk England. After his first year in sales he achieved 140% of target, placing him in the top 10% of the company for that year. So began his love affair with sales and business.

With stints as CEO for a number of businesses in the UK and US he remained at the sharp end of business and also runs his own B2B Social Media and educational and advice service for small businesses based on a simple subscription model. He calls it the Rainmakers Club

He attributes his success to the mistakes made along the way with people selection and leadership; these increased his learning and desire to drill further and further down into why people in business succeed and what makes success! He admits failures have been far more enlightening than successes. When asked what the most important advice is you would give to someone new to business, he offers these words:

"Make sure you are doing what you are most passionate about and Make sure you learn the art and science of successful business. When those around you say you can't, tell them you can and then go and prove it! Above all never stop learning, run lean test everything and always leave your ego outside!"

Lightning Source UK Ltd.
Milton Keynes UK
UKHW041136151119
353592UK00001BA/18/P

9 781728 394428